MUKTIFAUJ

MUKTIFAUJ

OR

FORTY YEARS WITH THE SALVATION ARMY IN INDIA AND CEYLON

BY

FREDERICK BOOTH -TUCKER

GYAN

ISBN : 978-81-212-1549-7(HB)

First Published, 1923

Published, 2018

Published by

GYAN

Gyan Publishing House
5, Ansari Road
Daryaganj, New Delhi-110002
Phone: 011-47034999, 9811692060
www.gyanbooks.com
E-mail: books@gyanbooks.com

Printed at: G. Print Process, Delhi.

COMMISSIONER AND MRS. BOOTH TUCKER.

CONTENTS.

ILLUSTRATIONS.

INTRODUCTION.

THE Salvation Army in India has followed a path differing from that of other workers in this vast Mission Field. There has been no desire whatever in doing so to reflect on the plans, or policies, pursued by others; but we have believed that our own path was the most direct, and that in choosing it we were guided by God. Certainly there was no idea that our path would be an easier one.

Looking back now on a period of forty-one years, we are able to realize that we have indeed been following the Pillar of Fire by night and of Cloud by day. Not one promise has failed of fulfilment. If we had to go over the ground again there is little in principle that we should propose to alter, and we think that we may humbly claim that the seal of God's approval has rested upon our labours.

True we have made some mistakes which a richer experience has enabled us to rectify. We have also spent some time in reconnoitring some highways and byways which proved to be fruitless and unprofitable.

But we think that apart altogether from the bunches of grapes of Eshcol, and other fruits of this goodly land, which we are able to present to our readers in these pages, we can claim to have given a general impetus to Missionary Work in India, and to have helped to bridge the gulf which divides India from Christ, for other feet besides our own.

When we landed in Bombay a leading Christian paper had recently stated that some of their readers had asked them to give an account of existing revival work in India. The Editor mourned that he could not report what, so far as he was aware, did not then exist. There was an atmosphere of depression resting upon the Indian Mission field.

From the day the Salvation Army landed in Bombay that complaint has never required to be repeated. Not only did our own work speak of rapid advances, but, catching the same forward spirit, many of the workers around us were able to tell of a surprising and extensive movement among large and increasing numbers of the population, till the now familiar term "Mass Movements" was finally coined to describe the position. The latest Census of India shows that during the last decade the increase has *averaged* no less than 87,787 per annum, or a total of 877,876 for the period between this and the previous decennial Census of 1911. To God be all the glory!

In the providence of God we have ourselves been able during the last forty years to launch out along new lines, and in doing so have learned many valuable lessons, which would not otherwise have been possible. Living for years as an Indian, and following at times, with other comrades, the extremest lines of sacrifice, such as begging my food from door to door, and sleeping in the huts of the poor, or under trees, I have had opportunities for observing India such as few have possessed. Our devoted Officers have also supplied me with much valuable information gathered from similar sources. We have got to know the Indian in his own home—not in the more or less artificial life of the city—but away in the villages where 90 per cent. of the population live and toil. We have thus almost unconsciously come to "think Indian." God has helped us to open, and enter, the door to her inmost heart.

I need only add that the entire plan of campaign had the whole-hearted approval of our beloved Founder, who followed every movement with the keenest interest. "*Get into their skins*" was the epigrammatic summary of his instructions to his representatives in India. It was heartily endorsed by his then Chief of the Staff, our present General, W. Bramwell Booth. Nor was the problem studied merely at a distance, and at long range, but visits were paid to India, both by the Founder and his Successor, particulars of which will be found in these pages.

The wise and far-seeing character of the instructions received by us will perhaps best be judged by the following letter received from the Founder, after the work had been in progress for about four years.

INTERNATIONAL HEADQUARTERS,
QUEEN VICTORIA STREET,
LONDON,
27th August, 1886.

MY DEAR COMRADES,

The recent visit of Commissioner Tucker and his brethren to this country, and the enquiries which that visit has stimulated, have greatly increased the interest and affection felt by myself and fellow-workers in the vast populations of your country.

The first proof of this interest is to be found in the money that has been contributed, and far more so in the devoted band of Officers, selected from among the most intelligent and self-sacrificing that we possess, who, while I write this, are on their way to Ceylon; and if the immediate results accomplished are in any way equal to the promise and the interest already awakened, the sympathy felt, and the help contributed, will go on increasing in the future.

That it may be so I want to point out my own clear impressions as to the methods that should be followed in carrying on the Indian War.

First, one thing is clear and incontrovertible, and that is, *that the Mission of The Salvation Army in India is to its non-Christian populations.* To raise and bless these is its work. For their miseries and sins we believe we have a remedy, and to reach them with it is our primary duty.

The other populations, that is the European, Eurasian and Native Christian, may need us as much, perhaps more so, inasmuch as guilt is in proportion to the measure of light possessed, and there is no doubt that these classes enjoy much more light than the non-Christians, and are therefore much more guilty before God, and in danger of much deeper damnation. Still, in consideration of their vast numbers, and the long night of sorrow and tears under which they have groaned, the non-Christians have by far the strongest claims upon our compassion. And to effect their deliverance, and bring Salvation to their ears and hearts, The Army is directly sent. Go, my comrades! Benefit the other classes, if possible, as you pass along, and form Branch Armies of European and semi-European Corps on the model of this country, if you have the opportunity. They will doubtless help you in supporting and carrying on native work. But do not undertake this, if it will in any way hamper your main operations, for, as emphatically and as positively as I can possibly put it, I want to say, *your mission is to the non-Christians.*

Nothing must take you off from this. Plenty of people with European notions and projects will try to divert you by all manner of difficulties and statements; but you must not listen to them, lest you be turned aside from your work. Do not try to kill two birds with one stone: if you do, you will assuredly miss both. Fix your eye, your heart and your aim upon the Indian, and go for his Salvation with all your might!

Now, with respect to the Indians, your work is plain, namely—

1. To attract their attention.
2. To gain their confidence.
3. To save their souls.
4. To train them up to live and fight for God and the Salvation of their fellows.

How this is all to be done must form your life study. We have learned something, not very much, perhaps, in comparison with what there is to be learned, but still it is something which has helped us to win some glorious victories. We must act upon it until we learn more.

Beware also of expecting too great results at the onset. We fancy some labourers in the Indian battlefield have expected success with the outlay of even less labour than has been found necessary to secure the same amount of success at home. If you want victory you will have to fight for it, no matter what part of the world you are battling in, and you must not expect results in India with less outlay of labour and anxiety than have been required to produce them in other lands.

Here I may remind you, that perhaps in no other country will there be a louder call, and a wider opportunity, for the display of that principle of adaptation which is a fundamental principle with The Army everywhere. In order to conquer you must stoop, becoming with the

Apostle all things to all men, in order that you may win them to your Master. This must mean, if anything at all, that to the Indians you must be Indians.

And yet in this adaptation there is to be no departure from the known and acknowledged principles of The Army. These alike fit all circumstances, and are adapted to the character of the humanity of every age and of every clime. These principles have succeeded wherever they have been faithfully tried, and persistently held on to. There can be no question that they will be found to apply to the millions of India, as they have to the millions of the English-speaking races.

1. More particularly, let me again revert to the four divisions of your work as previously stated. Let me begin with the first-named, that is, that which says our first business with the Indians is to *attract their attention.* This important end will be found by you to be comparatively easy, and wherever you appear, already accomplished. Your name alone brings you a crowd. The people have been made to feel, before you enter a town, that they must come to see and hear you. Your appearance, your music and your Indian uniform draw them to listen to your message, to enquire about your doings, and to wonder whether you may not be divinely sent to them. What an enormous advantage this gives you over every other form of Christian effort, I need not describe. Oh, that you may prove worthy of your opportunity!

2. The next part of your work demands that, having attracted the attention of the Indians, you should proceed at once to *gain their confidence.* A good beginning has also already been made here. You have a reputation with the Indians of being their friends, which has to be sustained and perfected. This is your mission. How most successfully to accomplish it is to be your life work. Without their confidence you will utterly fail. They must believe that you really care for them, not for the sake of any religious or worldly gain, but because you love their souls and truly desire their welfare. All then will be easy; having made them believe in you, they will be literally compelled to believe in your message. How will you do this? The way has already been laid open plainly before

you. Commissioner Tucker, Majors Bullard and Weerasooriya, and other comrades have discovered a path, which leads up to the Indian's heart, and have trodden it themselves.

Imitate their example, travel over the same course. Go to the Indian as a brother, which indeed you are, and show the love which none can doubt you feel. Go to him, eat and drink and dress and live by his side. Speak his language, share his sorrows, and make him feel that you have come down, if it is a coming down, to act after the fashion of that Christ, Whom you call Master and Lord, in order that you may raise him up out of his miseries and sins. If I mistake not this will bring such success as missionary annals have never recorded before, and will yet lead to a nation being born in a day.

3. Then as to the third part of your mission, which is to *save the Indian*. This will be accomplished with the Indian exactly as it is with the European, and that is just as it was with yourselves. You remember how you were converted. When you gave up your sins, and sought God, and cast your soul on Jesus Christ, He took your sins away, received you into His favour, gave you the spirit of confidence, love, joy, and hope,—you praised Him day and night. It will be just like this with the Hindus, the Mahommedans, the Singhalese, the depressed classes and every other kind of human being who has wandered away from God, when they repent and return to His feet, that is, if they are converted at all.

4. And then there remains the fourth part of your duty, which is to *train the souls so won to be saints, and to make them Soldiers* to fight by your side. And here let me say that your success can only be counted by what you keep. So many saved here, and so many at the penitent-form there, sounds very delightful, but it is the Soldiers you possess twelve months afterwards that I note as the true indication of advance. Moreover, it is not only what you have in numbers, but in quality, and the quality of true Soldiers is always measured by their fighting power. Your business as a branch and portion of The Salvation Army is to make warriors, to secure those you win, and to use them to the best advantage in winning others.

How most effectually to accomplish this is henceforth to be your constant study. Here you have many advantages. To begin with :—

You are not bound by any stereotyped or antiquated notions. What is being done in Europe or America, or what has been done in India in the past, or what is being done in the present, need not be any rule to you, unless you can see it is calculated to gain the end you have in view.

Go, my comrades, and pray and look about you, and thus acquaint yourselves with Indian modes of thought and feeling and action, and then adapt yourselves to them, so far as such adaptation shall be consistent with the doctrines of the Bible and the principles of The Army.

You will succeed! It will cost something to win India. Nay, to follow up, increase, and establish the success already attained, will require some considerable sacrifice. But this once done, I feel confident that such a wave of conquest will follow as the world has never before seen in connection with Salvation.

But this, I repeat, will cost something. It cost something to win you and me and the handful of Soldiers Jesus Christ has in Europe. Rivers of blood have been shed to gain this result, and somebody must be willing to suffer for India, and, I thank God, that I believe many will be forthcoming.

Only be prudent, and faithful to God, and to the principles of The Salvation Army, and our mighty advances in Europe, America, and Australia shall not only be repeated in India, but altogether surpassed and eclipsed! Farewell, my Comrades! Take all reasonable care of yourselves, and in dark and cloudy days remember that the sympathy and prayers and confidence of your General, and of tens of thousands of Comrades, are with you; that tidings of your welfare will be looked for by every mail, and that we will weep with you here, and triumph with you and rejoice with you there, when we meet you "*in the everlasting morning.*"

Believe me,

Your affectionate General,

WILLIAM BOOTH.

VOICES FROM AFAR.

O'er the palmy plains of India,
  Wailing voices come to me,
Like the voice of many waters,
  Like the whispers of the sea;
Even in my dreams I hear them,
  Faintly calling night and day;
'Tis the voice of India's children!
  Who will seek them, far away?

There the sun, in hottest splendour,
  Makes the weary eyelids droop;
See the old, the young, the tender,
  'Neath their heavy burden stoop;
With no voice to cheer them onward,
  With no hope beyond life's day,
Who will seek these dying millions,
  Far away, far away?

There beyond this night of darkness,
  Eager hands outstretched I see;
They're the hands of India's children—
  Comrade, they're outstretched to thee!
Can you calmly stand and see them
  Struggling, dying, 'neath hell's sway?
While you sit in ease and comfort,
  Far away, far away.

Listen to God's voice now pleading,
  "Rise, My child, and follow Me,
Where the millions now unheeding
  Sink in base idolatry.
You are Mine, with blood I bought you;
  Now I bid you lead the way,
O'er the burning sands of India,
  Far away, far away."

Captain G.

CHAPTER I.

THE INDIAN EMPIRE.

Thou thinkest, " I am single and alone ! "—
Perceiving not the great Eternal Spirit,
Who dwells within thy breast. Whatever wrong
Is done by thee, He sees and notes it all.

Mahabharata.

For the sake of those of our readers, who may not be well acquainted with the British Empire in India, it may be desirable for me to preface the narrative which follows with some brief description of our field of work.

1. ITS EXTENT.

The British Empire in India and Ceylon extends over an area of about 1,900,000 square miles. In other words it includes a territory larger than the Continent of Europe without Russia, thirteen times the size of Great Britain and Ireland, and more than thirty times the size of England. India proper is about 1,900 miles long, and 1,900 miles broad, in its extreme length and breadth. Starting from Bombay it takes 42 hours of incessant travelling by rail to reach Calcutta, 43 to reach Lahore, 35 to reach Madras, and 56 to reach Tuticorin in the extreme South. By steamer to Colombo, in Ceylon, takes three and a half days. To reach Ani, in Kulu, our northernmost station in the Himalayas, will occupy at least seven days. To reach our nearest Corps in Gujarat takes twelve hours by rail.

The Himalaya Mountains or Snowy Range (*hima* means snow), which form the northern boundary of India, contain the three highest peaks in the world. The chief of these is Mount Everest, which is 29,000 feet above the level of the sea.

India's plains are watered by many great rivers, such as the Indus, which is 1,800 miles long, and the Ganges, which measures 1,600 miles, and whose sacred waters are fabled as flowing direct from Heaven. Most of these rivers are worshipped, and their waters are supposed, at particular places, to be able to wash away the sins of those who bathe in them.

From a glance at the following figures, one may form an estimate of the importance of India's position in the British Empire.

AREA AND POPULATION OF THE BRITISH EMPIRE.

COUNTRY.	Area in Square miles.	Population.
Great Britain and Ireland ..	121,390	47,500,000
Australasia, including New Zealand	3,300,000	7,500,000
Canada	3,800,000	8,800,000
Ceylon	25,500	4,100,000
Other Dominions, Protectorates and Mandates	4,763,110	49,852,000
India	1,900,000	319,000,000
TOTAL BRITISH EMPIRE ..	13,910,000	436,752,000

2. ITS POPULATION.

The total population of India, including Burma, and the Colony of Ceylon, amounts to 323,100,000. Of these seventy-two millions belong to various Native States, and are only indirectly under the control of England. The remaining 251 millions are under the direct government of British Officers. The whole country is divided into numerous provinces and kingdoms.

The entire population of the British Empire amounts to 436,752,000, and of this all but 117,752,000 are to be found in India. That is to say, three-fourths of His Majesty's subjects live in India. On the other hand, the entire British Territory consists of nearly fourteen million square miles, of which India is only one-seventh. So that this large proportion of our fellow subjects is packed together in a comparatively small area. For instance, Australasia (including New Zealand), with an area of 3,300,000 square miles (nearly double the size of India), has a population of only 7,500,000! Similarly Canada, with an area of more than 3¾ millions, has a population of only 8,800,000.

3. MORTALITY FIGURES.

According to the Government statistics, the average death-rate of India amounts to at least 30 per 1,000 of the population yearly. Taking this figure as the minimum, we find that :—

3	in every	100
30	,, ,,	1,000
3,000	,, ,,	100,000
30,000	,, ,,	1,000,000
3,000,000	,, ,,	100,000,000
9,570,000	out of the total	319,000,000

pass into Eternity every year! If nothing else could arouse us to do our utmost for India's Salvation, surely this one fact should be sufficient to stimulate us to do all that lies in our power. Compared with the vast mortality, how paltry do our present efforts appear!

It is also interesting to note the *causes* of death, since India is peculiarly liable to certain scourges, which at times decimate the population of certain localities, while every year, as an ordinary matter of course, they sweep away hundreds of thousands. Annually smallpox, plague, and cholera, claim a heavy toll, while more than half the deaths are usually attributed to fever.

4. THE RELIGIONS OF INDIA.

The chief religions of India are as follows :—

Hinduism, with say	170	million	followers.
Animism, or Spiritism, with say	60	,,	,,
Mahommedanism with say	70	,,	,,
Christianity, with say	5	,,	,,
Buddhists, with say	11	,,	,,
Sikhs, Parsees, etc., with say	3	,,	,,

(i) *Hinduism* is remarkable for :—

a. Its elasticity and adaptivity. Hinduism has adapted itself to every nation and class with which it has come in contact, giving a religious sanction to the social distinctions which, with remarkable sagacity, it saw to be more or less inevitable, and throwing them as it were into a cast-iron mould, which the greatest reformers have vainly sought to break up. Instead of attacking Buddhism, it swallowed it wholesale, and absorbed it into its system in a way which to Christians would, of course, be impossible. It has conquered its enemies by adopting boldly their leading tenets, and thus robbing them of their distinctive power. A similar attempt to swallow Christianity and Mahommedanism is in these very days being made by the followers of the Brahmo, Arya and other Samajes. The immense antiquity and success of Hinduism has been largely due to this genius for assimilation. In this way it has taken the wind out of the sails of its adversaries.

b. Its self-support. By means of its system of endowments and begging, Hinduism supports the largest staff of religious ministers of any religion in the world, with an average of about one in ten to the entire Hindu population! This makes it extremely difficult for any other religion to compete with them. The Hindu priests can beat all competitors out of the market for numbers and cheapness. The majority of them are content with the sky for their roof, a ragged loin-cloth for their clothing, the coarsest grain for their food, and water for their drink!

c. Its versified scriptures and parabolic teachings are also admirably suited to the popular mind. Even its most intricate and subtle philosophies are embalmed in verse. Set to simple popular chants or lyrics, the religious teachings of the Hindu philosophers and saints are sung into the hearts of the people, or, honied with parables and romantic tales, they are accepted wholesale without question. The great Sanscrit Epic, the Mahabharata, is by far the longest poem that was ever composed, and leaves Homer and Virgil altogether in the shade. At the same time, each country has its own favourite vernacular poets, whose writings abound with the most admirable sentiments, couched in oriental imagery. The people naturally cling to these, and despise the plain unvarnished utterances, which they are accustomed to hear from the generality of Christian teachers.

(ii) *Animism.*

Animist is a polite name for Spiritist, or Demonolater. They call themselves Devil-worshippers. Their theory of religion is that God is good, and will do nobody any harm; therefore it is unnecessary to worship Him. The demons, on the other hand, are wicked and must be appeased, or they will cause some disease, or other calamity. Hence they practise openly the worst forms of demonolatry.

Up to recent years they have been included in the general term as Hindus, but Government now recognizes that this cult is really quite distinct. Moreover, the Animists are excluded from Hindu temples.

Their exact numbers are somewhat difficult to estimate. The Census enumerators, in the districts where the Animists are found, are mostly Hindus, and are anxious to include under that term as large as possible a proportion of the population. It may, however, be reasonably reckoned that the Animists and Depressed Classes are practically the same, and that they number about sixty millions, though the census places the figures at much less.

(iii) *Mahommedanism.*

Mahommedanism ranks next in numbers to Hinduism. The simplicity of its creed accounts largely for its popularity, and for its tenacity, where once it has taken root. The well-known "Kalima," or declaration of faith, "There is one God and Mahommed is his prophet," embodies all that any one may need to know and believe, in order to ensure him an entrance to Heaven. Its simplicity is the very opposite of Hindu complexity and mystery. Every one can understand and propagate the faith. Hence every believer *may*, and to a large extent *does*, become a missionary. I have very seldom been in the society of Mahommedans, without their making an effort to convert me to their religion!

(iv) *Christianity.*

The Census of 1921 shows the total number of Christians in India to be nearly five millions, being an increase during the last decade of 840,000.

THE RISE OF CHRISTIAN MISSIONS.

It is commonly believed that St. Thomas visited South India, and planted the Gospel on the Western coast, finally crowning a life of successful work by a martyr's death. There appear to this day to be distinct traces of his work in the still numerous Syrian Church of Malabar, while a hill near Madras is well-known as "St. Thomas's Mount," and is said to have been the scene of his martrydom.

Others of the Apostles are supposed to have visited Northern India, and evidence of their having done so may be gathered from some of the doctrines, ritual and legends of Hinduism, which appear to be distinctly traceable to a Christian origin. Amulets are to this day commonly worn with Syrian and Hebraic hieroglyphics, which the wearers themselves cannot now explain. The forehead marks, so commonly used all over India, are also believed by some to be an abbreviation for Jehovah. Again, the idea of washing away sins as typified by baptism is commonly known and practised by Hindus.

From 1500 to 1600 A.D. great efforts were made for the conversion of India by the Roman Catholics. Their priests penetrated boldly to the Court of the great Mahommedan Emperor Akbar, who seems to have received them well. One of his sons is said to have become a convert, and to have died a martyr's death. There are other no less remarkable traces of their work in the probable foundation of the two great Hindu dissenting sects of Kabiris and Sikhs, which sprang into existence about this time. There is some reason to believe that both these "new religions" were founded by priests in disguise. The originator of the Kabiris, knowing the instinctive hatred of foreign religions, transferred Jerusalem to Benares, gave the Saviour an Indian name, and in every possible way, and to a degree which we could not of course pretend to approve, Indianized Christianity. Al Kabir is the Arabic for the Almighty.

Similarly in Sikhism, which arose about the same time in the Punjab, there are many remarkable and more than accidental resemblances. They practise baptism, and the Lord's Supper, and on their pictures are seen crosses, tongues of fire, fishes, and other symbols of Christianity. Of course, it must be remembered that in those times the priests must have carried their lives in their hands. To go and settle in the Court of Akbar must have been even more difficult and dangerous than it would be now to commence work in the Court of the Amir of Afghanistan. Hence, the pioneer priests were careful to avoid everything that might serve to give unnecessary offence, and adhered scrupulously to native customs. Their chief successes were, however, won in the South, and especially along the coast, where they boldly claimed and received the protection and assistance of the King of Portugal, at the time when the Portuguese were masters of the Indian Ocean. It is sufficient to mention the names of St. Francis Xavier, Beschi, De Nobili, and Sancho Panza. Certainly for devotion and self-sacrifice, it would be difficult to find their equals.

Beschi boldly penetrated to the centre of the Tamil country, adopted a native name and dress, lived like a Brahmin, mastered the language, and wrote poems equalling the most celebrated compositions of the native authors. He wrote many books and accomplished single-handed results which have, perhaps, never been surpassed for magnitude. His work is the more remarkable that, unlike Xavier, he was cut off in a great measure from Portuguese support, and was obliged to cast himself upon the Indians themselves.

The first Protestant Mission that entered the Indian field was that of the Danes in Tranquebar on the East Coast. Ziegenhalg and Plutschau, their first two Missionaries, landed in India in 1706, being sent forth by the King of Denmark, and patronized by our own King George I, who did not consider it beneath his dignity to send them a letter of encouragement. In 1750 they sent out the famous Schwartz, who laboured in the neighbourhood of Tanjore for 48 years. So great was his influence with the natives, that the Hindu Raja of Tanjore built him a church, and assigned him a large piece of land on which to settle his converts. The church is still one of the sights of Tanjore, though it is kept closed, and only one Christian service is now permitted to be held in it every year.

Schwartz was the founder of the Tinnevelly Mission. Soon after his death the Danish Mission was discontinued, handing over its converts to other Societies.

In 1793 the first English Missionary, William Carey, landed in Calcutta, and was followed soon after by Ward and Marshman. So great was the opposition encountered by them from the East India Company, that they established their headquarters at the neighbouring Danish Settlement of Serampore. A footing was gradually established, and from that time to this the number of Missions went on steadily increasing.

5. THE LANGUAGES OF INDIA.

It is common to speak of India as if it were inhabited by a single nation, talking the Hindustani language. This is just about as far from being true as it would be to speak of Europe as being inhabited by a single race talking, let us say, the English language! It is true that in all the civilized parts of Europe may be found persons who understand English, but the fact remains that to the mass of the population it is wholly unintelligible. Similarly India is inhabited by races, whose languages and habits differ as entirely from one another as do those of the nations of Europe. The following table shows roughly the chief languages of India, with the approximate number of people speaking such languages :—

Hindustani	100,000,000
Hindi	50,000,000
Bengali	48,000,000
Marathi	19,800,000
Telugu	23,500,000
Punjabi	16,000,000
Tamil	18,000,000
Burmese	13,000,000
Gujarati	11,000,000
Singalese	3,500,000

Besides these main languages, there are, of course, numerous other languages and dialects. Many of these are, however, confined to small tracts of country. Again, a large number of them are more or less related to one another, and the characters in which some of them are written are the same, or similar. For instance, connected with the Sanscrit are Hindi, Marathi, Gujarati, Bengali and Punjabi, all written from left to right, while Arabic Persian and Hindustani are written from right to left. This adds, of course, greatly to the difficulty of mastering a language, there being no universally adopted character or script, similar to the Roman in Europe.

The people of India are famous for their linguistic abilities, and we have several Officers who can speak five or six languages. But we have found it necessary as a rule to confine our European Officers to some one country and language, insisting on their learning the language of the particular people to whom they are sent.

6. THE CASTE, OR LABOUR PROBLEM.

Every one has heard of the castes of India. There are said to be no less than 1,929 different Castes, Tribes or Labour Unions in India. Of these only

3	number	more	than	10,000,000
21	,,	,,	,,	2,000,000
47	,,	,,	,,	1,000,000
206	,,	,,	,,	100,000
472	,,	,,	,,	10,000
803	,,	,,	,,	1,000

Usually the members of each caste follow some one particular trade, or profession. In fact, caste is a sort of gigantic *hereditary trades-unionism* of the most elaborate nature, and public opinion is so powerful in this respect, that it is almost impossible for the son to follow any other profession than that of his father. Of course, there are many undoubted advantages in this system.

(*a*) Every member of the community is trained from childhood, in its own family, to some definite trade or profession. Hence, there is no such thing as "unskilled labour." Ask any Indian what is his caste, and you will know in what particular form of labour he is skilled.

(*b*) Each trade guild is responsible in a large degree for its own government, and for the care of its poor.

(*c*) Division of labour is carried to perfection, and in fact almost to the absurd. The agriculturist cannot trade, the merchant cannot plough, the waterman cannot sweep, the *washerman* (not *washerwoman*) cannot groom the horses, and the scavenger can only do his duty. Hence, a well-to-do household will commonly employ as many as ten to fifteen different servants, such as a valet (bearer), a butler (khidmatgar), a cook (khansama), a kitchen-help (masalchi), a groom (syce), a grass-cutter (ghasiara), a gardener (mali), a washerman (dhobi), a waterman (bhisti), a night-watchman (chowkidar), a messenger (chaprasi), a scavenger (mihtar), a nurse (ayah), and three or four "punkawalas" to pull the large swinging fans by night and day! None of these will do anybody else's duty!

The Priestly class is again divided into priests who officiate, and temple servants who minister. There are numberless orders of Evangelists, some of whom preach and teach, whilst others are astrologers, musicians, singers, etc. It is in some cases rather difficult to separate the secular from the religious, the one is so much interwoven with the other in Indian life. From a Government Compendium of Indian Castes and Tribes I have collected the following statistics:—

Brahmins	13,693,000
Temple servants, etc.	546,000
Religious medicants and devotees ..	1,240,000
Other religious "sectaries"	1,023,000
Dancers and Singers	141,000
Astrologers	72,000
Musicians	32,000
Total ..	16,747,000

It may naturally be asked, how so gigantic a system of priesthood can possibly be supported? Probably at least one-half support themselves by manual or clerical labour. The remainder are supported entirely by temple endowments, or gifts of food and money. At the lowest computation I should suppose that India supports directly ten million religious teachers, whose sole employment is to preach their various tenets. In comparison with this, how insignificant must appear the entire force which Christianity is able to put into the field, and how earnestly we should pray that in this, the world's greatest, and perhaps most hopeful, harvest field, the Lord will be pleased to send forth a sufficiency of Spirit-filled labourers to reap the golden soul-sheaves that await their toil.

Chapter II.

THE ARRIVAL IN INDIA.

Nothing could be more picturesque
than your entrance into Bombay.
William Booth.

When the P. & O. SS. "Ancona" passed through the Suez Canal on its way to India in September, 1882, the opposing forces of Arabi Pasha and Sir Garnet Wolseley were drawn up near its banks at Tel el Kabir, and the first news that greeted the passengers, when they landed in Bombay, was that of the famous moonlight charge and victory, which assured the fate and safety of that great waterway to the East.

On board the "Ancona" was another expedition of a very different character. The peaceful invasion of India was planned by a leader for whom Lord Wolseley had so great an admiration, that he said in later years that there was one man whose genius for organization was such, that he would prefer him to anybody else as his Chief of the Staff, though he could boast of no military training, and that was William Booth, the Founder and for forty-seven years the General of The Salvation Army.

It was the same brilliant expert in oriental warfare, who was credited with suggesting to The Salvation Army Commander-in-Chief, that he should despatch a couple of his Officers for the conversion of the Mahdiists, who were ravaging the Sudan and threatening the invasion of Egypt, offering to escort them to the borders of the troubled area, and then to administer a not-too-severe chastisement, which he felt sure would make the Mahdi offer, not only an asylum, but a welcome, to these messengers of peace, as the victims of British tyranny!

The Army, that landed from the "Ancona," and made its first "moonlight charge" upon the powers of darkness in India, was unconsciously putting into effect the very policy that Sir Garnet thought might serve to pour oil upon the troubled waters of Madhiism.

Indeed, the reception with which the party met on the part of the Government of Bombay, would almost be enough to make those who might have heard of Sir Garnet's plan for the Sudan imagine that his mantle must surely have fallen upon the shoulders of Sir James Ferguson, the then Governor of Bombay. Not that there was any such friendly intention on the part of the latter as was the case with Sir Garnet.

It was only a little band of four Salvationists that landed at Apollo Bandar in Bombay, on the 19th September, 1882. And yet the effect produced upon the whole of India could hardly have been exceeded had it been equal in numbers to the British force at Tel el Kabir.

There was not an English or Vernacular newspaper in the country which did not publish the story of their landing, and continue for months to chronicle their doings. Even the conservative *Times* of London thought the invasion of India by The Salvation Army deserving of column-long cablegrams from the seat of war.

The Press not only reflected the general attitude and interest of the public, but that of the Government itself, from the Viceroy in Simla, and the Governors of the Presidencies and Provinces, to the Magistrates and Police, who sought for instructions as to how they were to deal with this novel invasion of the land.

When it was known that The Salvation Army was coming to India, it was naturally expected that it would land in such numbers as would somewhat justify its claim to be regarded as an "Army." But the splendid audacity and faith of William Booth caused him here, as elsewhere, to send out so small a force that their presence, or very existence, might well have been ignored. "Where is your Army?" was a frequent question on the part of the puzzled audiences, who had gathered to witness its arrival, and who could not believe that the few representatives before them composed the entire force that was aiming at such large results.

Nor was there any attempt to make up for lack of numbers by profound scholarship, or worldly influence, or wealth.

The little party of Salvationists who landed at Apollo Bandar consisted only of four persons, three of whom knew little more about India's peoples, history, geography, or languages, than they did about those of Mars.

The following description of the landing of the party in Bombay is taken from *The Indian Witness*.

"The Arrival and March of The Salvation Army.

"The Indian Contingent of the above army reached this port by P. & O. SS. "Ancona," yesterday, September 19th. It consists of four Officers, viz: Major Tucker, Captain Bullard, A.D.C., and Lieutenants Norman and Miss Thompson.

"Those who have arrived are in fine spirits, full of faith and joy. On leaving the ship they struck up one of the salvation hymns sung in England. After this, Major Tucker suggested having a Prayer Meeting in the boat, as they were sailing toward the Apollo Bandar. The suggestion was no sooner beyond his lips, than Captain Bullard began to pray very earnestly, and was followed by one and another, until all had led in prayer.

"The Army marched most of the way from the Apollo Bandar to their Headquarters at 10th Lane, Khetwady, singing at intervals.

"Each member of the party is very happy, and all manifest the fullest freedom in their expressions of joy and faith in God."

The next day a procession in War Chariots had been publicly advertised in the local papers, together with a great open-air demonstration on the Esplanade. To this the police had given their consent, refusing, however, to allow the use of any music. For a procession in the streets of Bombay, this was in itself a great handicap in a city where the bazaar noises are often deafening, and where all religious and marriage ceremonies are accompanied with the beating of drums and clanging of cymbals.

We felt the order to be an unreasonable infringement of our liberties, and decided to challenge it. Lieutenant Norman was a good cornetist, and the procession, surrounded by immense crowds, had not proceeded far, when the notes of his cornet rang out clear upon the air. He was promptly arrested by the police, and removed to the Girgaum Chaukee (police station), where he shared his cell with a European who had been arrested for being drunk and disorderly. Both were brought before the Magistrate next morning and fined, the drunkard one rupee, and the Salvationist twenty, for the crime of blowing his cornet in a religious meeting.

Considerable interest had been aroused by the announcement of "War Chariots." These turned out to be the ordinary Bombay bullock-carts, across which planks had been placed as seats.

The procession passed through the heart of the native town from Khetwady to Dhobi Talao. Immense and interested crowds had gathered along the route, and on reaching the Esplanade there was found to be a great audience, estimated to number twenty thousand persons.

Here a halt was made, and an open-air meeting conducted. The crowd listened with the keenest interest, and there was no sign of any disturbance.

The procession then traversed the city by another route, and reached its destination without any mark of hostility on the part of the onlookers. This was not a little surprising, as it was known throughout the city by all classes that the English Officials and newspapers regarded the Salvationists and their proceedings with great disfavour, and Bombay contains a strong element of rough characters, who are only too glad to seize the slightest excuse for creating a disturbance.

The Governor of Bombay, Sir James Ferguson, now took the unusual course of insisting on further restrictions being placed by the police on our open-air meetings. Not only was music forbidden, but our Flag was taken away, on the pretext that it might arouse fanatical feelings, and that our motto "Blood and Fire" would probably be misunderstood. We were prohibited even from singing as we marched, and instructions were given that if we refused to comply, we were to be ordered to disperse, and in case of refusal to do so, we were to be arrested and prosecuted for "taking part in an unlawful assembly, which was likely to lead to a breach of the peace."

We were most anxious not to appear in any way to defy the authorities, and having reason to believe that the proceedings emanated from the Governor of Bombay himself, I requested the favour of an interview, in order that I might lay our case before him. This was refused.

I turned to the Commissioner of Police, Sir Frank Souter, but he assured me that he was acting under orders, and had no option but to carry them out, though intimating that, but for this, he would not have interfered with us.

There was nothing left, therefore, for us to do, but to challenge the order by disobeying it. We were accordingly arrested, and taken before the magistrate, Mr. Dosabhoy Framjee, who fined us Rs. 100.

We declined to pay, and the magistrate ordered the fine to be collected by the sale of our few belongings. The Police Officer, who superintended the distraint, himself bought our meagre possessions for Rs. 100 and returned them to us. We were deeply touched by his action.

As an illustration of the keen interest with which the attitude of the Bombay Government was followed, and of the strong tide of sympathy manifested throughout India, a few extracts from some of the communications received will be read with interest.

From Babu Keshab Chandar Sen, the well-known and eloquent leader of the Brahmo Somaj, we received the following telegram :—

> "One of the largest meetings ever convened in Calcutta was held in the Town Hall this evening, to protest against the unjust treatment of the Salvationists in Bombay. Every seat was occupied two hours before the time of meeting. Addresses were delivered by the representatives of various religions and classes, and resolutions adopted condemning the action of the authorities, and sympathising with those unjustly prosecuted. A memorial to the Viceroy was adopted, asking for religious neutrality and equal protection to all. Great enthusiasm prevailed."

A little later we received from the same leader, who was then at the zenith of his popularity, the following letter :—

> "My dear Sir,
>
> "In acknowledging your kind message, I am delighted to observe that you so generously appreciate our

humble sympathy in the hour of your trial and trouble. Such fraternal sympathy as we have given you, in spite of wide theological divergence, is the tribute which every man owes to God's persecuted servants.

"You have been most unkindly and unjustly persecuted, because your love for God and Christ exceeds the limits of conventionalism. And as you have been prosecuted and harassed in the name of the Indian Community, it is incumbent upon every Indian emphatically to assert, that, far from having any sympathy with your persecutors, he is ready to protest against the cruel and unjust treatment to which you and your coadjutors have been subjected. Against this treatment are arrayed both the law of the land and the spirit of the Hindu nation, while the Religion of Christ blushes, as it looks upon the humiliating spectacle of Christians in high places trying the faith and patience of their poorer fellow-Christians. . . . You have wisely resolved not to resent. Forgive and forbear, and meekness will triumph in the end. Accept for yourself and your comrades our fraternal love and cordial good wishes, and

Believe me,

Yours ever,

for the establishment of the Kingdom of Heaven in India,

(Signed) KESHAB CHANDAR SEN."

At the same time we received the following letter from the well-known authoress, A.L.O.E. (Miss Charlotte Tucker), an aunt of the writer of this book, then working as a Missionary in the Punjab :—

"Thanks for your very interesting paper. I am glad that you have shown so unanswerably that we can all—Native or European, Christian, Hindu or Mahommedan—find shelter under the White Wing of the Justice of our noble Empress Queen. You know that she thanked the Salvationists for their efforts to benefit her subjects in England. Their object is the same in India."

CHAPTER III.

THE BATTLE FOR LIBERTY.

A monarch has a real ally in him,
Who, faithful to his duty—disregarding
His royal master's likings and dislikings—
Tells him unwelcome salutary truths.
Hitopadesa.

The next arrest took place in the jurisdiction of Mr. Webb, the Chief Presidency Magistrate, on 20th October, 1882. Six of our Officers, including myself, were arrested, and the usual charge was brought against us. I was permitted to conduct the defence. The following summary of our arguments is of interest, as it was circulated widely through India, and resulted in our position being clearly understood in the other cities, which we were about to visit, and in our being granted all over India the privileges for which we were contending:

I. We are charged under section 151 of the Indian Penal Code, which runs as follows: "Whoever knowingly joins or continues in an assembly of five or more persons *likely to cause a disturbance of the public peace*, after such assembly has been *lawfully* commanded to disperse, shall be punished with imprisonment of either description for a term which may extend to six months, or with fine, or with both." Now it is absolutely necessary in the interest of public liberty that this section should be carefully and literally interpreted.

1. *There was no Likelihood of Disturbance.*

The first stile that the prosecution have to get over consists in the words "likely to cause a disturbance of the public peace." Now we contend that there was *no reasonable likelihood of such an occurrence.* In proof of this we rely (1) upon the evidence of the police. From this it was clear that there was no basis of fact upon which the police grounded their opinion that a disturbance might occur. Indeed the opinion itself was expressed in the vaguest possible manner. It was admitted that on our first arrival we had constant processions which were not molested, or in any way interfered with by either Mahommedans or Hindus, though they had at that time reason to believe that Government intended to put The Army down.

(2) *There was no disturbance at the time of arrest.*

The second point to which I would call attention in proof of my assertion that there was no real danger of a disturbance, is that though we were in a Mahommedan quarter, there was no symptom of an intention to attack us. Why could not the police have waited till they saw some real danger of a breach of the peace? It is wonderful indeed, considering the action of the police, that no attempt should have been made to molest us.

(3) *Our Witnesses prove the same,*

that is, that there was no likelihood of a disturbance. Two of these witnesses, at least, must be regarded as "experts," one of them having resided in Bombay for nearly 35 years, and both of them being well known as leading men in the Mission Field.

(4) *Twenty Native Newspapers*

prove the same. These I have not been allowed to put in as evidence, but surely their utterances are entitled to the greatest weight, as being the opinion of the very people of India on whose behalf Government, or rather the police, profess to have interfered. *The Hindu Prakash*, with the largest circulation in Bombay, says, "This is a question of liberty of conscience. Why should it be granted to some, and denied to others? It is alleged that there will be a disturbance, but there is really no chance of it. The Salvation Army having given up their flags and trumpets, the police should give up their obstinacy." *The Kaisar-i-Hind*, after pointing out that for years Christian Missionaries have preached and sung in public without any evil results, goes on to say that "beautiful faces, a fine procession and sweet tongue battery are not things to be afraid of. The Government is well able to protect The Salvation Army, and the excuses of the police are simply ridiculous." The *Subodh Patrika* remarks that while The Salvation Army has been reinforced from England, the police have been reinforced by *a fresh accession of Anti-Salvation fervour.* Besides these, the *Samachar*, *Dynanodaya* and *Satyavadi*, all Bombay papers, have taken our part, while from Calcutta I can quote similar passages from the following papers: *Hindu Patriot*, *Bengalee*, *Amrita Bazar Patrika*, *Liberal*, *New Dispensation*, *Brahmo Public Opinion*, *Christi Mohila*, *Anand Bazar Patrika*, *Sulava*, *Indian Mirror* and *East*. Now these extracts prove that the people are not against us, for the Editors would scarcely venture to write articles contrary to the opinions of their readers.

(5) *The Salvation Army Fathomed.*

Lastly with reference to the unlikelihood of any disturbance, your Worship must remember, that the present circumstances are very different from those of the previous case in Mr. Dosabhoy Framjee's Court. When we first came to the country, there might have been some reason to fear that the people would misunderstand our motives and oppose us; but we have now been in the country more than a month, and they know very well what we are. The Indians have fathomed us, and they know that there is no reasonable excuse for our being interfered with now, as we admit there may have been when we first arrived. The question now is, not whether the organization or methods of The Salvation Army are peculiarly calculated to arouse the hostile feelings of the people, but whether the singing of Christian hymns and the preaching of Christian truths are to be forbidden, and whether the fact that these truths might be undesirable to a certain part of the inhabitants is a sufficient reason to justify the police in withholding their protection.

II. The next point to which I would call your Worship's attention is to the fact that the order forbidding us to sing, or preach, or carry a flag in the streets is *not a "lawful command"* within the meaning of this section, and if not lawful, then the charge must fall to the ground.

In proof of this I would first quote (1) A Ruling of the

Madras High Court (See II. I.L.R. (Madras Series) p. 132), which is quoted by one of the magistrates in the celebrated Calcutta Preaching case, with the following comment :—

> "The Commissioner of Police has no power to declare a lawful act to be unlawful, and to interdict by anticipation."

III. WE ARE WRONGLY CHARGED.

Our offence is not that of assembling or going in procession, but of singing and preaching in the streets. *Why are we not charged with this offence?* Because there is no law prohibiting us from doing so! (Laughter). It is a mere twisting of the Law to take section 151 and hang it continually over our heads. It will do away with the liberty of the subject altogether. In fact, your Worship can easily see that if such a gross misuse is to be made of this section, every one's liberty will be at the mercy of the police, who are robbing people of their rights on every hand, without saying so much as "If you please" (laughter).

IV. THE ARMY IS ENTITLED TO PROTECTION.

Even supposing there was likely to be a breach of the peace, however, we are entitled to protection. In this case the arguments of the police are most flimsy. As one of the vernacular papers said, "the excuses of the police are simply ridiculous." These are not my own words. I should not like to use such strong language (Laughter). But the fact is our rights are to be taken away and never returned. It is a sort of pawnbroking concern, where everything goes into pawn, and is sold off immediately (laughter).

Now, even if matters were in a most serious condition, I would urge that we are entitled to the fullest protection of the Law.

V. THE QUEEN'S PROCLAMATION.

Perhaps this is one of the most important points in our defence, and I trust that your Worship will observe most carefully the wording of the following paragraph :

> "We declare it to be our Royal Will and Pleasure that none be in anywise favoured, none molested, or disquieted, by reason of their religious faith or

observances, but that all alike enjoy the equal and impartial protection of the Law; and we do strictly charge and enjoin all those who may be in authority under us, that they abstain from all interference with the religious belief or worship of any of our subjects, on pain of our highest displeasure."

Now your Worship, we claim the protection of this Court under the plain terms of this Proclamation. Perhaps the most important part of our "observances" consists in open-air work, especially in a country like India. It is here clearly laid down that we are entitled to the protection of the law, and the police and other authorities are forbidden, under pain of the severe displeasure of Her Majesty the Queen Empress, to interfere, or tamper with, the religious rights of any of Her subjects.

VI. POLICE USURPATION.

In utter defiance of the above Proclamation, and indeed of all law, stands out the high-handed action of the police, to which I would in conclusion call your Worship's attention. They began by alleging in the previous prosecution, that the peculiar tactics of The Salvation Army are calculated to cause a breach of the peace, but they now take a higher ground altogether. They admit that a month's experience has clearly shown that there is nothing in the methods, songs, words, or processions of The Army calculated to arouse hostility.

It is the fact that they sing Christian songs, and preach Christian doctrines, that is now objected to, and Sir Frank Souter boldly declares, that he will deal just as summarily with any Missionaries acting as we have done, as he has with us. Not only so, but it is openly stated that the Ganpati processions of the Hindus will be stopped, if any disposition is shown to attack them, and it is more than hinted that the police will be glad of an excuse to stop the Mahommedan Taboots!

Thus the police are recklessly making havoc of the very rights that it is their duty to protect. In fact they are putting their hands right and left into other people's pockets, and robbing them of their cash (laughter)—or rather of something infinitely more precious than cash—their religious liberties. For ourselves we do not wish to act in any way contrary to the orders of Government! Far from it! But we cannot consent to be robbed of our legal rights in this manner, and we have taken the only course possible for the recovery of those rights.

We feel above all that precious souls are at stake, and we dare not hold back for the sake of a little personal suffering. The police made up their minds to attack The Salvation Army, and deprive them of their rights. Encouraged by their success, and with the confidence that they are being backed up by the highest Government Officials, as well as by the Courts of Law, they have now invaded the rights of all Christians, and have openly avowed their intention of turning next to the Hindus and Mahommedans. In the end where will Religious Liberty be?

Echo answers, "WHERE?"

In reply to the above arguments the Public Prosecutor alleged that most of the arguments for the defence had no reference to the present case. He proceeded to quote from the London *Times* an extract, saying that it would be dangerous to allow The Salvation Army to pursue their methods in India. He did not consider that the Queen's Proclamation had any reference to The Salvation Army.

He then reminded the Magistrate that two of the accused, Major Tucker and Miss Thompson, had already been previously convicted of the same offence.

The Magistrate, after giving the whole case a most patient hearing, adjourned his decision till the following week, when he discharged the accused, after cautioning them regarding the importance of complying, as far as possible, with the orders of the police, and assisting them in the discharge of their difficult duties.

An Indian newspaper, in referring to the Magistrate's decision, remarked that the ends of justice would have been better satisfied, if the Magistrate had warned the Police, instead of the Salvationists!

The Indian Witness, a leading Missionary organ, comments as follows on the case:—

"We constantly hear people asking 'If these Salvationists are really good people, why do they refuse to obey the *law*?' We reply that they are most willing to obey the law, but when a public officer issues an arbitrary order in flagrant violation of the law, they decline to obey *him*—not the law. Major Tucker has, in point of fact, appealed to the law, and appealed successfully, against the usurpations of the Police Commissioner.

"The more we learn about this extraordinary prosecution, the more indefensible and shameless does it appear. The cause of religious liberty in India owes much to Major Tucker for this speech, as well as for the intrepid manner in which he has contended throughout for rights which are dear to all."

After the victory in the court of the Chief Presidency Magistrate of Bombay, Mr. Webb, the time appeared to have come for accepting the many invitations we had received from all parts of India. Accordingly a tour was arranged in which the following cities were visited—Allahabad, Delhi, Lahore, Cawnpore, Lucknow, Benares and Calcutta.

In none of these places was any attempt made to saddle us with the same restrictions as had been imposed upon us in Bombay. On the contrary, while receiving the most cordial reception from all sections of the Indian population, most of the Europeans residing in these centres attended the meetings, and the police were only present in small numbers to ensure order.

Writing about the meetings in Allahabad, one of the two capital cities of the United Provinces, the leading English daily, *The Pioneer*, observes :—

"The crowds seemed to enjoy the whole affair immensely. . . Almost every carriage in the station brought up the rear (of the procession). . . Never has such a bumper house been seen."

Similarly with reference to the Lahore visit, the principal Anglo-Indian daily, *The Civil and Military Gazette*, remarks :—

"Sir Charles Aitchison (the Lieutenant-Governor of the Punjab) wisely determined to act on principles of toleration. . . As in the North-West Provinces, so in the Punjab, the contingent of The Salvation Army under Major Tucker has been allowed to march and counter-march, and blow its trumpet, pretty much as it pleased. Lahore cannot boast of being, like Bombay, so nicely civilized that the sound of a drum must not come between the wind and its municipality. Major Tucker, therefore, and his myrmidons, have merely been required to refrain from flagrant breaches of the law; and the police were ready, as they usually are, to deal with any disturbance of the peace. And this is the best way of treating these fantastic fanatics. . . What is to be avoided is fussy interference."

Still more emphatic was the opinion voiced by *The Statesman*, one of the leading Anglo-Indian dailies of Calcutta :—

"We have watched their proceedings here with much interest, and the first remark we would make is, that personal observation has entirely confirmed us in the belief that the dread of hostilities arising between them and any class of natives in India was due to utter ignorance of their character and ways, and almost equal ignorance of the people, and that the repressive and watch-dog measures taken by the Bombay Police were a ridiculous blunder."

Needless to say that the Indian Vernacular Press were still more emphatic in the opinions which they expressed.

From beginning to end the tour was a great success. The last place visited was Mhow, where we received a warm welcome from General Sir Robert Phayre, and from the veteran Presbyterian Missionary, the Rev. Dr. Fraser (father of Sir Andrew Fraser, a former Governor of Bengal). While at this station an interesting incident occurred, which is culled from the pages of our Indian *War Cry*.

THE SURPRISE OF INDORE.

"Among all the wonderful scenes we have witnessed, few events have surpassed in interest our recent attack upon the town of Indore in the Maharaja Holkar's Territory. The Military Cantonment, Mhow, is about 14 miles distant, and in arranging to pay it a visit, we had great hopes that the way might open up for a visit to Indore. Our local friends, however, did not think it would be wise, so that on our arrival we found that nothing had been arranged, and we were almost abandoning the idea, when a copy of a circular note, addressed by Sir Lepel Griffin, the Governor-General's Agent in Central India, was placed in my hands.

"After saying that we could be permitted to hold meetings in Mhow, though even there they would be regarded with extreme disapproval, this letter went on to say that, with reference to Indore and other Native States, Sir Lepel would not tolerate this burlesque of the religion of the ruling power, and that should we attempt to preach, or hold any public demonstration, we were to be immediately arrested and removed to British territory. Of course we are always anxious to obey any orders of the Government, so long as they do not conflict with our duty to God. But that we should be flatly refused permission to preach at all, and this on the ground that we made a mockery of religion, was a dangerous and unlawful assumption of despotic power which we felt convinced must be resisted.

"There was no time to consider. A few minutes' prayer and the plan was settled. We received the letter about a quarter past two, sent immediately for our faithful friend, Dr. Fraser, drove off to fetch Captain Thompson, and were unexpectedly joined by her host, Mr. Drew. The train was just late enough to enable us to be in comfortable time, and as soon as we were inside and had started, I read Sir Lepel's letter to our little forlorn hope, and asked them if they were prepared to be arrested. Of Captain Thompson I had no doubt, but I must say that I was both surprised and delighted at the hearty way in which the Doctor and Brother Drew threw themselves into the plan. None of us doubted for a moment that we should be arrested, and as we reached Indore, we looked round to see if there were any police waiting to meet us. But no, every one seemed busy thinking about themselves, almost too busy to bestow a glance upon our little party as we hurried past and got into a shigram. There was a fine-looking European, who somebody said was the Political Resident, and we almost expected to hear him say those now familiar words, 'I command you in the Name of Her Majesty the Queen-Empress.' On this occasion, however, we were allowed to go on our way unmolested, and drove straight to the heart of the city. Our charioteer took us to a large open space, right in front of the Maharaja's Palace.

"It was a splendid pile of buildings that towered right away above us, and from its windows we could see a number of interested spectators watching us. The beat of the drum and the jingle of the tambourine, mingled with the sound of voices, soon brought a large crowd running round, and we commenced our meeting without delay. A party of the Maharaja's Sowars galloped past, but evidently did not know what to make of us. We couldn't be Padris surely! They never made such a noise as that, nor were they ever dressed as Indians. It was evidently a 'tamasha' of some kind, and really their very horses seemed to enjoy the sound of the music as they pranced past us. The meeting had continued for some time, when a constable came, and most civilly informed us that, owing to the death of Sir Salar Jang, the shops were closed, and the town was in mourning; would we come the next day? We promptly fell in, and invited the crowd to follow us to a place just outside the city, but in a thickly-populated locality. From here we could still see the great Palace of the Maharaja, and addressed a big and attentive crowd.

"The meeting over, we jumped into the shigram and disappeared from the town as suddenly as we had come. A Maulvi who wished to ask some questions, came with us to the station. As we were driving along, he quoted the saying of a Persian poet that 'the heart of man is like a flower, which quickly withers if exposed to the burning rays of the sun. Even so, if roughly handled, the heart of man will close up and droop.' Thank God we were enabled to shower some raindrops of love upon him, and his heart opened out so wonderfully, that before we went away he embraced me most affectionately.

"Not long afterwards we were enabled to go off in a goods train, and by half-past nine that evening we were back in Mhow."

On returning to Bombay the little party, who had been so warmly welcomed in the various cities they had recently visited, were not long in learning, that so far as Bombay was concerned, strange to say, the attitude of the Authorities, instead of relaxing, had hardened into a determination to inflict severe penalties upon the Salvationists.

CHAPTER IV.

PRISONER No. 331.

Opposition cannot put down the valiant Army of Christ.

Keshab Chandar Sen.

On the 18th February, 1883, four Officers and eighteen members of The Salvation Army were arrested by the police in the jurisdiction of Mr. Dosabhoy Framjee, who had, on two previous occasions, inflicted fines on the Salvationists. Mr. T. Lewis Ingram, a prominent barrister of Allahabad, kindly volunteered his services, free of expense, for our defence, and travelled all the way to Bombay for the purpose. Mr. and Mrs. Ingram proved to be lifelong and unswerving friends of The Army.

The Indian *War Cry* of 21st February, 1883, contains the following announcement of the proceedings in the Magistrate's Court, showing with what a cheerful spirit the Salvationists met their difficulties:—

LOOK OUT!

GRAND HALLELUJAH

FREE AND EASY.

On Friday, 23rd Feb., 1883, at 11.30 a.m.

BY SPECIAL INVITATION

OF THE

COMMISSIONER OF POLICE

at the

GIRGAUM POLICE COURT.

MR. DOSABHOY FRAMJEE

WILL PRESIDE

Addresses will be given by
THE PUBLIC PROSECUTOR,
THE DEPUTY COMMISSIONER
OF POLICE,
and Several other Police Officers
On the Work of The Salvation Army.
The Famous
BLOOD AND FIRE BANNER
will be presented to the Audience.
A Large Body of Police will be present
and will suppress with a Strong Hand any
ATTEMPT AT RIOT.
Everything will be done decently
and in Order.
Admission Free! Come and See!
NO COLLECTION.

The trial and judgment occupied five days. At an early stage in the proceedings the Public Prosecutor withdrew the charges against fourteen out of the nineteen accused, on the ground that they had been acting under the orders of Major Tucker.

In the course of the trial it was elicited from the Commissioner of Police that the prosecutions had been instituted under direct orders from the Government of Bombay. The two following telegrams were put in as evidence :—

"Procession Salvation Army announced for Wednesday, please take such measures as Law provides for stopping such processions. Inform persons that Government do not object to their holding religious services in any place of worship or building, temporary or permanent, but cannot consent to permit public peace to be endangered by processions of an aggressive nature calculated to offend the religious feelings of the people.

C. GONNE,
Chief Secretary."

"The same liberty allowed to Salvation Army as to other Missionaries, but preaching should only be allowed on large open spaces, such as Esplanade, and no processions should be allowed before or after.

C. GONNE,
Chief Secretary."

It was shown clearly by Mr. Ingram that such orders were illegal. In the recent cases of the Salem Riots in South India, Chief Justice Turner quoted with approval the following Resolution of Government in a previous case of riots in Tinnevelly :—

" The public high streets in all towns are the property, not of any particular caste, but of the whole community, and every man, be his caste or religion what it may, has a right to the full use of them, provided that he does not obstruct or molest others in the use of them, and must be supported in the exercise of that right."

Mr. Ingram went on to say that his clients did not desire to ask for any mitigation of any sentence that the Court might see fit to pass upon them, should such be the case. On the contrary he desired to reiterate on their behalf that, so convinced were they that these observances were in compliance with the command of the Bible, directing them to go out into the highways and byways and preach the Gospel to every creature, that they would most certainly go out again in procession, and would cheerfully submit to any penalty that they might thereby incur. They would do this in no spirit of defiance to the law, but purely as a matter of conscience.

On Thursday, 8th March, the Magistrate passed sentence on the five accused, as follows :—

" Mr. Tucker, who is the head and fount of the whole offending, is sentenced to simple imprisonment for a month, and the other accused, Mr. James Ingle, Mr. Chas. Cousins, and Mr. W. Glacken are sentenced to pay a fine of Rs. 25 each, in default of payment to suffer simple imprisonment for a week. As regards the accused Private Turner, of the 4th King's Own, of whose offence due cognisance will, I suppose, be taken by the military authorities, I order that he be kept in custody till the rising of the Court and then discharged."

The three Salvationists, having refused to pay their fines, were committed to prison for a week, while Private Turner, after being kept under guard for a few days by the regimental authorities was released, it being evident that they did not take the same view of the offence as the Court had done.

The Bombay Jail is a large forbidding-looking building in what is practically the centre of the native town. Attached to it is a workhouse for destitute Europeans. By a peculiar irony of fate, some thirty years later, during the Governorship of Lord Sydenham, then Sir George Clarke, The Salvation Army was requested first to open an Industrial Home for Stranded Europeans, and then to actually take over the management of a new workhouse erected by Government for the benefit of the few remaining vagrants, of whom the streets had been to a very considerable extent cleared under the operations of the Home. The Foundation-stone of a new Industrial Home was laid by Sir George's successor, Lord Willingdon, as part of a large Social Institution, which will be referred to later on.

It was not, however, in the European workhouse, but in the Jail for Indians that we were confined, the Superintendent, Dr. Partridge, placing us in an unoccupied ward of the Hospital. He also observed that the official, responsible for assigning prison costumes, had facetiously given me one which was ridiculously ill-fitting and patched up. I was ordered a new, and at least better-fitting, prison dress!

The joy with which we received and served our sentences was viewed with no little surprise by the jail subordinates, and by those with whom we associated. Writing of his experience at this time, one of my fellow-prisoners, Brother Glacken, said:—

> "The few days that I was in Chauki were the happiest days in my life. It was like Paradise there, for I felt the presence of the Lord Jesus greatly. I am willing to die to let the people know of this happy salvation."

"While in jail," wrote Brother Ingle, "we still continued to have our meetings and prayers. I must not omit to mention that we were treated very kindly by the Jail

Officials. . . I never expected that I would have an opportunity of going to jail for the cause of my Saviour Jesus."

An appeal had been lodged with the High Court of Bombay against the sentence of the Magistrate, but it was not till I had been in prison for a fortnight that I was summoned to appear. I conducted my own defence, and in order to make the experience, I suppose, as disagreeable and humiliating as possible, I was brought before the Court in my jail costume, as Prisoner No. 331.

The application to the High Court had been accompanied, as is usual, with a written statement giving the grounds for appeal, but the interval of a fortnight in prison had given me an opportunity for considerably strengthening my arguments for the defence. The promise that when for the sake of Christ His followers were brought before Authorities, they were not to feel anxious, or worried about results, and that the Holy Spirit Himself would be mouth and wisdom to them, was indeed literally fulfilled. I had not much hope for a favourable decision. I had noted for one thing that the two Judges had brought with them a written judgment, so that it was doubtful whether the further arguments would carry much weight. Moreover, in a previous appeal, while the Judges had hinted strongly that the police had exceeded their legal powers, they had refused to interfere with the decision of the Lower Court.

Before, however, proceeding to pass judgment, one of the Judges said to me, "Well, Mr. Tucker, we shall be prepared to release you, if you promise not to do it again."

"My lord," I replied, "if I had a rope round my neck, and were going to be hanged the next minute, I would not make such a promise."

The Judges then proceeded to read their judgment, rejecting the appeal, and I had to return to prison to serve the rest of my sentence. It happened to be my 30th birthday, and I have ever since looked back upon it with unmingled joy and satisfaction. My stay in jail was a time of rich spiritual refreshment. I seemed to hear the Saviour saying, "Come ye apart into a desert place, and rest awhile, for there were many coming and going" (Mark vi. 31).

It was in this jail that I learned the useful art of being able to sleep without the mosquito curtain, which, as a

European, I had always hitherto looked upon as an absolute necessity!

While I was in prison the work was in charge of my chief assistant, Captain (now Commissioner) Bullard. A more energetic, capable and devoted helper I could never desire to have. After the decision of the High Court rejecting my appeal, the police decided to take further proceedings against The Salvation Army. Captain Bullard and two of our women Officers were accordingly arrested. This time the jurisdiction was that of Mr. Ryan. Greatly to our surprise, the Public Prosecutor, Mr. Cleveland, said that after reading the depositions of the police, he thought that it would be "unfair" to say that the present case came within the section of the Penal Code, under which the Salvationists were being prosecuted. He did not wish therefore to press the charge, but had no objection to the police proceeding with it.

Mr. Ryan: "I hold that view of the law myself."

Mr. Cleveland: "Perhaps your Worship will be able to see your way clearer if the evidence of the witnesses be taken."

The European Inspector, who made the arrest, then proceeded to describe what had taken place.

Mr. Ryan: *"How is it that they were arrested? There is no law to prohibit singing."*

In his judgment dismissing the charge, the Magistrate said that he knew of no law which empowers the police to stop persons singing in the street.

The final stage in the controversy had, however, not yet been reached.

I was released from prison at 7 a.m. on the 8th April, and was met at the prison doors by a large crowd of Salvationists and others. The *Bombay Gazette* thus describes the proceedings:—

> "Precisely at 7 o'clock the outer door was set ajar, and Major Tucker passed out. 'Amen' was the first word he uttered on beholding his friends, and 'Amen' was the loud response of the crowd. The Major and his comrades immediately adjourned to a piece of land in close proximity to the jail, and there they held a thanksgiving service, prayers being said and

hymns sung. Afterwards they formed in procession and marched to the headquarters in Khetwady, singing hymns *en route*. The police authorities did not interfere. Indeed, there was no need of their interference, there being no sign of hostility towards The Army on the part of the natives.

"In the evening a demonstration of the Major's friends and sympathisers was held in the Framjee Cowasjee Institute to celebrate his release. The hall was crowded in every part by Europeans and natives of all castes, all of whom were most orderly and respectful in their behaviour. The fervid eloquence of the speakers had a manifest influence on the audience. arresting the attention of the curious, and commanding the respect even of those who had sympathy, neither with the end which they had in view, nor with the means by which they sought to attain it."

On Saturday, 11th April, three days after my release from prison, the sixth and final prosecution took place, four Officers and six other Salvationists being arrested and brought before the Chief Presidency Magistrate, Mr. Cooper.

I was again permitted to conduct the defence, but before the case had come on for hearing, the magistrate sent for me to his private chamber. The Commissioner of Police, Sir Frank Souter, was seated beside him. I took a seat at the opposite side of the table.

Mr. Cooper opened the conversation by saying, "Now, Mr. Tucker, it is surely time that these disgraceful proceedings should come to an end." I replied that I and my Comrades would be glad if such could be the case. The Salvation Army were law-abiding people. The magistrate then said, "The Commissioner of Police has consented to withdraw this prosecution, if you will undertake, on behalf of The Salvation Army, that you will obey the orders of the police in future."

It was barely a fortnight since I had received a similar proposition from the Judges of the High Court. Lifting up my heart to God for guidance, I replied,

"Will your Worship be so good as to give me in writing exactly what you wish me to promise, and I will then be able to say whether we can agree to it or not. To place the religious liberties, not only of The Salvation Army, but of all Christians, entirely at the discretion of the police, would obviously be unreasonable, and would only open the door to future disputes and difficulties."

Mr. Cooper: "I think, Sir Frank, that is a fair proposition."

Sir Frank Souter assented, and the clerk was sent for and took his seat beside me.

Mr. Cooper commenced to dictate the terms, but was evidently at a loss what to say. Turning to the Commissioner of Police he said, "I think, Sir Frank, that as you are familiar with the whole controversy from the beginning, you had better dictate what you wish The Salvation Army to promise."

Sir Frank agreed. I felt very much as we may suppose Daniel to have felt in the lions' den, when, to my surprise, the Commissioner of Police turned to me, and said, "I think that the best plan will be for you to say what you are willing to accept, and we will then consider how far we can agree to the same."

If ever I had realized the presence of God, it was in that room. Just as He had seemed to close the mouths of the Magistrate and Commissioner of Police, so He seemed to open mine. I turned to the clerk, and dictated the following—

> "Considering the police authorities are of opinion that it would, under the present circumstances, endanger the public peace for the members of The Salvation Army to pass down the strictly Mahommedan quarter of the town in procession with singing, I will undertake on behalf of the members of The Salvation Army in Bombay not to sing when passing down such quarters, while such danger continues to exist; provided that such processions are allowed in non-Mahommedan streets, unless some special emergency should arise."

Somewhat to my surprise the Magistrate turned to the Commissioner of Police and said:—

"Well, Sir Frank, I think that is quite within their rights."

The only amendment suggested by the latter was the

insertion of the words, "while the police consider that there is danger of a disturbance."

I argued that this was a question which would have to be decided by evidence in each case, and with this view the magistrate concurred. With a slight modification in the wording of the last sentence by the magistrate, these terms were agreed to, and a copy was submitted to the Public Prosecutor, Mr. Cleveland. It was an open secret that he had only consented to prosecute us at the point of the bayonet, under strong pressure from Government. Hence no difficulty was anticipated in regard to his acceptance of the proposal.

However, to our surprise, whatever may have been his motive, he returned the paper with an endorsement to the effect, that while he had nothing to do with any agreement the police might subsequently enter into with The Salvation Army, yet so far as the present case was concerned, the Salvationists had broken the law, and he could not consent to withdraw the proceedings.

It was necessary, therefore, for the case to continue, and the witnesses for the prosecution were duly called and examined. When I rose, however, to present the case for the defence, the magistrate said that it would not be necessary for me to do so. As I took my seat the Public Prosecutor rose and, in closing the case for the prosecution, harangued the Court with great vehemence, demanding a severe sentence upon the Salvationists for defying the law.

The case was then adjourned to the following day, when the magistrate delivered his judgment. Producing the agreement, which was acceptable, he said, to the police and the Court, he proceeded to acquit the accused.

Thus ended—permanently as subsequent events have proved—this long and painful controversy, which finally established the rights not only of The Salvation Army, but of the entire Christian community in India, to procession and hold open-air meetings with singing and music—a right which has never since been challenged.

CHAPTER V.

THE GUJARAT REVIVAL.

Go straight for souls, and go for the worst.
William Booth.

Among the Cadets who entered The Salvation Army Training Home, just opened in Madras, was a young Singhalese, belonging to one of the leading families in Southern Ceylon. When Arnolis Weerasooriya was still a child, his mother used to take him to the Pansala (temple), where his uncle was the Chief Priest, and place in his hands flowers to offer at the shrine of Buddha. The grandmother of Arnolis was a staunch Buddhist, who had performed the most meritorious actions called for by her religion. She had dedicated one of her sons, then a boy, to the priesthood. Another of her sons, who had perverted to the Christian faith, she had treated with great cruelty, and outcasted from her family. She had also been painfully conscientious in the performance of penances, and votive offerings. Her death made a profound impression upon her family.

Instead of the peaceful death-bed, which they had anticipated, for one who had been so strict in the performance of her devotions, she was seized with despair, and cried out that she was a lost soul, going to hell. Her priest-son was in attendance at her side, and had drawn up a long list of her meritorious actions, and presented them to his mother, reminding her that they far outnumbered and outweighed* any sins that she might have committed. But she pushed them away, reiterating that there was no hope for her. She was a lost soul. And then she became

* The theory of Buddha was that at death a person's good deeds were weighed against his sins, and, if they outnumbered the latter, the soul passed to a higher state of existence, finally culminating in Nirvan, or Annihilation.

unconscious. The priest could not bear to see his mother die in such despair, and requested the medical attendant to jerk the lock of hair on her forehead, a custom which is sometimes resorted to, when it is desired to bring back a dying person to consciousness for the signing of a will, or a last farewell word. The eyes opened, and the son said, " Mother, look here at the list of your good deeds." But again she pushed them away, and with the words, " Lost ! Lost ! " upon her lips, she expired.

The father of Arnolis had been converted to Christianity some years previously, and had endured much persecution. At first his wife and children had deserted him, but his persistent love and patience had finally won them over. The family was a large one, but the father was determined that his children should have the fullest benefits of modern education. Arnolis was sent to Trinity College, Kandy, for his education, and after passing through successfully, became a teacher there.

One day there fell into his hands, *From Death unto Life*, by Haslam. As young Weerasooriya read this book he became convinced of the fact that, though he was a nominal Christian, he had never been truly converted. He passed through a season of great agony of soul, but at the morning service in the chapel, he suddenly realized that his burden of sins had rolled away, and that he was in very truth, born again.

" I am a child of God," he said to himself, and as he uttered these words, his heart was flooded with joy. He looked at the clock and noted the very moment the change had taken place.

In the following letter Weerasooriya writes to tell his father the news of his conversion.

20th July, 1882.

" My dear Father,

" The first and the chief news I have to tell you, is that I have found *Jesus*, fully and truly. I cannot express how happy the mind is. It is a great reality and a treasure not to be given up for the world. The change took place last Sunday morning. This love I wish to be telling always of. All difficulties sink in the bottom of the ocean. *All sins forgiven*. No weight on the mind (Prov. xvi. 3; Psalm xxxvii. 4). Realize these words, and you will no more be unhappy. It is a peace of mind which cannot be expressed. I will tell you, when I come, the wonderful things God has since done for me."

And now commenced a wonderful work of grace in the College. Out of the fullness of his heart, he spoke to the students, and one after another was converted, until the revival swept through the school, to the surprise and joy of its teachers and leaders.

Writing the name of JESUS in large letters on separate pieces of paper, he pressed each letter to his lips in passionate adoration.

"Is there anybody who loves Jesus more than I do?" he would ask himself. "Let me sit at their feet and learn from them, whether it be in books, or in living representatives, that I see it. Nobody shall love Jesus better than I do, cost what it may."

That was his self-appointed standard, when news came that Captain Gladwin of The Salvation Army was visiting the town and conducting meetings. Young Weerasooriya was present, and was smitten to the heart. "Here," said he, "is someone who loves Jesus better than I do. A white man has discarded his usual dress, and adopted that of India for the love of Jesus, and to win the people of the East, whereas I, a son of the East, have discarded my native costume for that of the foreigner. How then can I say that I love Jesus equally well? I have found someone now who loves Jesus better than I do. Can I rest satisfied with taking a second place? Never!"

His decision was quickly made. He hurried to his home in Dodanduwa, near Galle, and told his father and mother that he had decided to cast in his lot with The Salvation Army. The storm of opposition which had met David Weerasooriya, when he renounced Buddhism, was reproduced on a smaller scale in that Christian home. For a fortnight he was confined to his room, but it was not a wasted season, for it was spent in prayer, which finally prevailed, Arnolis wringing a reluctant consent from his parents, and joining The Army in Madras, which was then the nearest point to which our operations had reached.

After enlisting as a Cadet, he wrote to his father as follows:—

MADRAS, 16*th February*, 1883.

"Bless the Lord, all the time He is with me. I have fully tried The Army and its modes of work. These modes have the touch of the Apostles very much. I have signed the papers of The Army, and sworn allegiance to it. May God help me to stick to it till I die!"

During a brief visit that I paid to Madras, I realized that our newly-arrived Cadet possessed remarkable natural gifts, as well as a special baptism of the Holy Ghost, which would make him extremely valuable for the salvation of India. I felt that God had sent us the kind of man who would help to unlock India's heart for the Saviour, Whom he so passionately loved himself—a prophet, and more than a prophet. I was not disappointed. From the day we first met to that of what seemed to us his too premature death from cholera but five years later, he proved to be unfaltering in his devotion, as he was capable and intelligent in his leadership. Although not a Brahmin, he had the noble commanding appearance of one, and when we were travelling together, the people would often gather round him, and ask if I was one of his chelas (disciples). If at a railway station he happened to go to the filter for water, high caste travellers would call out to warn him that the water was polluted.

Further reference is made to Weerasooriya in Chapter VIII, but these few words of introduction seem necessary to explain what occurred during the early months of 1884. Our first eighteen months in India had been occupied in visiting the principal cities of India and in establishing a permanent work in Bombay, Calcutta, Madras, Poona and Colombo. More than two thousand persons had publicly professed conversion, but only a small proportion of these had actually joined our ranks.

In the cities, where we were working, persecution was keen, and the converts from Hinduism and Mahommedanism, though numerous, disappeared almost as soon as they were made. It was in most cases impossible to find any trace of them. They had been carried off by their relatives and friends.

We were well aware that almost all the converts of Christianity in India had been secured from the ninety per cent. of her village populations, and that the cities constituted a specially hard, and for the moment almost hopeless field, for which our small force was as yet insufficient.

Where and how to strike out into the heart of the rural population was to us a difficult problem. The entire country had been mapped out and divided up amongst the great Missionary Organizations as their own peculiar reserves, which must not be invaded or interfered with with by new bodies, or individuals, seeking to find a field for labour. However vast the territory they might profess to occupy, and however small the number of their workers, and however limited might be their operations or success, owing to lack of funds, or for other reasons, it was regarded as an act of sacrilege to invade the sphere of influence for which they happened to have given each other and themselves a " mandate."

The unoccupied fields were few, and those that existed were barren and unfruitful. Sometimes health conditions were unfavourable. But as a rule it was the sparseness, or peculiarly bigoted character of the population, that had compelled the workers, who had attempted to occupy these fields, to abandon them as being for the moment impracticable and fruitless.

It was in March, 1884, after a memorable half-night of prayer for special guidance at our Bombay Headquarters, that I sallied forth with Weerasooriya in quest of some rural area where we might plant our workers. If we had a preference in our minds, it was for the Punjab, where I had a special knowledge of the villagers and their dialects and customs, gained while I was in Government service. But we resolved to follow the leadings of the Spirit.

The first point at which we halted, for what we intended to be but a brief stay of two or three days, was Ahmedabad, the capital of British Gujarat. We had no knowledge of the people, or of their language, and hence did not propose to make a survey of this field, when one of those providential incidents occurred which serve to lead God's people.

A telegram from Bombay recalled me to attend to some urgent business, which had arisen since our departure. I left Weerasooriya to accept a warm invitation, which we had received, from a Christian village named Ranipur, in the vicinity of the city.

I had scarcely reached Bombay, when he telegraphed to say that a revival had broken out among the Christian villagers, urging me to return at once, and take part in the same. The simple recital of his own experience as a nominal Christian, and of his remarkable conversion, had taken powerful hold of the people, and had led them to search their own hearts, with the result that many, if not most of them, confessed to never having experienced a real change of heart.

Never can I forget the wonderful scenes that followed! Tears rained down many of their faces as they confessed their past sins, to be followed by shouts of joy as the burden of their guilt rolled away. The first of the converts was a notorious character, who though nominally a Christian, had been a drunkard and had lived a wicked life. On one occasion he had tied a rope round his wife's waist, and let her down into the village well, till the water reached her chin, when she was rescued by the villagers. On another occasion he would not allow her to cook the family meals for seven days in succession, pouring water on the fire each time she lighted it. At other times he would dress up in his wife's clothes, and go about the village insulting the people.

Extraordinary confessions were made, amongst others that of lying in wait to shoot one of their European Missionaries. The mutilation of cattle, which had strayed into their fields from adjoining villages, was a form of cruelty which was regarded with peculiar horror by their Hindu neighbours.

Naturally their frequent misdeeds had caused much distress to the leaders of their Mission, and they had received many warnings, and even punishments. But nothing in the form of a revival had taken place.

About this time a great gathering had been arranged for the Christians of the whole province at one of the Mission centres, the small country town of Borsad. We were earnestly invited to attend. The converts of Ranipur told us that what had been true of themselves was largely true of the other Christians in Gujarat. Few, if any, of them really knew what it was to experience a change of heart, and much open sin was rife amongst them.

We were present during the services, but it was not till these were concluded, that late at night the people gathered round us in the open-air, and begged us to conduct a meeting. Then followed a scene that could never be effaced from the memories of those present. It was Easter, and the beautiful Paschal full-moon shone down upon us from a cloudless sky, almost turning night to day, and rendering unnecessary any artificial illumination. The hot weather had already commenced, and all were glad of the comparative coolness of the night breeze, which was scarcely sufficient to stir the leaves of Gujarat's noble peepul trees.

Our hearts were deeply stirred as we gazed upon that sea of perhaps a thousand upturned faces, so eagerly drinking in every word. The difference between a true and nominal Christian—a Nicodemus who had been born again, and one who had not yet experienced the glorious change—one who was indwelt by the Saviour, and one whose heart was destitute of His personal presence, had only to be mentioned to evoke an immediate response. I can still see Weerasooriya pouring out his heart upon that crowd and urging them to claim for themselves what he, himself a son, if not of India, of the East, had received. The fact that he came from Lanka (Ceylon), the fabled Island, famous in Indian mythology, where the Demon Rakshas and their monarch Ravan dwelt, added to the dramatic character of the scene and to the power of his eloquent appeal.

Surrounding us sat the converts from Ranipur, burning with the fiery zeal of their first love. To describe the prayer meeting which followed would require an angel's pen. The invitation for decision was no sooner given than scores, and then hundreds, rushed into the space which we had cleared for seekers in the centre. They flung themselves on their knees, bowed their faces to the ground, and with tears streaming from their eyes, confessed their sins and sought definite forgiveness, and received Christ into their hearts as their Saviour from sin. And then followed a wonderful period of rejoicing, mingled with songs and testimony, such as in all my Salvation Army experience, stirring as it had been, I had never witnessed. The simple and sincere faith with which the people received and rejoiced in Christ as their Saviour from sin made us feel that surely the time had arrived when a nation should be born in a day.

It was not a little remarkable that in this meeting the way was led by a venerable Christian named Girdhar Bhai. Forty years previously he had heard of Christ, and had travelled south some two hundred miles to the then nearest Mission station to beg the Missionaries to come to his country, where he was sure that a rich harvest of souls awaited them. The invitation was accepted, and resulted in a large number embracing Christianity.

That he should lead the way produced a profound impression upon the rest of the community, who regarded him with reverence and affection as the one who had introduced Christianity and the Bible to their country.

Asked afterwards by a European whether, during all this long period, he had been a hypocrite, he replied nobly in the figurative language of the East, "No, Sahib! I have not been a hypocrite. I have been like a match in a closed box. The Salvation Army has opened the box and struck the match and now I have the Fire!"

"Mind," said his interrogator, "that you do not lose it."

"Sahib," he replied, holding up the stick which he carried to support himself, "wherein is the strength—in this stick, or in the hand that holds it?"

"In the hand that holds it," was the reply.

"Sahib! I am but a feeble stick," said the aged veteran, "but I am in the Hand of an Almighty Saviour, and He is able to keep that which I have committed to Him." Girdhar Bhai remained faithful to the end, and has long since passed to his reward.

CHAPTER VI.

THE GARDEN OF INDIA.

Though the whole city be on fire,
  What do the song-birds care?
The wingless cats and rats lament,
  Who cannot cleave the air!
Heed not, my soul, the fires of care!
Rise Godward on the wings of prayer!

Akha, a Gujarati poet.

Gujarat has sometimes been called the Garden of India. A tract of country stretching perhaps for some two hundred miles from south to north, and about one hundred miles from west to east, is famous for the fertility of its soil, and consequently also for the density of its population. It is sometimes said that not a stone is to be found in the entire region, except such as have been imported. A rich alluvial soil, watered by several large rivers, and with an abundant underflow, tapped by countless wells, rewards the toil of the dense agricultural population which inhabits this area.

The model primeval Indian Village, divided into water-tight compartments, is to be found here in its perfection. In its central and most aristocratic quarter dwell the Patidars, the hereditary ancestral landowners of the domain, resembling very closely the old feudal lords of ancient Europe, with their tenants grouped around them. Physically they are a tall, well-built, noble-looking race, accustomed to rule, expert farmers, owning large herds of some of the finest cattle and buffaloes to be seen anywhere in the world. The buffaloes are unrivalled for the richness and quantity of the milk they produce, whilst the cattle are devoted to draught purposes, all the milk of the cows being given to the young stock.

A sad and depressing feature of the buffalo production is that, while the male buffalo is a powerful beast and capable of useful work, it is so completely outclassed by the Gujarati bullock, that the young male buffalo is unwanted and is allowed to die of slow starvation. The Mahommedan butcher would be glad to take it, but strong religious sentiment prevents this. They could be obtained by thousands free of cost, and transported to other parts of India, where the labour of the buffalo is valued and utilised, but it can only be done on the definite condition that it is not to be made over to the butcher. We made inquiries in this direction, but found the cost of transportation to be prohibitive. We have never, however, abandoned the hope that some arrangement of this kind may ultimately be carried into effect.

Next in rank and importance to the Patidars come the Kolis, who are the hereditary cultivators, but not, as a rule, owners of the soil. Physically they too are a fine race, but noted for their turbulence, and very considerably addicted to crime, causing the Government and police constant trouble. Another important and very numerous group consists of Weavers, who are here known as Dhers. At one time they supplied their own villages with all the cloth that was required, and were extremely prosperous. But the introduction of Manchester and Indian mill-made goods has reduced them to a condition not far removed from extreme penury.

The Potters, Chamars (leather workers), and Sweepers constitute three other communities, which complete the self-contained village system from time immemorial. Each village was able to produce its own food, clothing, shoes and crockery. The interchange of goods and labour made cash payments unnecessary, and the little money that did circulate was only required for the purpose of paying taxes, or to be turned into jewellery, the Indian Savings Bank for a rainy day. Any further superfluity of cash was buried in the ground.

This village arrangement was very convenient for agricultural purposes. The landowner was supplied with an abundance of cheap labour, an important consideration, especially during harvest, in a country where animal life is considered sacred, and where in consequence birds, monkeys and squirrels abound.

As the crops begin to mature, the ordinary industrial operations of the village artisans cease, and Weavers, Potters and Chamars join Kolis and Patidars, first in protecting, and then in gathering, the vast crops that beautify the fields.

The grain once gathered is divided into great heaps, and assigned to the various communities, being distributed amongst their families by the headmen of each group. Originally one of the largest heaps used to be set apart for the payment of the land-tax to Government. It was a fixed proportion, amounting to about one-fifth of the total crop. The substitution of a cash tax for a grain payment has created an opportunity for the moneylender to step in, and at times his exactions have led to serious difficulties, which Government has tried to meet with legislation, with only moderate success.

Coming in as strangers into the midst of this communal life, our temptation would certainly have been to aim at the noble-looking Patidars and Kolis for our next revival. In this we should have made a serious mistake, from which we were fortunately guarded by our Indian Christian friends, who let us know that it was the Dher, or Weaver Community that was by far the most prepared to accept Christianity. It was from their ranks that the largest accessions to the Mission had hitherto taken place, and it was this class that the most readily opened their hearts and homes to us and to our Officers. It was no uncommon thing to see from thirty to fifty, or even more, kneeling at the penitent form.

While poor, they were intelligent. No one who saw the deftness with which they operated their antiquated hand-looms could doubt this. They were the artisans of the village—the very class from which Christ recruited His Apostles, and The Salvation Army in every land has obtained the bulk of its recruits.

In going to them we practically cut ourselves off from the Patidars and Kolis, who regarded them as polluted, and refused them admission to their homes and to the quarters inhabited by them. Their very touch was defilement, and it was only in later years, after we had come to be well known and believed in by these so-called higher castes, that even our European Officers could freely approach them, as we are able to do to-day.

There was, however, no disposition amongst either Patidars or Kolis to accept, or even listen to, the Gospel, and our time would have been wasted had we devoted ourselves to their salvation, superficially promising as the material might have seemed to be.

Much time and money have been ineffectually expended upon what may be called perhaps the "attractive" classes. It has been argued by workers in the Mission Field that one convert made from these classes will be of greater value than hundreds, or even thousands, from the depressed classes. But the correctness of this dictum may well be questioned. They do not, as a rule, make good apostles to the depressed classes, who prefer leaders of their own caste, and are tempted to believe that those of the better-off and better-educated classes will misunderstand and look down upon them.

We found the Dhers of Gujarat to be an exceedingly fruitful field, and devoted ourselves heart and soul to their salvation. As a result we have built up amongst them a solid, spiritual and well-organized work.

It was also in Gujarat that we first developed our Educational system, which has undoubtedly helped largely to strengthen and consolidate our work in India.

1. It was created wholly and solely for the benefit of our own converts.

2. It limited itself almost exclusively to rudimentary education, taking advantage where necessary in exceptional cases of existing Government or private institutions, where the higher branches seemed in the interest of our own work to be desirable.

3. It made religious teaching, not only an essential part of our instruction, but its very backbone. In later years our Young People in Gujarat were formed into "Gayan Tolis," or Songster Brigades, and "Faliadars," which became the agency for conducting family prayers in village streets among groups of families, besides forming a very attractive feature of our evangelistic work. Many of them composed their own songs to popular Gujarati tunes.

4. Connected with the Village Day Schools were central Industrial Homes for Boys and Girls, with a view to preparing the best of our children for their future careers as Officers, Teachers of our own Village Schools, or Foremen in charge of our various Industries. Those who proved to be unsuitable for either of these avocations gravitated back to their own homes. Hence there was no blind alley education, and no training of all our children to clamour for Government positions as clerks and baboos, one of the greatest drawbacks to the modern system of education in India.

The boys are taught various useful handicrafts, which will be advantageous to them in after-life, while the girls are trained to be good housewives, and adepts at needlework. Corresponding to every Boys' Home there is always a Girls' Home of about equal numbers, and the training given to the latter is as thorough and systematic as to the former. This relieves the parents of a great anxiety. It is ingrained in their minds that the first duty which they owe to their children is to get them suitably married. Hence the increasing tendency to early engagements and marriages. A child is no sooner born than the parents begin to look around for a suitable match. To obtain such becomes increasingly difficult. Unmarried boys and girls are exceedingly hard to find and are much sought after.

To prevent an engagement once made from being broken, money usually passes, and in order to tie the knot with increasing firmness the village Brahmin of the particular caste is called in to perform ceremonies of a mystic and binding character. Although the children return to their parents, an engagement is treated as if it had been an actual marriage.

Our Boarding Schools for girls enabled us to cope effectively with this difficulty. The parents realized that there was no need for premature action, nor was it necessary for them to plunge into debt to raise the necessary money. For every boy and girl a suitable partner was being trained, and would be in the highest sense a " help-meet."

Our Girls' Boarding Home in Gujarat is picturesquely located on the wall of the city of Ahmedabad on the bank of the river Sabarmati, The Boys' Home is situated in

Anand, a great and prosperous railway centre, from which branch lines radiate to all parts of the region.

In connection with our song books, Indian tunes, *War Cry* and publications of Gujarat, Brigadier Dayasagar (Burfoot) has done yeoman service. His familiarity with the Gujarati language has been of great value to The Army, and has been further supplemented by his study of other Indian languages. He has also very successfully acted as "*liaison Officer*" for placing The Army and its work in close touch with some fifty or more vernacular papers, which have evinced the keenest interest in us, and have gladly placed their columns at our disposal.

This again has served to familiarize the leaders of Indian thought with the aims and objects of The Army, and when our annual Anti-Drink *War Cry* has been published, leading Mill-owners and employers of labour have circulated thousands of copies amongst their work-people, not infrequently contributing a few warm words of commendation from their own pens.

Another valuable form of help has been the sinking of wells. The high caste quarters of the Gujarat villages are usually supplied with a sufficiency of excellent wells, but access to these is as a rule denied to Dhers and other depressed castes, who have either to resort to the open tanks, in which the cattle drink, the buffaloes wallow, and the people bathe and wash their clothes, and which frequently dry up in the hot weather; or their water has to be fetched from distant wells in the fields.

It is difficult for those who have been accustomed to draw an abundant supply of water from a tap every time they need it for bathing, washing, drinking, cooking or other purposes, to know what it must mean in a hot country like India to fetch water from a well, for the daily needs of a household. Let us suppose that the water-level is from thirty to fifty feet from the surface of the ground, and as a matter of fact, it is not infrequently from sixty to eighty feet. A large brass or earthen vessel is tied to the well-rope, and let down into the water. When the vessel is full, it is drawn up and the contents emptied into the two or three other similar vessels which contain the household supply for the day. When the vessels are full, each one is hoisted on to the top of a woman's head, or tucked under her arm. It is not unusual to see a woman with two, or even three, of these great heavy vessels balanced on the top of her head. This work is relegated to the women of the village, and my wife often says that had this been the duty of the men, pumps and taps and cisterns and windmills would have been introduced long ago!

There is only one thing worse than a village well, and that is not to have one available, or to have it at some distant point, whence every drop of water requires to be daily carried in this laborious manner! To the poorer classes amongst whom we labour, the possession of a well is a boon, which is the most precious of any, next to Salvation.

It so happened that when the late Colonel Balwant (Spooner) was in charge of the work in Gujarat, he became personally acquainted with one of the Raises (merchant princes) of Ahmedabad. He suggested that as a memorial to some departed members of his family, it would be an excellent plan if he would have some "Memorial Wells" sunk, with a tablet commemorating the dead. The Colonel's suggestion met with a ready response. One of the favourite charities of India is the sinking of wells, or supplying of water to travellers. For a thousand rupees each, three wells could be sunk at villages where they were greatly needed. The order was given, and in due course, the Colonel called upon the generous donor and offered to accompany him on a trip to the villages concerned. When the motor car brought the giver and his guide to each village, there was a grand turn-out of all the Salvationists. The gratitude of the people, their unalloyed joy at the possession of such a treasure, hitherto unknown in the history of that particular caste, the garlands and addresses that were presented, the songs, and village music, the enthusiasm, deeply touched the heart of the giver. As a result of his tour a further order for more wells was generously given.

Chapter VII.

LANKA, THE PEARL OF THE OCEAN.

> Of one thing I am quite satisfied, and do not need a single fact or argument to convince me, and that is that we have no more right to impose Western notions on the Eastern peoples, than the Eastern peoples have to impose their notions on the Westerns.
>
> *William Booth.*

The news of the Gujarat revival, and of the prominent part played in it by Weerasooriya, had reached Ceylon, where a promising work had already been commenced in Colombo. It was only natural that Weerasooriya himself should urge the claims of his own native land. Familiar as he was with its condition, people and languages, he felt satisfied that, in the rural districts, we could obtain results at least equal to those which had been witnessed in Gujarat.

The following beautiful description of the Island is from the pen of one of our early Officers :—

" Delicate tints of violet and gold line the skies that canopy fair Lanka's Isle, while fringing its borders, like a phalanx of plumed warriors, is a wilderness of coconut trees, with a ridge of yellow sand begirdling them from the wash of the in-rolling sea. Bamboos rustle and shake out their ribbony foliage at the touch of each passing breeze. Broad-leaved fruit trees soften with their shadows crimson flowers, springing beneath, while the breath of dawn is sweetened by the perfumed touch of cinnamon and other spicy shrubs, and the evening is be-starred by myriads of fireflies gemming the tangled vines and moonless trees.

" In the streets of its cities, especially Colombo, mingle races from the uttermost parts of the earth. There we behold the white, or red and white robed Moorman, the yellow-garmented Buddhist priest, the picturesquely-attired Singhalese, the half-naked Tamil coolie, the industrious Burgher and the Englishman.

"The Singhalese are a frank-hearted, courteous people, to love and be desired. We desire them, and seek to win them. And as the ocean with its moving, throbbing waves, encircle Ceylon, so we in the name of our Christ mean to begirdle it with a living wall of Salvation."

Of the old Singhalese capital, Kandy, the scene of Weerasooriya's education, conversion, and revival, the same writer says :—

"Kandy is one of its most charming places inland. The native town has long straight streets, lined each side with pretty little whitewashed houses. Emerald hills, covered with equatorial vegetation, surround it, from whence flow streams, which unite with each other, forming a lovely lake, sheltered and draped by beautiful trees. Charming drives run round it, and footpaths, if followed, lead into most delightful openings. Here the giant bamboo rears its head a hundred feet or more, while the tall silk cotton bush is a pleasant contrast, crowned with crimson flowers, and climbing plants twine and twist themselves in endless profusion, shading the earth, till its damp breath moistens all around.

"Here stands the famous temple, where a large tooth is kept, supposed to be Buddha's. This temple is kept very carefully, and surrounded by the usual votaries, male and female, who buy flowers from the flower-sellers, who throng the temple, and thus give their simple offerings, which every morning are cast out from the temple by the priest—but the perfume of the gift remains, to tell it has been there. Here the young priests are trained, and a very charming sight it is to see this brotherhood, in their saffron robes, walking or sitting 'neath the shady trees, meditating, and preparing for their calling."

It was on the 1st January, 1885, that I arrived in Ceylon, whither Weerasooriya and another Officer had already preceded me.

The rural district which had been selected for our operations was inhabited by a Singhalese caste known as Paduas, and was situated at the base of the mountain range leading up to Kandy in the centre of the Island. Rice-growing was the chief occupation of the inhabitants. Paddy fields stretched in all directions, whilst clumps of coconut palms and other trees grew on the higher grounds. Rainfall was abundant and water plentiful for irrigation. The scenery was beautiful, but the climate was extremely malarial, and at certain seasons it seemed as though the entire population was prostrated with fever. Living, as it were, with one foot always in the grave, the people seemed peculiarly ready to welcome the Gospel.

It is true that the first village visited, that of Talampitiya, regarded the visitors with suspicion, and even went so far as to refuse them their hospitality. A cave is still pointed out where the Officers spent the night, and outside which in the morning were seen the footprints of a leopard that had prowled around.

But the adjoining village of Hewadiwilla sent them a cordial invitation, and they had a wonderful "break," and witnessed similar scenes to those which had taken place in Gujarat. The Holy Spirit was outpoured among these simple people, and the work spread rapidly to the surrounding villages.

When news of these happenings reached Talampitiya, they sent an earnest invitation, and similar results were repeated in their midst. We cull the following extracts from the reports of these meetings written at the time by Weerasooriya himself :—

Hewadiwilla.

"About three weeks ago, we commenced to enlist Soldiers here. Hallelujah! As we look at these three weeks we feel sure of winning Ceylon soon.

"More than one hundred Buddhists saved and testifying! Only the other day the village headman said that there was indeed *very little room for the devil* now in the village. This headman is fully saved. He weeps at the meetings, and speaks of talking to the Lord often till after midnight. You could at times see big drops of tears running down the cheeks of a young Buddhist, saved only a few days ago, because Jesus had made his heart white like milk—("kiri vage una,") and he loves Jesus so much. (Snow is unknown in these tropical regions).

"One who sells appas—a kind of bread—in the village is in a rage, and has once or twice disturbed our meetings.

For six thieves, who have been in the habit, for months past, of stealing arecanut and selling it to him at a cheap rate, to his disappointment, did not make their appearance with arecanut and other stolen property as usual before dawn. On inquiry, he found that the whole gang had got saved the previous night at our meeting.

"I am particularly thankful to God for the blessing that the Lord is pouring upon the women of this district. Their simple hearts when touched by the Holy Spirit, seem to brighten up wonderfully. They say that they love the Song Book, because they understand it. Some of the Christian women, to whom it has been for long years a burden to be present at a meeting for two hours once every week, now say that it would be a great pleasure for them to be at our meetings, if possible, from morning till night. Men, women and children shew by their happy faces that they really enjoy our singing, praying and talking, and this with an increased interest.

"We had told them that the Loku Mahatmaya was coming, meaning our "Headman"—that is, our Major. Many, I observed, were filled with anxiety for a time. They wanted to make special arrangements. When I told them that he was bare-footed, slept under trees, ate the poorest village food, carried his own luggage, either in a box or in a bundle on his shoulders, or on his head—in short, that he was in no way bigger than a white Singhalese man, they seemed to be delighted and came to him as freely as they would come to any of us natives.

"The visit was a gloriously blessed one to the Officers and Soldiers in the village. The power that I had often seen in Gujarat, came pouring down now, and filled our souls, and the Soldiers for the first time began to see that there was a great deal more than getting saved and testifying to that all the days of their lives.

"The meetings were devoted to free, straight talks about 'Sampurna gelavima,' or Full Salvation and Power. On Sunday we had five meetings. If there had been time they would have arranged for more.

"There was not much talk for the unsaved, still about five came forward for Salvation during the day.

"We had one little meeting in a small mud hut. It

was in the house of a Buddhist family saved during the month. About twenty saved Soldiers were present besides ourselves.

"The Major commenced singing in Singhalese a line which runs as follows:—

> "Ma nissa devlova sepa at eriya,
> Yesu tamai mage Swami!"

> "For my sake He abandoned the joys of Heaven,
> Jesus indeed my Lord!"

"As we went on repeating this one couplet our souls began to feel the baptism of love. Our hearts became very tender suddenly, and our voices trembled. All knew that it was the presence of the Master.

"Have you ever felt Jesus' presence? Have you ever wept simply because you love Jesus? Have you ever wept for the perishing world?"

Soon after my arrival in Ceylon, I proceeded to visit the work in this newly-opened district, and was greatly cheered by the manifest evidences of its deeply spiritual character. The following account of this trip was written by me at the time, and gives some interesting particulars as to the nature of the work, and our plans for making it self-supporting.

"We find ourselves in a densely-wooded country inhabited by a race called Paduas. Cadet Rice and his Hallelujah wife are in charge of Fort Billigodapitiya, and report over thirty Soldiers enrolled and well-saved, besides others of whom they could not be quite so sure. We slept at Jemadar Patrus' home, and went over in the morning to the Officers' quarters. It beats any that we have got even in Gujarat, size fifteen feet long by about ten feet broad. One room, about eight feet by nine feet, served as kitchen, dressing-room and bedroom. The rest is an open space enclosed only on three sides, which does duty as parlour. No chair or furniture of any kind. Cadet Rice was chopping wood for the fire when we arrived, and then went off to get water from the well down the hill. We could not help praising God for the courage and devotion which enabled him and his wife to stick bravely to such a difficult post.

"A country walk along a narrow footpath, through beautiful green rice fields and dense woods, brought us to Fort Hewadiwilla. We went direct to the Officers' quarters, a small hut something like the other, but nearly twice the size and more substantial. Both places have been given to us, rent free, by the Soldiers, who are arranging at both of the villages to put up rather more substantial huts, where we shall be able to have our meetings as well.

"After our arrival we took our palm-leaf baskets and went out begging for our morning meal. The people were rather surprised, but evidently very pleased, as we said 'Api pinapati ava.' ('We have come to beg for food.'). They quickly loaded us with enough for at least eight persons, though there were only five of us, and we afterwards found that the other party had been stopped at a house, where they insisted on providing them each with a full meal.

"The custom of 'pinapati' is in some respects peculiar to Ceylon, and is commonly practised by the Buddhist priests. About ten or eleven o'clock they may be seen going singly from house to house with a vessel under the left arm, and their shawl thrown over it. They will stand silently before a house. If the owner has got nothing ready they pass on. Usually, however, you will see in a few moments one of the women come out with a dish containing rice or vegetables. It is emptied into the vessel and then the giver falls down and worships the priest, who gives his blessing and passes on. Large temples with scores of priests and without endowment are thus supported cheerfully by people, who could not afford to give them money, and the priests are thus also saved the trouble of cooking.

"Huge torches are made about six feet long from palm branches and serve to light us along the narrow difficult paths on dark nights. They are necessary too to keep away the snakes which are common in these jungles. One of our Soldiers has just brought a very venomous one which he has killed close by. It is about three feet long, and is said to be a great enemy of the cobra, which is also found in this country. When the two happen to meet, they are said to have great fights, the one swallowing the other. Fortunately this kind cannot see well in the day-time and are therefore easily killed. The boa constrictor is also occasionally met with. Not far from here there are also tigers, bears and elephants. Most of the people are armed with guns in this neighbourhood, so that these animals keep at a respectful distance, but a little further in the interior we are told that people never go out without taking a sort of hatchet with which to defend themselves in case they should meet with bears.

"However, our interest centres not in the beautiful scenery and trees, but in the human beings who inhabit this Paradise. Here too we find the hell of sin in their hearts, although outside there is everything to draw them nearer to God. However, we have been having some grand times among them. Many are saved and give a clear bold testimony. Others are still hesitating, but the fire spreads and we are having constant invitations from other places.

"A party of Buddhists are walking along the road. We overtake them and urge them to get 'Gelavima.' They decline, and as we walk on we hear one of them say, 'The days of man are one hundred and twenty years. If a man lives in sin for sixty years, then if he performs works of merit for the remaining sixty, the good works will counterbalance the bad ones. Then instead of being sent to hell, or doomed to pass through many existences as an animal, he will obtain the bliss of "nirvan" and will cease to exist.' He did not explain what would be the case if the man died before reaching his one hundred and twentieth year. Still this was a rather more comfortable idea than that of another Buddhist, who said to us plainly, that there is no forgiveness of sin. For every sin that a man commits he must be punished. God cannot possibly forgive. He must continue to receive the punishment of his sins till the term of punishment is exhausted.

"'There is no God!' This is commonly alleged by Buddhists in Ceylon. 'Where is God?' said a Buddhist the other day. 'I cannot see Him. I do not believe He exists. It's all a fable.'

"'Gelavun Karaya' is the name by which we are best known among the Buddhists in the South. It means simply 'Saviours.' Sometimes they call us 'Hamadru, a title of respect which they only give to their own priests."

Chapter VIII.

COLONEL WEERASOORIYA.

"The Cross is the attraction!"

Weerasooriya.

At this juncture we received what we could not but regard as a "Macedonian cry" from some Christian friends in Moratuwa, a densely-populated district some fifteen miles south of Colombo. It could hardly be called either a town or a village. The inhabitants were nearly all carpenters or fishermen. Whilst there were considerable numbers of Christians to be found among them, by far the greater number were Buddhists, with a large admixture of Roman Catholics.

The people were well off, and had substantial and comfortable homes, quite different from the mud and palm-leaf huts to which we had now become accustomed. Each cottage had its little plot of land. The soil was sandy, but the coconut, jack-fruit and bread-fruit trees flourished. Indeed, so did everything of a vegetable character, and the cottages were embowered in a wealth of greenery, while the moist climate, tempered with the soft sea breeze from the Indian Ocean, made it the home of a healthy, vigorous, stalwart race, the very backbone of the Singhalese nation.

The whole coast-line from Colombo to Galle, and on thence to Matara is occupied with a long string of similar villages, one of which, near Galle, was the ancestral home of the Weerasooriyas.

After our experiences in Gujarat and the Hewadiwilla region, we should have felt inclined to refuse the invitation. But the friends who invited us would not take "No" for an answer. The question of finance need not trouble us. They would erect immediately a palm-leaf "Maduwa," or hall, capable of holding four or five hundred persons, and this in due time should be replaced by a solid substantial building constructed with the red "kabuk" stone which abounded in the neighbourhood.

The Fernando family, who headed the invitation, had a prosperous carpentry business, and held a leading position among the Christian community. They were men of their word, and their promises were more than fulfilled. One of them became a prominent and earnest Salvationist. All of them stood by us with unswerving fidelity, and proved to be a tower of strength. They knew the district well and were confident that the time was ripe for a revival. They were not mistaken.

The campaign commenced on the 17th January. The hall was packed to overflowing, and in three weeks there were more than 100 professed conversions; during the third week there were numerous surrenders among the women, and the awakening extended to the surrounding villages. A month later we were able to telegraph that, since the opening of the work, there had been about 350 seekers, and that the women converts were taking part in the marches and open-airs and were testifying boldly.

It must be remembered that the idea of coming forward publicly to the penitent form to seek Salvation was as completely repugnant to the tastes of this community as it would be to a respectable Church of England congregation in the West End of London. Still more distasteful, especially to the women, was the idea of speaking in public and testifying about the blessing they had received. But it was a repetition of the glorious scenes spoken of in the Acts of the Apostles, when the Holy Ghost fell upon the converts and they immediately began in the joy of their hearts to "speak with tongues!"

During the commencement of this campaign we made the Maduwa our home, as well as the Headquarters and meeting-place. The benches consisted of planks sawn from the trunk of palm trees, attached to sections of other trunks which were cut transversely and fixed in the ground. With a tambourine for a pillow, and nothing softer than the plank for a bed, we became such experts that we could balance ourselves on the narrowest of them.

After a few weeks, however, we transferred our Head-

Sketch of the Headquarters in Moratuwa, Ceylon, with the Author in the doorway.

quarters to a tiny palm-leaf hut under the coconut trees. It was about ten feet long by about eight feet broad. In the evening, after the meeting was over, we would refresh ourselves with a bath in the sea. This led to our striking up a friendship with the fishermen who ply their trade along the coast.

The following account of how this came about was written at the time, and gives an interesting glimpse of what occurred :—

> " Simon Peter saith unto them, I go a fishing. They say unto him, We also go with thee ! "

" It is a beautiful moonlight night. The meeting is over and our hearts are full of joy, for we have had a glorious haul of fish—human fish—about seventeen of them in the net, as we pulled it to shore. We felt ready for anything the Lord might want of us. I told Him so. The Lord took us at our word and gave us a surprise.

" Captain Weerasooriya and myself went down to the beach for our customary bathe. It was the only spare time we could get. When we reached the shore we found that the net was being pulled in. We could hear the shouts of the fishermen, as they pulled it to land. ' Let us go and help them,' said Weerasooriya. It was a new idea altogether. We looked at one another. We were in regular fishermen's costume, stripped (except waist-cloth) for our bathe. It would just suit. We lost no time in arguing or considering about it.

" Soon we were right in among them, pulling away with all our might—no sham about it. At first they are not quite sure whether we are making fun of them. Soon they can tell we are in real earnest. We shout louder than any of them, only instead of their ' Hoi, hoi,' we shouted ' Hallelujah,' ' Gelavima ' (Salvation). After a little time in the excitement of the pulling, we find them almost unconsciously repeating the same words.

" At last, after an hour's hard work, the end of the net is brought to shore. It is in the shape of a huge bag. All this time we had been pulling in the two long arms which stretched out about a quarter of a mile to sea, and obliged the fish to find their way into the bag at the end. At first, no doubt, the fish would feel but little alarm, as the sides of the net were so far apart, that they had plenty of room to swim about. But gradually, as they found themselves drawn closer and closer to shore, they would struggle to escape. We found the whole catch right at the very end of the net, where it was so strong that there was but little chance for them to get away. Probably it was a very similar net that was used by the Galilean fishermen in the times of Christ.

"As the fish were drawn to land, gasping and struggling to the last, we could not help thinking of the nets that the devil had spread to catch unwary souls. A little fancied liberty at first, but the strong meshes of sin pressing closer and closer, till at last the sinner is dragged to shore, only to be cast into the flames of hell. We thought, too, about the other net, which we were casting into the seas of sin to drag sinners to a place of safety.

"The fishermen told us that at times they would have such a huge haul of fish that the net would burst and all would make their escape. When they did succeed in bringing them to shore, they would be able to get as much as £40 for a single haul. At other times they would have to toil for days and nights together, and yet catch scarcely anything. For six months in the year they would have to stop fishing altogether, owing to the roughness of the sea.

"We rejoiced that our Salvation boat could go out in all sorts of weathers, and that we could have some of our biggest hauls when the sea was roughest."

In the year 1886, the first International Congress of The Salvation Army, took place in London, and India was invited to send representatives. These included converts from Hinduism, Mahommedanism and Buddhism. Weerasooriya was one of the party.

We were warned by our Headquarters that, while we were heartily welcome as delegates to the great Congress, we must not expect or plead for reinforcements of men and money, as the resources of The Army had been taxed to their utmost by the many extensions already carried out, and by the needs of other lands.

However, the detachment from India carried everything before it, and such was the wave of enthusiasm that was aroused by their appearance, and by their impassioned appeals, that our hopes and prayers were more than realized, and when the contingent prepared for its homeward journey, it was accompanied by one of the largest missionary reinforcements that had ever been dispatched for the conversion of the heathen.

Weerasooriya's life and influence had made itself felt, both in public and in private, wherever he appeared. None could gaze into that noble countenance, or meet those flashing eyes, or listen to those burning appeals, without realizing that the nations whom he represented were indeed worth saving. It was decided by the General that fifty Officers should be at once sent out.

While the majority of this reinforcement was set apart for the extension of the work in Ceylon, a small nucleus was also formed for the purpose of commencing a campaign among the Tamils of South India. These had scarcely reached Madras, when a pleasant surprise awaited us in the form of a generous donation from a friend in China.

A few weeks previously we had forwarded to London India's contribution of £100 for the annual Self-Denial Appeal of The Salvation Army. At that time Rs. 1,500 had seemed indeed a large sum for India to contribute, remembering the extreme poverty of the people among whom we worked, and the severe hardships and sacrifices endured by our Officers. But we had sent it without deductions, and with a willing heart, although it left our War Chest empty.

About the time we were signing the cheque for London, that was to take our Alabaster Box of Ointment to the feet of Jesus for the salvation of other nations, another cheque was being drawn up, unsolicited, by a friend in China for £5,000. The two cheques were probably written about the same time, and must have reached their respective destinations on nearly the some date. The generous donor was none other than Charles Studd, the well-known founder of the Heart of Africa Mission, then working with the China Inland Mission, and formerly famous as one of England's leading cricketers. "I feel mysteriously impelled to send you this amount," he wrote, "though to do so I shall have to draw upon my capital."

He would surely have felt gladdened could he have

witnessed the scene, when his letter was opened, and its contents were disclosed. It proved to be one of the turning-points in our Indian history.

It enabled the Founder to arrange for the dispatch of another reinforcement of fifty Missionary Officers, and Colonel Weerasooriya was summoned to London to assist in their selection, preparation, and despatch.

In describing his journey to England, on an Italian Liner, Weerasooriya wrote as follows :—

"Everything so far has been beautiful, excepting the food. I could not at all take the Italian food, so I spoke to one of the Officers and arranged with the cook of the Mahommedan sailors. The ship is like a little city or kingdom. We have got the Hindu, Mahommedan, Parsi, and Christian quarters. We have got one Nawab (Indian Prince) and his staff.

"The Nawab is really a prince in every way. He called me near, and got all the information he could about salvation and The Salvation Army. I was struck with his happy smiling face. I thought because he was a native prince he will be very proud, and won't have much to do, especially with poor natives. He was very patient, and not only listened when I explained, but (he being the only one of the party present that knew English) took the trouble to translate every sentence carefully to his staff, who gladly drank in every word that fell from the lips of the noble interpreter. They got me to sing, and quite enjoyed it. They were not satisfied until I sang to them 'Hae, mere waste' (Alas, and did my Saviour bleed !) over and over again, to that Persian tune, 'Taza ba taza.' 'How do you get your living?' asked the Nawab. 'Very often we go begging for our meals, and people give us food and money.' His Excellency gave me two Mahommedan silver coins before leaving.

"Next morning I was reading my 'Guide' when the Nawab, staff, and several European gentlemen, came and wanted me to sing. When I had sung one or two verses in English and Hindustani, I had to sing the Nawab's favourite, 'Hae, mere waste.'"

Weerasooriya was at this time my right hand. The Founder and the present General, then Chief of the Staff, had come to know him personally and had formed a high estimate of his abilities, and he was promoted to the rank of Colonel and second in command of the work in India and Ceylon. It was a unique and daring innovation in the history of Missions, being the first instance, so far as I am aware, of an Indian being placed in command of European Missionaries. He had under him at the time about 150 European, and 150 Indian Officers. He was accepted and followed with equal alacrity and cheerfulness by all, and I cannot recollect any instance of our European Officers objecting to his authority.

They loved him and regarded him, not only as a man of God, but as a born leader of his people.

The influence wielded by Weerasooriya was something truly remarkable, and certainly without parallel in the history of missionary work in India. The secret of his power is perhaps disclosed in the following description of how he settled a difficulty which had arisen between two Officers.

The Lieutenant thought she ought to be Captain. Explanations seemed useless, so he arranged a private meeting with them. He got one of them to fetch some water, and began to wash their feet. They burst into tears, and tried to stop him. But he declared that unless they allowed him to do it, they should have no part or lot with him in the Heavenly Kingdom. While he washed, they wept. Then they had a melting time before the Lord, and he heard no more of any ill-feelings. Afterwards, the Captain took to washing the Lieutenant's feet, and love was the conqueror.

A still more striking example is related of the way in which Weerasooriya overcame the opposition which he sometimes encountered. The incident took place in Kandy, while the revival which followed his conversion was at its height. The striking conversions that then took place, not only amongst Christian students, but amongst Buddhists, caused an outburst of hostility among the rougher elements of the Buddhist community. The life of Weerasooriya was threatened.

Weerasooriya met the opposition in his own characteristic fearless way. He announced that he would conduct an open-air meeting, outside the city in a jungly place, and invited those who wished to do so to accompany him, thus affording the roughs just the sort of opportunity they required for wreaking their vengeance upon him. A number of them accepted his invitation to attend the meeting, and there can be little doubt that they had evil intentions towards him in doing so. Taking only one or two of his friends with him, he proceeded to the spot. Arrived there, he produced a rope and a knife. The rope, he explained, was for the purpose of binding him securely to a tree, so that he could not resist them. The knife he had provided to enable them to execute their intention of killing him, in case they had not brought any of their own. The lonely place had been chosen because, had they made an attempt to kill him in the town, the police would probably have interfered, and they might have been captured and punished.

Here in this lonely spot none could see or interfere. As his Master and Saviour had died for him, so he too was willing to die for them. The scene of Weerasooriya bound to the tree, offering them the knife with which they could execute their threat, awed and conquered those turbulent characters. One after another slunk away, without accepting his challenge! He was left alone with his one or two friends, who released him and returned with him to the city. No more was heard of the threats against his life.

Weerasooriya threw himself heart and soul into the Tamil campaign in the cities of South India, but did not live to see the subsequent answer to his prayers in the glorious revival in Travancore, where the scenes which had taken place in Gujarat and Ceylon were afterwards repeated.

The Colonel's father, Mr. David Weerasooriya, gives the following account of his meeting with his son, upon his return to Ceylon, after joining The Salvation Army:—

"I found them to be regular fakirs, and I thought I must, at any rate, make my son change his dress. Mr. Tucker, Arnolis, and myself got into the coach together. On the way, I said to him, 'Son, look at your hair. It is very shabby. You are very foolish to let it grow so long.

But he said, 'Father, don't look at the outside, but look at my heart, how clean it is!' I talked no more.

"When we got down from the coach at Dodanduwa, hundreds of people rushed to see this wonderful mystery. In one of those meetings I and my daughter felt our sins and got properly saved. Praise God!

"Arnolis was called to the Buddhist temple, to see his uncle who was then the High Priest of South Ceylon. His uncle said, 'I don't like to see you in this awful dress,' and asked him to have another, to which Arnolis replied by enquiring whether his uncle would like him to put on the robe of a Buddhist priest, and talk about Jesus, who had cleansed all his sins away. 'No, no,' said the uncle. He then said, 'Arnolis, you are living just the same as our Buddha said you ought to live. You have no lust for the world. Also you are humble and patient. But you must not say it was Christ who altered your mind. You must say that you acquired it by your own exertions.' There were at that time twenty priests present, and I asked him if any of them possessed these good qualities by their own power. They looked at one another, but no one answered.

"From our village they proceeded to Galle, where a wonderful work broke out. Many souls were saved. One thing most beautiful occurred here. A rough knocked Arnolis down, kicked and beat him. Instead of striking back, he kissed the hands of his persecutors, and, kneeling down in the road, prayed that God would forgive and save them!"

In connection with this visit to his uncle, it is interesting to note that Arnolis had himself been dedicated to the Buddhist priesthood by his father, previous to his conversion to Christianity. As a token of his consecration a thread had been tied round his arm by his uncle, the High Priest. This thread was broken by his father, when he became a Christian. Arnolis, then a boy of twelve, was so angry at his father's action in breaking the thread, that he got hold of his father's Bible, tore it and trampled upon it.

Writing to welcome Commissioner Rahiman to India, he says:—

"I imagine to myself how grand you will look in the

native dress, and become one among the millions of native women. I should like to be the one who will wash your feet all the time you are in India."

It was while I was on a visit to England that a cable reached me from India, on 18th May, 1888. It was indeed like a bolt from the blue. It announced that Weerasooriya had died of cholera.

Born on the 20th September, 1857, he had not yet completed his thirty-first year at the time of his death.

A European Officer had been stricken with cholera, and Weerasooriya, with his usual intrepidity, had hurried to his side to nurse him. As is well known, the disease is very infectious, and Weerasooriya caught the dreadful contagion, and while the one he had tended recovered, he himself succumbed.

All the Officers on the Indian Field felt that they had lost a more than brother. He had endeared himself alike to European and Indian. To myself personally the blow came with crushing force. From the day I met him first in the Madras Training Garrison our hearts had been knit together, and we had seen eye to eye on the great questions which concerned the salvation of India's millions.

He had especially endeared himself to our Founder, and to the present General during his brief visits to England, and all had anticipated for him a long and brilliant career crowned with a great harvest of souls. But God's ways were not as ours.

His death was triumphant, tenderly his comrades nursed him, regardless of the risk to their own lives. The following is a description of his death by one of our Officers who tended him devotedly to the last :—

" He died like a Soldier, with no sign of fear, and amid the most terrible agony, his face lit up with such a strange brightness, as he said with a smile, '*It's nice to be saved !*' As the weary hours of night wore on, and our hopes grew fainter, we learned how much we loved him. Never before did I realize what a hold our gentle and loving Colonel had on my heart. We each felt, 'Lord, if it be Thy will, take us, but spare Him.' He didn't talk much. He wanted to know if we had written to England. His thoughts were evidently with you. Then *he asked if we were neglecting the work by being in his room?* As time wore on, he spoke of trust being trust, and when a comrade began to sing softly his old favourite hymn, 'Blessed Lord, in Thee is refuge,' he joined in singing the chorus, over and over, 'I will trust Thee. All my life Thou shalt control.' He sang it both in English and Singhalese. The translation of the hymn into the latter language was by himself.

"Near the end I thought he was unconscious. I asked him if he knew me. He said, 'Very well!' The dear hands had grown very cold. We strove to warm them all we could. I held them to my own warm face, but all in vain. He then thought he was dictating a letter, and signed himself, '*Yours for the salvation of India.*' After a little struggle, he passed calmly away. I felt that the Lord had taken our bravest and best. I closed his eyes, and kissed him for you and his loved ones. *Then we dressed him in full uniform, and he looked every inch an Army Officer*—just as *if he was only tired and had fallen asleep,* with The Army flag which he had carried so bravely, spread over him.

"Next day at 4 p.m. crowds thronged the Esplanade—rows and rows of carriages. With band playing, we marched him to the cemetery, and in the beautiful Army funeral service over two hundred comrades and friends took part, and followed him to the grave. As we laid him to rest, we felt as if no sorrow was like unto ours. I give you most of the details, because I think you would like to hear everything about your loved one. God bless you! He is not dead—only gone before."

Chapter IX.

FAKIRISM.

I am made all things to all men, that I might by all means save some.—1 *Corinthians* ix. 22.

Get into their skins.
William Booth.

The general rule having been laid down that we should adopt Indian costume and customs, the application of the rule to such practical questions as uniform, food, housing, and self-support engaged our earnest attention from the very first.

At the time of our arrival in India we had very vague notions on the subject, and it is interesting to observe the various stages, first of experiment and modification, and finally of definite regulation, through which we passed. Our original uniform for men consisted of a long white jacket and scarf, with ordinary trousers, and European boots, and turban with "Muktifauj" badge. The women wore white sarees, the end coming over their heads. Both men and women were supplied with double sun-umbrellas.

While we confined ourselves to City work, this way of dressing was fairly satisfactory, but as soon as we turned our attention to the rural districts, it was open to considerable objection.

Halls with chairs, or benches, and bungalows with the usual paraphernalia of tables, chairs and other furniture, seemed quite all right so far as the cities were concerned, being very largely adopted by most of the middle and upper-class Indians, while charpoys (beds) were frequently made use of by even the poorest classes.

But it was quite different in the villages, where pure nativism of the crudest character not only prevailed, but was preferred.

Our English boots were the objects of the keenest criticism, even in the cities, and we soon began to realize that this badge of Western civilization would have to go. At first we retained stockings and adopted Indian shoes. The usual kind worn in Bombay are of an ornamental, but most uncomfortable pattern, intended more for show than for use. When entering an Indian house, shoes are left at the door, It would be as rude to wear them indoors, as to keep one's hat on in entering an English home. When walking any considerable distance an Indian who possesses shoes will commonly take them off and carry them under his arm.

There was another difficulty about wearing Indian shoes. Every time we went out, our stockings became hopelessly soiled, besides developing large holes. We simply *had* to give up wearing stockings. But then came a still worse perplexity. Instead of wearing holes in our stockings, the shoes cut holes in our feet, or created sores and blisters of a painful character.

I can remember very well discarding for the first time my Indian shoes, and going out barefooted for a march in Bombay. The Corps Officer, Captain Hawthorne, a warm-hearted Irishman, nearly wept. He was sure I could not do it, and insisted on carrying my shoes himself, so that I could put them on at any time. But I came through the ordeal successfully, without having to take advantage of his thoughtfulness!

That was not always the case, however. At times in the heat of the day the roads became absolutely unbearable, and on one occasion a short walk over burning sand resulted in my being laid up for several weeks. However, this was only in the hottest places during the hottest parts of the day, and most of our open-air work was carried on at night, or in the mornings and evenings. Hence, to go barefooted was found more convenient than to wear the only kinds of Indian shoes with which we had then experimented.

At a later stage in our history we discovered that sandals, made of good leather, would entirely do away with the above difficulties, and these became an essential part of our Indian uniform, and involved no hardship.

It is important to bear in mind that ninety per cent. of the population of India—290 out of 320 millions—live in villages, and only 10 per cent.—about 30 millions—in the cities. The habits of the two classes are diametrically opposed to each other, and methods which are quite suited to the city, are altogether unsuitable for the villages. The tendency is for European Missionaries, including those of The Salvation Army, to settle in the cities, where European comforts are within easy reach, and do not attract any special attention. The same tendency exists with all classes of Europeans, whether officials or otherwise. When duty carries them on inspection, or for other purposes, to the villages, they usually make special arrangements to carry with them as many as possible of their city comforts, which get to be regarded by them as absolute necessaries, though they are by no means regarded as such by the villagers.

I was myself very much saturated with the notions commonly prevailing among Europeans on this subject, and it required no little effort on my part to throw aside my long-established prejudices. However, I said to our Officers—a beautifully devoted band—that the only way to find out where the line could be fairly drawn between the possible and the impossible, or rather perhaps between the expedient and the inexpedient, was by boldly crossing to the other side and finding out by actual experience which plans were to be retained and which rejected as unnecessary, or undesirable.

The wonderful baptisms of the Holy Ghost which obviously accompanied our first daring departures from the beaten track, both in Gujarat and Ceylon, satisfied those of us who were acting as pioneers in these matters that God's peculiar blessing was resting upon us. Nor were those revivals a mere flash in the pan. The children and grand-children of the converts of those times are with us to-day, and after the lapse of nearly forty years, the permanent character of those glorious awakenings leaves no room for doubt.

However, we were very largely influenced in our plans by the pressure of circumstances. Satisfied that our greatest results would, could, and must be achieved in the villages, we threw ourselves heart and soul into this branch of our work, and spent most of our time in looking after our newly-made converts, and in extending the work. Let it be remembered that in doing this, we had to depend entirely upon the people to whom we were ministering. We had neither halls, nor homes, nor money with which to buy any. We accepted their hospitality, which was always generous, provided that we were willing to take what they could offer. Occasionally we might meet with a rebuff, and they would close their doors against us, but we found that it was no great hardship to sleep under the trees, and in Ceylon, where the climate was damp, we could always make use of the "amblamas," or Buddhist shelters, which were everywhere to be found, and were free to all.

The more whole-heartedly and unreservedly we threw ourselves upon the people, the more cordial was their response.

I was myself by no means the inventor of all our advances. Indeed, we seemed to vie with one another in thinking out new plans to help forward the work One of our pioneers changed his name. The Indian *War Cry* dated 1st June, 1885, contains the first announcement of the change. It was not long before the rest of us followed suit. Hitherto we had kept to our English names, and it had not occurred to us that it would be very helpful to the work if we adopted names that were more Indian, and had something of a war significance.

The same Officer suggested that instead of a blanket for our bedding, we should find sacking more convenient and suitable, and more easy to keep clean. The idea was quickly accepted, as it helped to lighten the few belongings, which each one carried for himself. Mine were contained in a small tin box, which I called my Headquarters, as it contained the few papers and writing materials which I required to take with me on my tours.

We all travelled third-class, and usually chose the crowded Indian compartment in preference to those set apart for Europeans. This was perhaps the most trying part of our cross, as we could seldom get room to lie down even on the floor of the carriage, and the journeys were often long and wearying.

But there were so many compensations and consolations. The people, wherever we might go, simply showered kindness upon us.

The following extracts from my diary give some interesting experiences from our journeys at this period :—

Monday, 4th April, 1885.

" Bombay to Vasad. Only just in time for the train, having quite forgotten that Bombay keeps two different times, the railway, or Standard time for all India, being half an hour ahead of the Bombay City time. This is like some people's religion, fast and go-ahead, and glad to add an extra half-hour to their day, while others are such slow-coaches, they are behind the rest of the world. I never could make out why the business people of Bombay made such a fuss to prevent Standard time being kept by everybody. In religion, however, it is common enough.

" When we came to India we put our Salvation clock half an hour faster than the other religious clocks in India by adopting native dress. This was not fast enough to suit us, and so we soon put on another half-hour by adopting the fakir costume. This was still too slow, so we put on another half-hour by going barefooted. Too slow still, so we went in for Indian food. Not fast enough yet, so we started begging and living under trees, and then began to twist the hands of our clock to see if we couldn't get another half-hour extra. English shirts were next discarded, and nothing but a light cloth kept for the shoulders. If we can find any fresh way of adding another half-hour we are determined to do it. People may say, 'How ridiculous and extravagant to have our clocks three hours faster than everybody else's.' Some would like us to keep Church of England time, and others Methodist or Baptist time, but we take our quadrants and have a good look at the Sun of Righteousness, so as to find out the correct time which is kept by the clocks of Heaven. No differences up there—all the clocks agree with the great 'Thy-will-be-done' clock-tower. Only the earthly clocks are a long way behind. We are getting ours regulated, and are only sorry it has taken so long.

" What a crowd at the station! What a tight pack!

What shouting and squabbling! Are you fully saved? Are you quite sure about it? Take a third-class ticket any day by the B.B. & C.I. Railway* to any station in Gujarat. A capital test for your Salvation! If you can smile your way sweetly through the jamming and shoving and squeezing and quarrelling, and then sit or stand in a compartment for twelve hours with ten to fifteen travellers packed in with you, and a good lot of baggage as well—if you keep your sanctification through all this, you would certainly not think much of the difficulties that would meet you at the other end, when you come to see for yourself whether The Army really thrives in Gujarat, or whether it exists only in the imagination of the Major and some of his fanatical followers.

"You would at least be sure of getting a nice soft piece of sandy ground on which you could stretch yourself full length at night.

Tuesday, 5th.

"Vasad to Borchasan. At Vasad we found our Comrades Grundy Bhai, Narain Das, Janji Bhai, Musa Shah and others ready to welcome us. After walking nearly half-way to Borsad, we were glad to get into the bullock-cart, which they had kindly brought for us, as the sand became so hot under foot that we could not walk over it with our bare feet. On our way we were glad to stop and get a drink of water at the different spots where some charitable person had posted a servant to give water to thirsty travellers, reminding one of Isaiah's 'Ho every one that thirsteth! Come ye to the waters! And he that hath no money.'

At Borsad we had a hearty welcome from Captain Valji Bhai and Lieutenant Jita Bai and all their family, and went on the same evening to visit our outpost at Borchasan. This was the first place where we had a smash among the Hindus, and we found some of those first saved still standing and still determined to fight on to the last. We had a good meeting among them, and then went outside the village and slept in an open space. We did sleep! So soundly that we could not remember having such a sleep for ever so long, and all voted that the open-air was

* Bombay, Baroda, and Central India Railway.

better than any palace. The Staff Captain had just introduced sackcloth in the place of blankets. Two sacks sewn together only cost six annas, whilst the cheapest blankets we can get are one rupee. Besides they are stronger, and more useful and will not easily spoil. Then, too, as the Ninevites of the present day will not sit in sackcloth and ashes for themselves, we may well do it for them. If there are any Jonahs, who prefer to sit comfortably under their gourds in their bungalows and look on to see what will happen, we would rather keep out of their company. If they love their gourds better than perishing souls, so much the worse for them. Only let them take care that their gourds do not wither."

Before leaving Gujarat I was able to realize fully that the work in Gujarat had not been by might, nor power, nor human wisdom, but by the Spirit Himself. Begun by Weerasooriya and myself more than a year ago, it had been carried on by others and was still flourishing, in spite of all the efforts that malignity could invent to blast the work. There were the same faces, only brighter, holier, and happier; the same testimonies, only full of greater courage and confidence. Best of all, the Officers themselves had developed along thoroughly fakir lines, had wonderfully improved in their knowledge of Gujarati, and had added many new songs, choruses, and some first-rate native tunes to their previous stock.

There was a delightful spirit of unity and love among us all. Everyone was confident of victory. Things which had before seemed so difficult and even impossible now came quite as a matter of course. We slept in the open air, begged for our food, bathed at the village well, cleaned our teeth with a bit of stick, washed our hands and rinsed our mouths before meals, poured water over our feet after journeys, dipped our fingers into the dishes, and even ate chillies, just as though we had been Indian villagers all our lives.

The following letter will give some idea of the impression created even in places where our visit was only of the briefest character:—

"I have great pleasure in sending you to-day a postal order for sixty rupees. I want to tell you that Rs. 24.4

of this is given by the orphan girls and native teachers. I told three of the older girls that if they would like to give something, we at the house would supplement it, and that they might ask any of the teachers they chose, provided the teachers understood that it did not come as a 'hukm' (order), or even request, from me. I knew you had won their hearts, and I wanted them to be left free to act as they chose in the matter.

"Three of our girls receive Rs. 3 and four others receive Rs. 1 monthly, out of which they furnish their clothes and meet any incidental expense. These each gave *a full month's pay*—all that they had. Others gave one anna, two annas and four annas, which they happened to have received as gifts from friends. One Hindu teacher gave Rs. 2.4. A Maulvi gave Rs. 1, and some Hindus receiving Rs. 7 monthly salary, gave Rs. 1 each. Another Hindu on Rs. 6 salary, gave eight annas. One girl asked if she might cut her hair and sell it, as she had no money otherwise to give. She was allowed to earn her mite by doing some extra work.

"I tell you this that you may see how the Lord gave you the hearts even of the children of the heathen. A Pandit (who is not a Christian), remarked, 'If Major Tucker should remain a year, the whole city would become Christians.'"

I have a vivid recollection of one of the rare occasions on which we were turned down by the people of a village. Weerasooriya and myself had been visiting them. It was the early days when we were little known. The people told us plainly that they neither wanted us nor our religion, and that it was useless for us to remain, as they would never change their minds. Going out of the village we settled under the shade of an adjacent tree for prayer and rest.

It was the heat of the day, and it had become impossible for me to walk further across the scorching sands with my bare feet. I fell asleep, and it was only afterwards that I learned from Weerasooriya how the villagers, who had gathered around us, had been feeling the soles of my feet to see whether they were hard and horny like their own. When they found that they were soft and footsore, the tears had sprung to their eyes. In after years I used sometimes to remark that I had preached one of my best sermons when asleep. We have now a large and flourishing work throughout the district where the incident occurred.

The exchange of coat and trousers for shoulder-cloth and dhoti appeared to be no cross, when we were living, sleeping, eating and holding meetings among the swarming multitudes who did the same. To eat with our fingers the khichhri of Gujarat and the more savoury curries of Ceylon, seemed to us to be as natural as it was for the people whom we had come to save. It put us on a level with them, and made them feel that we were really one with them.

The life teemed with touching incidents. We were visiting our Soldiers in a village where there had been dreadful persecution. It seemed as though they must give way and could no longer resist the pressure brought to bear on them.

We announced at the conclusion of the night's meeting that we would devote the next two days to fasting and prayer, going away into the jungles for the purpose. They were deeply touched and begged us at least to remain with them until the morning. We refused, left the village and walked for some distance across the fields.

Gujarat abounds with thorn bushes, and it is sometimes said that, but for these, there would be no crops, as they are largely used to protect the fields from the cattle. The roads are strewn with thorns, and in the darkness of the night, with our bare feet, it was difficult for Weerasooriya and myself to make much progress. We found a secluded spot where we had a precious season of prayer, and at break of day we walked on for a distance of several miles. Finally, on the bank of a river, under the shade of a banyan tree, we settled down for our two days of prayer and fasting.

About noon we heard a shout in the distance, and saw several of the villagers running towards us. They told us that the people had spent that night in tears and prayer. In the early morning, knowing that we had taken neither food nor water with us, they had gone out in parties to try to find us, to tell us that our prayer had already been answered, so that we could return to the village. At all costs they were determined to be faithful. They pressed us eagerly to return with them, but this we declined to do, nor would we take the food which they had brought.

They reluctantly left us and carried the news back to their village. Not long after we saw all the people come streaming across the fields. They had resolved to spend the time with us under the tree. It was a wonderful season of prayer and praise that followed.

"The disciples were filled with joy, and with the Holy Ghost"—Acts xiii. 52. Consecrations were renewed, praise followed prayer, and prayer followed praise in quick succession. They were indeed two days and nights which could never be blotted from our memories. During the short intervals of sleep, while some of the people had to return to their village for home duties, many slept around us, unwilling to leave us even for a few hours.

Nor was this a solitary instance of such prevailing prayer. We literally prayed our way through our difficulties, and they were many. The answers which we received were truly remarkable.

There can be no doubt that the adoption of fakir lines at this time helped to throw wide open the door of India before us, and it was beautiful to watch the way in which our pioneer Officers responded to the opportunity. The words, "Behold, I have set before you an opened door, and no man can shut it," seemed to ring in our ears like a clarion call. It seemed as though we were putting our feet in the blood-besprinkled footprints of our Master. He had said, "Foxes have holes, and the birds of the air have nests, but the Son of Man hath not where to lay His Head!" How near we felt Him to be in those days, and how many were the doors that opened before us, and how we literally gloried in each so-called sacrifice.

CHAPTER X.

NORTHERN INDIA.

> The Lieut.-Governor of the Punjab (Sir Louis Dane) . . . has paid a high compliment to The Salvation Army for its efforts of reclamation. . . His Honour has impressed on all Deputy Commissioners and Police Officers the necessity of close co-operation with The Salvation Army.
>
> *Civil and Military Gazette, Lahore.*

Many flying visits were paid by me and other Staff Officers to North India, but the great distance from Bombay, and the urgent demands made upon us by the Gujarat, Madras and Ceylon fields, made it difficult for us in the early days to give it the attention which it deserved.

As early as 1883, a Corps was opened in Lahore, but the visible results appearing to be small, our Officers were withdrawn.

We, however, continued to pay constant visits to the Punjab, and to keep in touch with our friends there. The following account of one of these journeys was written by me at the time, and the tour proved to be full of interest. At some stations the most earnest entreaties were made for us to stop, if only for a few hours. After passing through one station, a telegram was sent after me asking me to return. It was addressed to—

"A Beggar,
3rd Class Compartment, Down Mixed Train."

At another place, a Brahmin Station Master told me that he was anxious to get saved, and wanted the Muktifauj to come and tell the way of Salvation. On reaching Firozpur station, a Hindu gentleman who had been travelling with me, slipped a rupee into my hand. Another gave me a seat in his "ekka" to the place where I wanted

1. Portion of The Army's Hospital at Moradabad.

2. Jemadars, or local officers, raised from amongst The Army's converts in a Northern Province. Such men have proved of great assistance in the advance of the work in the villages.

Representative of thousands of little girls cared for by The Salvation Army in India. Many Officers have been recruited from such as these, and have gone forth to proclaim the message of the Saviour.

to go. A native Christian official gave me a hearty welcome.

On the following Saturday, I paid a visit to Batala, a town in the Punjab, where my Aunt, "A.L.O.E." (Miss C. M. Tucker) lived and laboured as a Missionary for some twenty-six years. She lived about half a mile outside the city, in a Boarding School for Indian boys. I wanted to see her as she had taken a keen interest in our work, and with her facile pen had sent valuable contributions to our Indian *War Cry*.

Before turning my steps in that direction, however, I entered the city, and had not gone far when a Hindu gentleman stopped me, and asked me to what "pant" or sect I belonged. I replied, "To the Jiwan Mukti Pant (Get-Saved-while-you-are-alive Religion), otherwise called Muktifauj." And then came the question, where was I staying? "Under some trees, where I can speak freely to the people, and deliver my message from God." "Would I accept the hospitality of his home?" I declined with thanks. "You are a high caste gentleman, and the poor could not have access to me if I went into your house." "Indeed," he replied, "my door shall be open to all. Nobody shall be shut out." On that condition I accepted his offer. It was meal time, and the best that the home could produce was set before me. The house was quickly packed from end to end. Above my head was a trap-door, leading to an upper room. That too was crowded with the ladies of the house. The meal finished, after the customary mouth and finger cleansing, for it had been eaten, of course, Indian fashion, with my hand, my host said, "And now, let us hear your Message. Give us *gyan*—spiritual instruction."

Oh, how they listened! Soul-hunger was written on those eager faces. Could it be really true that there was a Saviour, Who could and would save them then and there?

After a time we heard voices at the door. Some Christians from the Mission had heard that I was in the town, and had hunted for me high and low. Now they wanted to take me there. The crowd would not budge an inch to make way for them. This Sadhu had nothing to do with the Mission. He belonged to the Jiwan Mukti Pant, or the Muktifauj!

Finally I was appealed to. How it recalled the scene, "Thy mother and brethren stand without desiring to speak with thee." I felt indeed that that eager listening crowd were in a special sense my "Mother and sisters and brethren." I informed the Christians that I intended to spend the day under a tree in the city, so that all could have access to me, but that in the evening I would visit my Aunt before taking the train for Amritsar.

The crowd followed me from the house and helped me to select a suitable spot—a chabutra, or raised platform, beneath the shade of a tree. I had not been there long, when an invitation came from Munsiff Sher Singh, an Indian judge, whom I had known while in Government service, as a warm friend and sterling Christian, inviting me to his house. I declined the offer with thanks, but soon after the Munsiff himself came riding up, dismounted, embraced me, and took his seat beside me on the ground.

When the time arrived for me to visit my Aunt, the crowd followed me from the city. It was an unusual sight. It had been always necessary for them to go to the people—now the people had come to them. My Aunt was not slow to see and seize the opportunity. Fetching her guitar and calling to the boys to come and help, she sang Punjabi bhajans, Christians hymns to popular Indian tunes, of which the people are very fond.

It was the last opportunity I had of meeting her. A few years later she passed to her reward, and by her own direction was buried without a coffin, near the scene of her labours. She had noticed the growing tendency for expensive funerals among the Native Christian community, often involving their families in debt, and sought in this way to impress upon them the lessons of economy which she had taught them in life. She left behind her a sweet fragrance of Christian influence. Her grave has become a sacred spot often visited alike by Christian and non-Christian.

From Batala, I took the train to Amritsar, a distance of some twenty miles. It was dark when I left the station and entered the "Hall Darwaza" (Gateway), so named after Colonel Hall, who had been my Deputy Commissioner some nine years previously, when I was sent to Amritsar as an Assistant Commissioner, my first Government appointment in the Punjab. What memories chased each other through my mind! Colonel Hall had always shown me great kindness as a young civilian. He made no profession of religion, but he was a "strong" man, and more than once championed my cause when a newspaper correspondent, who was in the station, wrote to the papers to complain that I was holding religious meetings and endeavouring to make converts to Christianity. When in the station, my bungalow was a centre for prayer meetings and other religious activities, and when touring among the villages I usually devoted the evenings, after my work for the day was concluded, to lantern scenes with pictures of the life of Christ, or Bible stories from the Old Testament.

Complaints in a newspaper regarding the conduct of any official always resulted in an immediate letter of inquiry from the Punjab Government. Colonel Hall, through whom such enquiries came, was always ready to take my part, saying that he looked upon me as a zealous and efficient young Officer, and popular with the people. He considered that I had a right to spend my spare time as I might wish, and assured Government that no undue official influence was brought to bear on the people. My own position was that, as a Covenanted Civilian, there had been no pledge on my part that I would abstain from holding religious services, and that I was certainly not prepared to make any such pledge, be the consequences what they might.

I knew several friends in Amritsar who would gladly have put me up for the night, but this would have spoiled my object, so I walked along through the "Hall Darwaza" looking for some suitable open-air spot where I could spend the night. It was not long before one of my fellow travellers recognized me in spite of the darkness, and came up to ask me where I was staying. Finding I had nowhere to go, he volunteered to take me to a Dharamsala belonging to the Golden Temple, where pilgrims were accustomed to be accommodated. This just suited me.

The fakir in charge of the place received me kindly, and insisted on spreading a "razai," (a padded quilt) for me on a raised place in the courtyard, as he did not think my sackcloth was sufficient.

My guide was a soldier in a Sikh regiment, and he looked after me with great kindness, while a Mahommedan merchant, who had known me as an official, brought me a bowl of nice hot sweetened milk. He afterwards told me that as he carried it, his tears had fallen into the milk as he thought of the sacrifice which I had made. He watched me drink the milk, tears and all, with feelings that he could not describe.

Early next morning, my friends took me round to see the "Darbar Sahib," as the Golden Temple is called. Here I was recognized by several people, and a large crowd soon collected and followed me through the streets of the city. One of them, a kindly Hindu, guessed that I had not breakfasted that morning, so he seated me at a sweet-meat shop, and gave me some very tasty sweets. It is a great mistake, yet a common one among Europeans, to suppose that Native food and sweetmeats are not nice. Many of their dishes are excellent, and for vegetarians nothing could be better.

After returning to the dharamsala, large crowds assembled and listened earnestly to the story of Salvation. Some gave me pice, and others food. My mid-day meal was provided by another fakir who lived next door to my host. Afterwards they took me to a larger room, where the Granth Sahib (Sikh Scriptures) were usually read, and placed me on the gaddi (throne) of one of their priests. Here again I had another opportunity of speaking. My old friend, Babu Rallia Ram, a highly-respected Christian Pleader of Amritsar, whose brother, Captain Narain Das, is with us as an Officer, found me here, and with some difficulty persuaded my hosts to allow him to take me to his home for a few hours, promising to bring me back in the afternoon, when it was arranged that a meeting should be held in the "Guru ka bagh," a garden attached to the Temple.

This was one of the most remarkable events that has yet occurred in our Indian history. So far as I am aware no Christian meeting has either before or since been held here. A friendly crowd awaited me on my arrival, and conducted me to an empty water tank, on the steps and in the body of which most of them sat or stood. They gave me a place on the edge of the tank, where I sat down, with crossed legs, Indian fashion, and taught the people. A friendly and learned Pandit, who sat close beside me, asked me several questions and raised some objections to what I had said, but it was done in a kindly spirit. The meeting lasted for more than two hours, and there must have been about three or four hundred people present all the time, while coming and going there could not have been less than eight hundred.

The evening was spent in talking and praying with a few whose hearts seemed to have been specially touched. Many were the entreaties for me to prolong my visit. I promised to return quickly, if they would write or wire me that they had made up their minds to be saved, but told them that it would be useless for me to stay unless they did this, and that if they wanted time to make up their minds I must hurry away to those who were already prepared to settle the question.

My heart yearns over these Punjabis. They are a grand race, and when saved will make us splendid Soldiers. The fields seem ripe for the harvest, and we are praying the Lord to send forth more labourers to enable us to occupy it.

It was not until 1895 that a small party was dispatched to attack the Punjab villages, on the Boom March plan. In the course of a few months, they were able to report the opening of 61 Corps and Outposts, and had raised up about 100 Officers and Cadets.

A little later Colonel Yuddha Bai (Bannister) was transferred from the Maratha country to the Punjab. Under her experienced and sympathetic leadership, the work in the Punjab made rapid progress, her Headquarters being established in Gurdaspur, the centre of a densely-populated village area. The districts of Amritsar, Dehra Nanak, and Sialkot were successively occupied, and the Headquarters were finally transferred to Lahore, the capital of the Province.

The following touching story of the death of one of our little Punjabi Juniors from the pen of the late Colonel Yuddha Bai (Bannister), gives a vivid glimpse of the powerful influence of the Gospel in the lives of these simple villagers :—

" Our dear Subadar Ditt, of Daburjee Village, has had his home literally emptied by death. It would be impossible to see a more holy and beautifully resigned expression than his rugged face bore, when he came into the Headquarters to ask us to hold a memorial service in the village. We went, and our hearts were filled with wonderfully mixed feelings of joy and sorrow.

" Daburjee was only an outpost, but by the constantly repeated earnest entreaties of Ditt, we made it into a Corps, and sent an Officer there and opened a Day School.

" The Subadar's three children, a boy of twelve named Munshi, a girl of nine, and another boy of six, were all pupils in the school. Little Munshi was a boy of much promise, and as he was getting on well in the day school his father had entertained the fond hope of presently sending him to the Industrial School with a view to his becoming a Salvation Army Officer. The Lord accepted the father's offering of his son, but not as Ditt had expected. The angel, disguised as death, entered the humble but satisfied dwelling, and in two short days had snatched away the mother and the three children.

" The bereaved father himself gave me an account of little Munshi's triumphant death. There was no fear, he said, no terror at the pain or approach of death. He asked him, ' My boy, do you want anything ? ' and he answered, ' Bring me the Testament and the dolak ' (drum). They were brought and placed on his bed. ' Now,' he said, ' I will say my lesson,' and he repeated some Bible lessons he had learned by heart. Then he sang the chorus :—

" Mera Premi Rab Yisu !
Mera dil ka pyara Tu !

" Which means :—

" Oh my loving Lord Jesus !
Thou art the beloved of my heart !

" Then as his father anxiously asked if he wanted anything, he replied triumphantly, ' No, that's enough, what more can I want? Now I am ready, I must go!' and the anguish of the desolate father's heart, as he laid his four loved ones in the dust, seemed turned into a wondering joy at the remembrance of his boy's triumphant death-bed, transferred from the dirty little jungly village and the mud hut to a mansion in heaven."

From the Lahore Industrial Home for Girls we cull another touching incident:—

"If Jesus should come for me to-night, He would say, 'Sophie where are you?' and I would answer, 'Here I am Lord Jesus; take me!'

"A few days after little Sophie, the second daughter of Captain Sant Masih of the Punjab, gave the above testimony to a group of her playmates of the Lahore Girls' School, she suddenly took ill, on the 20th May, and passed away within two days, leaving the school stricken with sorrow. For Sophie, during the three and a half years of her stay at the school, had grown into the hearts of both Officers and children through her exemplary life.

"Captain Cooper, speaking of her, said, 'Although only nine years of age at the time of her death, Sophie was ever ready, in order to shield a playmate, to take any blame upon herself, and was the first to plead for forgiveness on behalf of anyone else.'

"Motee, her elder sister, endeavouring to comfort her sorrowing parents, wrote, 'Tell darling Mother not to grieve, Father; little sister is with Jesus in Heaven.' And we know it to be so."

The work in the United Provinces of Agra and Oudh had a similar commencement to that in the Punjab. In the early years we had no regular work there, confining ourselves to visits by touring Officers. The first of these took place soon after our landing in Bombay at a time when the first persecutions had aroused much interest and sympathy. We were everywhere accorded a reception which might fairly be described as overwhelming. Not only did the European community flock to the meetings, but the Indian leaders, both Hindu and Mahommedan, usually met us at the station, escorted us to the meetings, and received us with the most affectionate cordiality.

In Naini Tal I was the guest of the leading Hindu, and during my stay he threw open his home to all classes of Indians who might wish to meet me. During the final evening of my stay he sent out an invitation to the leading members of the Indian community, and after an intensely interesting meeting, a silver salver was taken round among the guests and a generous amount raised for The Salvation Army.

The same gentleman presided for me at a public meeting in Almorah, and made a speech warmly commending the work of The Army. The English District Magistrate afterwards said to him, "Sadar Amin Sahib, you have always been known to be a strict Hindu. How is it that you presided at The Salvation Army Meeting?" "Had I seen Christianity before like this," he replied, "I should myself have been a Christian."

Similar receptions were accorded to us in Lucknow, Allahabad, and Benares. If Officers had been available for us to take advantage of this flowing tide, the same scenes which were witnessed in Gujarat and Ceylon would doubtless have been repeated in the United Provinces. But our hands were full, and it was impossible for us to enter the many doors of opportunity that presented themselves to us.

It was not till ten years later, in 1892, that our first Boom March* was arranged. It met with considerable success, but we were again unable to take full advantage of it through the shortage of Officers, and the urgent needs of other fields.

In February, 1895, another Boom March was arranged under the leadership of an able and energetic European Officer, assisted by a party of forty Gujarati Officers. More than thirty Corps were opened, and a work organized which has been maintained ever since. While not equalling other parts of India, owing to the scattered nature of the population among whom we work, our Officers have plodded on with a persistence and courage beyond praise.

*See Chapter VII for an explanation of Boom Marches.

CHAPTER XI.

THE POLICY OF PARTIES.

All that is old is not on that account
Worthy of praise ; nor is a novelty
By reason of its newness to be censured.

Kalidasa.

The work in India had been watched with keen interest from the Homeland, and when the Founder announced his intention of sending reinforcements, and called for volunteers, no less than 150 Officers came forward, undeterred by the severities and hardships of the fakir lines, about which they had heard so much. From amongst these a party of forty was chosen.

A special ship was chartered on which third-class passages were engaged at extremely moderate rates. We had the ship entirely to ourselves, and could therefore make arrangements to suit our own convenience for spiritual meetings, language lessons, lectures on India and Ceylon, or music and band practice.

By the time the party reached Ceylon, they were able to pray, sing, and testify in Singhalese, and had gained a rudimentary knowledge of the people, their language, and customs, which was most useful to them after their arrival.

The following account of the voyage and landing was written at the time by one of the party :—

"The life we are having on board is indescribable. The Lord is indeed blessing us with the joys of self-sacrifice. The pangs of parting with parents and friends have been taken entirely away, and the richest blessings have filled our souls. We are carrying out to the letter the injunction given in our Song,

'There'll be meetings all day
Our experiences to say.'

"On arriving at Port Said the whole party landed, our band played and marched round the town; we stirred the whole place, and finished up with an open-air meeting on the beach. There was perfect order, while Salvation was preached to the crowd in five languages. As our party was returning to the ship, they were followed by three or four who professed to get saved.

"The following programme will give some idea of the work done during the voyage.

"Engagements for the Day:—

6.0 a.m. Bugle call—Rise, wash, bathe, dress, tidy bunks, private reading and prayer.
7.45 a.m. Extension drill.
8.0 a.m. Breakfast.
8.30 a.m. Chapter from Soldier's Guide, and pray for Officers in the Field.
9.0 a.m. Language Lesson for Lads, Major Weerasooriya in charge.
10.30 a.m. Band Practice for Lads, Captain Voisey in charge.
10.30 a.m. Language Lesson for Lasses, Major Weerasooriya in charge.
12.0 Dinner.
12.30 p.m. Knee-drill, prayer for the General and the Army and chapter from the Field Officer.
1.30 p.m. Exercise in Language.
2.30 p.m. United Meeting on poop.
5.0 p.m. Tea.
5.30 p.m. Chapter from Soldier's Guide and prayer.
6.0 p.m. Band Practice.

"A lecture was given daily by the Commissioner or Major Weerasooriya on India, its climate, its peoples, its religions, its customs, its languages, etc. A blackboard was used to assist in giving language lessons and lectures, and proved to be of great service.

"On the voyage all the officers adopted native names, which the people can pronounce and understand much better than English names.

"An Officers' Band was organized on board, and although many of them could not play any instrument when leaving England, great progress was made before reaching Ceylon.

At Colombo, one of our friends, Mr. Buckney, met the party in his own steam launch. At the landing jetty they were met by the Officers and Soldiers of the Colombo Corps. After hearty greetings, all fell in for a grand march through the town, and at night the Salvation Hall was packed out, all sitting and standing room being taken up, and many unable to gain admittance. The party had so far advanced in learning the Singhalese language that the singing at the Officers' Meetings was all in that language, and some of the talking and praying too!

"'I thought when I was saying good-bye to England, that I was saying good-bye to home, but I now feel I have got home again,' said one of the Officers; while another said, 'At some of my stations I loved the people truly, but I feel I love these people more dearly than ever I loved any one in my life.' These two experiences seem to represent the feelings of all present, and to reveal the secret why it is they have been so happy ever since.

"The reception at Moratuwa was a grand affair. Both Corps were marshalled outside the railway station, with a large banner, on which was inscribed, 'Ceylon for Jesus.' Of course, there was a large crowd also eager to give the reinforcements an out and out welcome. On alighting from the train the party, followed by the Soldiers, fell in for a march, and swept through the streets bringing nearly every one to their doors. The playing of the band delighted the people, and with the exception of a few stones thrown by some 'skeletons,' all went well. A triumphal arch was erected outside the *maduwa*, while inside the decorations were beautiful. The meeting was enthusiastic, volleys of Amens being fired for the new arrivals. The entire district was aroused, and more than eighty seekers came forward during the first month after our arrival."

The success which attended this new departure was such that it led to the adoption of what might be called a *Policy of Parties*. Instead of sending our Officers in driblets, they were grouped together annually, in large parties, under the leadership of someone experienced in Indian conditions and methods, and the voyage was utilized in the manner above described in preparing the Officers for their future tasks.

The various parties were usually known by some special name, such as the Jubilee Fifty, the Wedding Fifty, the Memorial Fifty, the Founder's Memorial Party, the Swedish Party, the Calypso Party of 120—(not all of these last, however, were destined for India).

There were many obvious advantages in this Policy of Parties.

The first was in regard to the Officers themselves. They were enthused, and filled with a zeal and devotion, which were infectious and particularly helpful to those who might be lacking in faith and easily discouraged.

Again, the arrival of these large parties helped to attract the interest and attention of the people to whom they were sent, and secured larger and more immediate results in the way of both crowds and conversions.

Amongst those who have been transferred to other countries may be mentioned Commissioner Jai Singh (Bullard), who has rendered valuable service in Japan and in the West Indies, where he is now in command.

Commissioner Ruhani* (Mrs. Booth Hellberg), after commanding the work in India, together with her late husband, for several years, is now in charge of the work in Norway.

Commissioner Sena Singh (Sowton), after a very successful term of service as Chief Secretary in India for six years, ably assisted by his wife, was transferred as Territorial Commander to Canada West, then to Sweden, and lastly to Canada East.

Lieut.-Commissioner Nurani (Case), one of our veteran pioneers, has now retired, and is in the Homeland.

Lieut.-Commissioner Yisu Ratnam (Stevens), is now in charge of Chosen (Korea), assisted by his devoted wife.

In addition to the above many others might be mentioned.

One important influence which the coming of these successive parties exercised consisted in the modification of the fakir lines. It was thought desirable and necessary to introduce special safeguards for the health of the incoming Officers, and to regulate questions of uniform, food, house accommodation, salaries, education of children, homes of rest for sick and convalescent Officers, etc.

A number of the new arrivals were married, a few had

* Youngest daughter of the Founder.

families, the marriages of others were being arranged, while other volunteer families were waiting in the background for the settlement and regulation of these various questions.

The present attractive uniform, with its red jacket for both men and women, helped to supplement and stamp the hall-mark of The Army on the fakir-coloured turban, dhoti and shoulder-cloth of the men, and the sari of the women, for whom, when exposed to the sun, a topi was considered to be necessary as a protection for the head, in addition to the double umbrella.

In regard to salary, the question was at first met by a weekly minimum grant for each Officer, whether European or Indian. The following memorandum on the subject was issued to the Officers :—

"INDIAN TERRITORY.

Allowances for Officers.

No Guarantees.

1. As in the case of Salvation Army Officers all over the world, it must be distinctly understood that no salary or allowance is guaranteed to any Indian Officers.

Self-Support.

2. Similarly every Officer will be expected to make his Corps *self-supporting*. It is specially with a view to this that Native food and clothing have been adopted. The majority of the Town Corps are already strictly self-supporting.

Indians and Europeans.

3. The following rules apply equally to Indian and European Officers, who shall continue to be placed, as in the past, on the same footing with each other.

Minimum Allowance.

4. Officers in poor Corps (especially in low-caste villages), shall receive a *special weekly food (or subsistence) grant* according to the following scale :—

Each Officer	8 annas.
Each child under 3	2 ,,
Each child under 8	4 ,,
Each child over 8	8 ,,

Divisional Officer Pays.

5. The D.O. in command of the District or Division shall decide whether Officers are entitled to receive this grant, and shall see that the necessary amount is received by them weekly.

Clothing Grants.

6. The D.O. may also grant to Officers in charge of poor Corps such blankets, clothing and medicine as may be necessary, and shall be responsible in these respects for watching over the temporal needs of his Officers.

Postage Allowance.

7. A special postage allowance shall be given to European Officers in charge of poor Corps, not exceeding the sum of nine annas each per *month.*

Town Corps.

8. In towns experience has proved that, while living in such places is more costly than in villages, yet it is comparatively easy for an active Officer to pay all his personal and Corps expenses. Now, however, that the number of our Officers has so greatly increased, it has become necessary for their guidance that a maximum limit should be fixed for personal expenses. This will have the double advantage of checking extravagance, and of preventing Officers from being troubled with doubts and conscientious scruples on the subject.

A Maximum Limit.

9. In such cases no Officers shall be entitled to exceed the following *weekly* scale of allowances, such amounts being only drawn in full when all the other Corps liabilities have been duly met.

Single Officer living alone ..	Rs. 2	8	0
More than one Officer living together, each	2	4	0
Each child under 3		4	0
Each child under 8		8	0
Each child under 14	1	4	0
Each child over 14	1	8	0

Personal Expenses.

10. Officers drawing the maximum allowance will be expected to pay their personal expenses, such as food,

clothing, postage, etc., but not for their quarters. They will still be at liberty to receive gifts of food."

The above arrangement, which might seem to those acquainted with India as ridiculously insufficient, was cheerfully accepted at the time by all concerned as meeting the requirements of the situation.

The Founder, who gave much personal time and consideration to these questions, was anxious to maintain a careful balance between the two contrary currents of opinion which now existed—the one being the tendency to extreme fakirism, while the other would have quickly developed, unless checked and controlled, to equally extreme Europeanism.

There was also the very real danger that the gulf which had long existed between Indians and Europeans, even in Missionary circles, might creep into our own ranks. It was only to be expected that relaxations, which had been granted to European Officers, should be claimed on similar grounds by their Indian comrades, resulting ultimately in the separation of the Indian Officer from his Soldiers, who would be unable to provide him with comforts and advantages which they did not themselves possess. This would mean the creation of Indian, as well as European, Officers, who would be more or less "foreign" in their way of living, and dependent upon "foreign" funds for their support.

The numerous conversions, which took place after the arrival of the Clan Ogilvie Forty in Ceylon, gave rise to considerable opposition amongst the Buddhist community. In some places a Buddhist Salvation Army was organized, and this novel innovation attracted for a time large crowds. But it was difficult for them to maintain the interest. The doctrines of Buddhism did not lend themselves to its success. The only hope of ceasing to sin was to cease to act. The accidental crushing of an insect in sitting down was sin. To drink insects in one's water was equally sin, however unintentional. Nirvan, or annihilation, was their only hope of salvation, and this could only be achieved by a tedious balancing of good works against sin at the end of many, indeed countless, existences, and a gradual process of purification extending over numberless ages.

When the name of God was mentioned, Buddha placed his finger on his lips. He was an agnostic and refused to discuss the question.

This indefinite teaching seemed to lead to nothing, and quickly palled on the crowd.

But the opposition was none the less brisk. Not infrequently a shower of stones would greet our procession, though we were marvellously preserved. I can remember a stone bounding off my head. I had nothing but an Army handkerchief wrapped, Singhalese fashion, round my head. The blow did not even produce a bruise. Another time we were holding an open-air in Angulana when a Buddhist ran up with a staff and struck me a blow across my back which ought to have felled me to the ground. It was as if an angel hand repelled its force, and I scarcely felt the blow.

On some of our converts the persecution fell with special severity, and it was beautiful to witness the courage and constancy with which they endured their sufferings.

The following story of a young woman convert, named Pavistina, created a profound impression at the time :—

" One of our Moratuwa lasses has been severely stabbed. The Buddhist young man, to whom she had been engaged, met her as she was leaving a meeting, and stabbed her in seven places. The doctor gave his opinion that each stab was intended to kill her ; almost every wound had to be stitched. This operation was so trying that Major Weerasooriya said he was not strong enough to look at the painful process. Amidst all this she could rejoice abundantly in her Saviour, who marvellously sustained her, and gave her grace to glorify His Name. As the stitching was going on, her face was lit up with joy. A big crowd gathered around, and occasionally opening her eyes, and lifting her head, she preached Salvation to them, pleading with them to give their hearts to God at once, declaring her determination to fight for Jesus till the last.

" The man was arrested, tried, and sent to prison for five years. As the time for his release drew near, he renewed his threats and announced his determination to kill some Salvationist. But just a day or two before his term of imprisonment was over, though apparently in excellent health, he suddenly fell dead."

It was about the same time that the conversion of a young Mahommedan in Kandy created great excitement amongst that community. He was the son of a leading Maulvi (priest), and had been constantly attending our meetings for some months. One night he came forward to the penitent form, and sought and claimed salvation. The news flew like magic through the town, and in a few minutes our hall was besieged by a great crowd of Mahommedans. Fortunately, we were near the Police Station, and with some difficulty the Police were able to rescue the young man and shelter him for the night. In the morning he was taken before the Magistrate. The court was crowded with Mahommedans, and the aged father pleaded with his son to abjure his new faith, and to return to that of his ancestors. The Magistrate advised him to do the same. But he was firm, and though the attitude of the crowd was threatening, and he knew it would probably cost him his life, he never wavered. He was taken back to the Police Station with considerable difficulty, and we were able that evening to get him away to Colombo.

The news spread through the city that he had come, and it was believed that he was in our open-air procession. A crowd of Mahommedans quickly gathered around us, and our position became perilous. Stones were flying and sticks were brandished, when the Buddhists heard that the Mahommedans were attacking the Gelavima Hamudava (Salvation Army). In a few minutes they had swarmed around us, and bidding us march on, they turned upon the Mahommedan rioters and cleared the streets of them. There is no love lost between the Buddhists and Mahommedans of Ceylon, and on this occasion they were glad to pose as our champions and defenders.

On another occasion when the Hindus attacked us in the streets of a South Indian town, it was the Mahommedans who came to our help, and formed a nightly bodyguard for our procession. So that from the most unexpected quarters we received unsought help and deliverance.

CHAPTER XII.

THE BOOM MARCH.

Call us not out-castes! Only wicked men,
And those who harm the good are true out-castes.

Mrichakatika.

The next field which we diligently explored was that of Southern India. It is here that by far the largest proportion of Indian Christians may be found. But this did not facilitate our task, and a longer period elapsed before we found our feet in this Presidency than had been the case in either Gujarat or Ceylon.

We made our first start in the City of Madras, and here we received a warm welcome. During the first three months after our arrival there were some 400 professed conversions. But to enroll any considerable number as Soldiers was quite a different matter, and we soon discovered that the same difficulties existed here as in the other large cities of India in regard to securing the kind of results we desired, with a view to creating a permanent fighting force.

Neither Weerasooriya, nor any of our European Staff, including myself, had any practical knowledge of this part of India, its languages, or of the extreme rigidity of its upper castes. Moreover the old difficulty met us in an intensified form of all the most hopeful fields being claimed and occupied by Missions, who had been long in the country.

Ninety-nine-hundredths of the Christian converts of South India probably came originally from the depressed castes of the rural areas. But many of them were the children, grand-children, and still more remote descendants of their original ancestors. One hundred years of education, civilization, and moral and social advancement had made a vast difference in their appearance, habits and customs. The thirst for education had almost developed into a mania. Europeanism had made rapid strides. Government positions had often become the rewards of their industry, thrift, reliability and honesty. They could fairly compare with the best, most reliable and intelligent classes of Christians in other lands.

While they were extremely friendly to The Salvation Army, our methods were never intended to meet their tastes any more than those of our English compatriots. Moreover, they were all bound to their respective Missions by the strongest ties of gratitude and affection, and felt that they owed them what they could never repay for their spiritual and social uplift. They admired and praised The Salvation Army for its self-sacrifice and Indianism, but there was scarcely a corporal's guard amongst them who were prepared to imitate the example of Weerasooriya, and the isolated ones and twos had usually, like him, to cut themselves adrift from their own homes and relatives.

Nor did we change our tactics to induce them to join us. We feared lest their previous training and surroundings might make them become rather a hindrance than a help. We had, however, warm friends among them, and not a few who owed to us the blessings of conversion and sanctification, and they were always ready to help us generously according to their means, and to advise us in regard to the Southern field.

The introduction of the Policy of Parties at this time placed at our disposal a considerable influx of European Officers. Our friends thought, and we thought, that the time had now come when we could make a definite attack upon the many large cities in South India, which were the veritable strongholds of Hinduism. Their mammoth temples, often towering far above the palms, and dominating the entire city and surrounding country, with their myriad swarms of worshippers, seemed to offer a worthy target at which we might aim. We should at least be trespassing on no Missionary Society's domain. It was a matter of common knowledge that, so far, these citadels of castely power had successfully resisted all attacks of Christian warfare.

Accordingly we launched our efforts, and opened successively the cities of Tanjore, Negapatam, Kumbakonam, Trichinopoly, and Coimbatore, establishing at the last-named place a Tamil Training Garrison. The assault upon these strongholds of Brahminism were made with a courage, faith, and persistence, which could not fail to produce considerable results. In several cities converts were made of a really remarkable character, but the tornadoes of persecution that burst over their devoted heads usually swept them out of our sight, and we could seldom find out what had become of them.

Our tactics at this time were intended to reach and attract the castes whom we were endeavouring to capture for Christ. We even adopted their system of caste marks. Those who are familiar with Hinduism in South India will be aware that it is divided into the two great sects of Vishnavites and Shivites—the followers respectively of Vishnu and Shiva. They are distinguished from each other by distinctive caste-marks, which they place on their foreheads. The Shivites have three horizontal white stripes across their foreheads. The Vishnavites have two white vertical marks with a red central mark, the two white marks meeting in a single line along the nose.

There can be little doubt that in past and long-forgotten ages, both were originally intended to typify the Trinity, while the Vishnavite further accentuated the Unity of the Godhead, and the blood-red mark probably signified the blood of Christ. In confirmation of this may be mentioned the legend regarding Vishnu. A dove, pursued by an eagle, is said to have taken refuge in Vishnu's bosom, where he afforded it shelter. The eagle demanded that its prey should be surrendered to it, but as a substitute Vishnu gave permission to the eagle to tear the equivalent of flesh from his own bosom—thus inculcating the doctrine of Substitution and Sacrifice of a sinless Incarnation of the Deity for sinful man.

To meet this condition of things, and somewhat to the horror of our Christian friends, we boldly adopted a system of caste marks, The Army colours, red, yellow and blue being transversely painted across our brows. For this purpose we carried little paint-pots and oil colours, which would not run, owing to either perspiration or rain. There can be no doubt that the plan served its purpose admirably, and helped to place us on a most friendly footing with the people we were after, while the marks were a constant text from which we could preach and enforce the three great Salvation Army doctrines of Pardon, Purity and Power—of Salvation, Sanctification and Soldierhood—fixing them upon the minds and hearts of our hearers in a way that perhaps nothing else could have done.

However, after a prolonged effort, covering a period of about three or four years, we gradually came to the same conclusion as we had done in Bombay some ten years previously, that it was to the sixty millions of Depressed Castes that our mission lay, and not to the high-caste Hindus, who represented very much the Pharisees and Sadducees of the days of John the Baptist and of Christ. We reminded ourselves that Christ Himself had said, To the poor the Gospel is preached, and How hardly shall the rich enter into the Kingdom of Heaven, while the great Missionary, Paul, had written, "Not many mighty, not many noble, were called"; but God had chosen the foolish, the weak and the base to confound the wise and mighty, that no flesh might glory in His presence. Above all we realized that the same blessing was not attending our city policy as had attended the attacks we had previously made on the vast rural population of India, where we had by this time succeeded in raising up a Soldiery of some ten thousand members.

We had now become familiar with the Southern field, and had pushed a few outposts into some of its rural districts. At the invitation of Mr. Cox, a Christian planter of Travancore, we had sent a few Officers to his estate and to some of the neighbouring villages.

In May, 1892, the Divisional Commander of the Southern Field decided, with the approval of the Bombay Head-quarters, to apply to South India a novel system of warfare, which had been introduced with remarkable success during the last two years in Gujarat for the opening up of new and hitherto untouched districts, and for the extension of the work.

Introduction of Boom Marches.

The introduction of the Boom March was surely one of those inspirations of the Holy Spirit to those who live in constant touch with His leadings, the importance of which was not at the time fully realized.

The plan was briefly as follows :—

The leaders ascertained, by careful enquiry among our own people, which of the neighbouring districts and castes were the most approachable and likely to surrender to a concentrated attack.

An experienced Pioneer Officer was then selected to visit these Districts along fakir lines, without appearing, however, in Salvation Army Uniform, as we were anxious to avoid giving a clue regarding our intentions to hostile castes, and to those who were likely to oppose our coming. The Pioneer visited the most likely villages, interviewed the leading people of the caste we were aiming at, and after explaining to them the objects and purposes of The Army, said that it was proposed for a party of Salvationists with music, flags and other attractions to visit their district—would they send them an invitation and would they help with the food arrangements ? It was not long before the curiosity of the people was aroused, and the way was thus prepared for the coming of the party. It was invariably arranged that it should be at the slack agricultural season, when the people could most conveniently spare the necessary time for day and night meetings.

Meanwhile the party had been getting ready, and there had been special seasons of private and public prayer arranged among its members. Usually a target of time and results would be fixed, in order to give a definite point to their faith and prayers. At first we were more than pleased if we could aim at and reach a target of three or four hundred converts, but our faith gradually increased till it usually aimed at a minimum of one thousand seekers in the three or four weeks during which the Boom March lasted.

The composition of the party was very carefully considered. It always included two or three of our most experienced and successful Indian soul-winners, of the type of Weerasooriya, with, if possible, the local touch, which we found to be so valuable. These were not necessarily Officers. They were often picked from the best of our Sergeants and Soldiers, among whom we had many who were remarkable for their power of prayer and speech. The bulk of the party consisted, however, of the Officers who were to be left in charge of the newly-made converts and newly-formed Corps. They were to become the shepherds of the sheep, whom they had themselves helped to gain, and there were to be a sufficient number of villages and converts grouped together to compose a reasonable fighting force, both for mutual self-help and for aggression.

There were also certain attractions of a kind likely to strike the public mind and draw the crowd, such as the testimony of notorious converts, songs to popular Indian tunes, musical instruments such as the villagers love and appreciate, flags with appropriate mottoes, with sowars (mounted Salvationists) on horses and camels.

The arrival of the cavalcade was looked forward to with increasing expectation by the group of villages selected for the campaign, and generous preparations made for their reception, each locality vying with its neighbour in showing them hospitality. The fact that the party included white "Gurus" (religious leaders), who had dispensed with all the trappings of Sahibdom, and were willing to accept of their crude comforts, helped of course greatly to add to the curiosity and interest with which the campaign was regarded. The news having spread far and wide, many visitors came from villages which were not included in the programme.

It must not be supposed, of course, that the whole of the above plan was produced cut and dried at the onset. Constant improvements were suggested by individual Soldiers or Officers, who took part in the Boom Marches, until the above plan was reduced to a perfected system.

In Gujarat where the plan was first introduced, and became an annual feature of the work for some years, its advantages may be judged from the following account written of a series of Boom Marches which took place in the month of March, 1892, when the Founder had called for a simultaneous soul-saving campaign throughout the world:—

"The number of souls seeking Salvation in the Gujarat Division amounted to 13,328, being the greatest number in any division in the world. One special feature of the Campaign, which resulted in great blessing, was an All-Night of Prayer for the whole Division in a central Corps."

A month later another Boom March was organized, of which the following description was written :—

"Filled with enlarged desires begotten in the glorious seasons of spiritual blessing during the General's visit, some of our leaders concerted an attack on the heathen darkness of Gujarat on a scale hitherto unattempted, boldly announcing their intention of compassing the conversion of a thousand Gujaratis. A hundred Officers were collected, with horses, camels, war-chariots, flags, drums and a brass band to sweep through the country. Twenty-eight villages were to be attacked and fifteen days occupied in the onslaught, companies were told off for special attacks and for visiting and dealing personally with the sinners and the convicted souls. It was a bold announcement, and those who believed, believed with trembling."

On Tuesday, 19th April, 1892, the mobilization of the troops took place at Atmapur near Khaira, and on the 4th May a special despatch announces the close of the campaign with the following magnificent results :—

Total number of people seeking Salvation during the fifteen days 3,300

Patidars	102
Kolis	107
Dherds	2,950
Bhangis	61
Chamars	80

In May, 1892, the Officer in charge of the Madras Division left that city for Travancore with a large reinforcement, which had been gathered together for the purpose. The following brief summary of the campaign was written at the time :—

"Some forty-six Officers mustered for this campaign at Miladie, on Sunday, 27th May, and on Monday the column started on its triumphant course. Slowly rose the tide of conquest until, by the 13th June, the capture of 1,391 prisoners was wired, and as a somewhat new feature, the building of barracks for some of the newly-formed Corps was begun while the march was still in progress, ground being given by the converts. By June 20th, a grand total of 2,001 souls sought Salvation, three new districts were formed, and what had been previously a mere handful of village Soldiers was suddenly transformed into a large and important centre of Salvation activity, instinct with all the enthusiasm and go belonging to a brand new concern."

By the month of November the work had assumed such proportions that it became necessary to form it into a separate Division, which was placed under the charge of Major Jeya Kodi (Johnston). By the end of September, 1893, the Major was able to thus summarize the results of the year:—

"Much time has been spent raising Cadets, erecting cheap buildings, and otherwise consolidating the work done on the first Boom March (June, 1892). Nevertheless, soul-saving has gone steadily on, and preparations made for a great extension during 1894. About 1,500 souls have professed Salvation in new openings and old Corps, among them being many noted for devil-dancing and wickedness. During the year about 800 new Soldiers have been enrolled, but making allowance for some losses, our increase would be about 600 Soldiers."

Speaking of this Travancore Boom March, Staff Captain Sukh Singh (Blowers), who is now Commissioner in charge of the Southern India Territory, said:—

"The number of available Officers that can be left behind to carry on the permanent work fixes the limits of the march. It is no use going any further when there are no more Corps Officers. We could have gone on and captured village after village, almost without limit, if we had had more Officers. The reason we did not have so many people saved as during some other marches was simply because of the lack of Officers. We went on until every available Officer was stationed, then we had to stop."

Chapter XIII.

PERSECUTIONS AND PROSECUTIONS.

"Great spiritual harvests are not gathered by the fireside."
Railton.

Both in the Marathi country, and in Travancore, the success of these Boom Marches gave rise to bitter opposition on the part of the high-caste Hindu population. They had successfully defeated our efforts to make inroads among their own castes, and they now viewed, if not with equal alarm, at least with hostility, the rapid progress we were making among those whom they had for countless ages regarded as hereditary serfs. They felt that the ground was slipping from beneath their feet. Already a considerable proportion of the population of Travancore had openly professed Christianity, the last Census of 1921 showing the number of Native Christians to be 1,172,934 out of a total population of 4,006,000.

The following account of these persecutions was written at the time, and will give some idea of the storm of suffering through which both Officers and Soldiers passed:

"During the next month or two great advances were made. Many sites of land for barracks-building were given by the villagers. About a dozen schools were started for the children of the converts. Many new Corps and Outposts were opened. Scores of Soldiers were enrolled. Temple after temple was given up for Salvation purposes. A Training Garrison for men Cadets and another for women Cadets were opened, and in every possible way the work was consolidated and the foundations well laid for unlimited extension.

"A time of severe persecution now began, and in December the high-caste burnt down one of the barracks and also trumped up a false charge against the Soldiers of one of the Corps. A little later there were altogether nine false charges lodged in the courts against our Soldiers. A great number of the converts were devil-dancers, and their changed lives became monuments of God's saving power. At two seasons of the year great devil-dancing festivals are held and are a means of much temptation to the converts, for continual attempts are made to get them to take part in the scenes of devilry. One of the two seasons falls about the beginning of December, and the following description, written by Ensign Jeya Thebam, will give a good idea of a devil-dance.

"'We at the Cape have been passing through a very trying season lately. It has been the devil-dancing festival, and all our converts have been more or less tempted to join in the celebrations, but, glory to God, they have stood firm. Have you ever seen a man possessed of the devil? The tom-toms beat, the cymbals clash, and a weird, uncanny song is chanted. Presently the devil-dancer begins to move, his body sways, and he begins to shout, and the dance goes on increasing in vehemence and intensity till he leaps to an incredible height, and dances at a speed that makes one giddy and sick to look at. Undoubtedly he is possessed of the devil.

"'At Kadacheri the other night an attempt was made to perform the above rites before the temple which was some time ago given over to The Army. A great crowd of Hindus collected and the music began. A devil-dancer from another village was brought and prepared for his performance. A few Salvationists who were present prayed very earnestly to God to defeat the devil, and it really turned out so. In spite of all their exertions and shouting, no devil would come upon the man, and after an hour or two they retired discomfited.

"'The devil-dancer of the village, who is now a saved man, stood by and remarked: "For nine years past I have been possessed of the devil, and danced before that temple at this season of the year; but now all that is gone, for I worship the true God." Our meeting commenced just afterwards, and he and many others gave similar testimonies. In this Division I should think there cannot be less than one hundred devil-dancers like the foregoing, who through The Salvation Army are now bright, happy worshippers of Jesus.'

"In January the caste people became more and more desperate in their attacks upon The Army. Besides bringing all manner of false charges against our Soldiers—in one case employing four lawyers to prosecute, but yet lost their case—burning several barracks down, and in many other ways trying our people to the utmost. They got up a foul plot which, if successful, might possibly have ended in very serious consequences.

"About four miles from Cape Comorin is the large temple of Suchindra, which is of such importance that even the Rajah of Travancore has to fast during certain of its festivals. The plot was to capture some Salvationists and carry them into the precincts of the temple, which would desecrate it, then to call the police and charge the Salvationists with wilfully invading the place with intent to attack and destroy the idol. But Adjutant Yisu Ratnam (now Lieut.-Commissioner in charge of Chosen, Korea), who was then in charge of the work in this district, heard of the plot, informed the Government, and, of course, saw that the road to the temple was carefully avoided.

"The plot was arranged to have taken place during a special ten days' festival. When the festival was over the Sudras became enraged at the failure of their plans, and determined to have their revenge. They laid in wait for Adjutant Yisu Ratnam when they knew he would be returning from a certain village at night after holding a meeting. It was nearly midnight and very dark when the unsuspecting Adjutant started on his homeward journey. He had not gone far before the ruffians sprang out upon him. He ran back for his life, but the gang swiftly followed him, ran him down, beat him unmercifully and left him lying helpless and alone on the road. After a time he managed to get back to the village, and had just reached the Barracks when his persecutors came in a crowd yelling out, 'Where is he? Kill him!' The Adjutant jumped out of the back window, and just as he did so the crowd burst open the front door, and, finding their prey gone, wreaked their vengeance upon the lamps and fittings of the building, smashing everything to pieces.

"An incident of a very different kind comes in the record of the same month. A District Officer, Adjutant Deva Sundram, and some Field Officers, were going home one night after a meeting, when they were surprised by hearing sounds of singing and a Salvation Army meeting going on in a village in which they knew no work had been started—'We have no Corps in that village and have never held a meeting in it,' exclaimed the D.O., 'what can this mean? Let us go and see!' After crossing some fields they came upon a villager leading a meeting. They fired a ringing 'volley' on seeing the Officers, and explanations followed. The man who was leading the meeting got saved at an adjoining Corps and had started meetings to get his own village saved.

"At the beginning of March about 400 Soldiers and all the Officers in the Division met in Nagercoil to welcome the Maharajah who was passing through the town. A large and artistic arch was erected, with a large painting of the Maharajah in the centre of The Army crest. The Soldiers were drawn up on both sides of the road and the Maharajah and suite passed through them and saw for the first time some of the results of the two years' work of the *Ratchaniya Senai* in his State.

"At the end of March the court cases against the Soldiers had all been settled except one. Several of those decided against us were afterwards reversed on appeal to the High Court. The one case outstanding afterwards became notorious. A Tamil Lieutenant, Manikam by name, entered a caste street in Thalakudi during a festival to buy some plantains. The lad was of the Vellala caste, members of which are allowed in any Brahmin street except on the occasion of a wedding when the Brahmins are eating. But having in The Army worked among Pariahs, this was quite enough—the lad was seized and carried off to the police court. After some trouble he was released on bail for the sum of Rs. 500. Appeal was made to the Diwan of Travancore and to the British Resident, but while the case was being considered by these authorities the lad was dragged up to the court no less than sixteen times, lost sixteen days, and was put into prison twice, and travelled more than 200 miles over the affair. In the end he was sentenced to twenty days' imprisonment.

"Several South Indian newspapers spoke out strongly about the affair, and pointed out its injustice. After the Lieutenant had gone to serve his sentence, a telegram was sent to His Excellency the Governor of Madras, asking him to interfere. Lord Wenlock in reply said that instructions had been telegraphed to the British Resident to enquire into the case, and that he had given orders that in future all such cases should be dealt with by the District First-Class Magistrate only. But after all, the Lieutenant had to serve his twenty days, and received very harsh treatment from the jail authorities.

"Before this case was over the high-caste burnt down the Katkad barracks which cost about Rs. 150. But the Soldiers immediately set to work to get the place rebuilt, and about Rs. 150 were raised on the spot and in a few surrounding villages.

"At the end of July the Cape Comorin Division was working fifty-one villages and the number of scholars in the schools amounted to 461.

"About this time there were six devil temples promised to The Army on condition that *Ratchaniya Senai* temples would be put up in their places.

"As one of the many proofs of the love of the people towards the *Ratchaniya Senai* may be mentioned the fact that all through the year the cry has come from untouched villages for work to be begun in their midst. Major Jeya Kodi writes: 'Invitations to open new villages pour upon us, making us sick at heart. Oh, for Officers and money that we might seize all these opportunities!'"

The following story is told of one of the converts in Travancore, and throws an interesting sidelight regarding the persecutions which were so patiently endured:—

"He was an old man—how old no one knew—but his white hair and tottering gait proved that he had passed his threescore and ten. He was a Pariah, and had in his day been the leader, or chief man, in a wide district, though his son had now stepped into his authority and power. By dint of careful saving and laborious toil, he was rich—that is, he owned fields—had a tiled-roof house, and had rice to eat all the year round ; also like most of the elder men he was superstitiously attached to his devil-worship. He had built a private devil temple of his own, where he regularly propitiated angrily-inclined spirits and devoutly offered thanks when they abstained from mischief. But though thus sunk in very deep darkness, he clearly saw the misery and helplessness that his fellow-villagers were in.

"The Army came. Staff Captain Deva Sundram visited the village, described the victories that had already been won by The Army, and old though he was, bound by every tie of custom and superstition to his devil-worship, in spite of having to face certain persecution through the step, he came to Jesus, simply like a little child. His family followed, and then the storm broke. Persecution, false law cases, annoyance of all sorts, showered upon the hapless Salvationist. The caste people used their utmost power to crush his budding faith—but all in vain. Serenely cheerful the old man endured it all, and with his plucky son fought successfully through.

"It was not long ere the temples were given up, and levelled to the ground, the instruments being taken to our Headquarters as trophies. A few months ago the old man—still a Soldier—lay down to die. No terrors now of the Dark River, no going forth into the Unknown, but a triumphant entrance into Heaven!"

"Let me die in my uniform," said another of these warriors, a wonderful trophy, being converted from drunkenness and devil-dancing. So they put on him his red jacket, and he passed triumphantly away.

Many of these converts endured terrible persecutions. "They have burnt my house, my supply of grain, and my red jacket. But they could not burn the salvation out of my heart," was the testimony of one who had literally been burnt out of house and home.

On another occasion I was called to visit a village of our converts which had been burnt to the ground by the high-caste Hindus. Yet there was no wavering, though their enemies offered to rebuild the village and give them all the food they required, if they would give up salvation and return to their old religion.

The work in Travancore has continued to steadily develop. At an early date it was extended to the Northern districts, where the Malayali language is spoken, including Trivandrum, Tiruvellar, Mavalikarai, and other districts. More recently the neighbouring State of Cochin has also been opened.

The annual Melas, or Mass Meetings, which are held every year in the principal centres, form an important feature of the work, and are greatly looked forward to, not only by our own people, but by increasing numbers of Hindus belonging to all castes. The numbers assembling usually range from 3,000 to 15,000 persons, and during the recent visit of the General to Travancore, it was estimated that no less than 20,000 people were gathered to welcome him at Nagarcoil.

These annual Melas are a great feature in the religious life of India, and it is extremely encouraging to know that the vast crowds which have hitherto flocked to Hindu Temples and Bathing Places are now beginning in real earnest to turn to Christ. Nothing about these immense gatherings is so remarkable as the intense earnestness and spirit of prayer which pervades them. At times the whole congregation will burst unitedly and unanimously into a torrent of prayer, which can only be compared to a Spiritual Niagara. With eyes closed, and tears rolling down their cheeks, all the men, women, and children will pour out their souls to God. And when the invitation is given for seekers to come forward, hundreds will deliberately make their way to the open space cleared for them before the platform. The meeting will usually continue to a late hour, and when it is over, little groups will gather under the palm trees for further prayer.

The story of Travancore would not be complete without mentioning the name of Colonel (now Lieut.-Commissioner) Nurani (Case). For fourteen years she wisely directed this ever-growing work, and has left behind her, as well as in Gujarat and Ceylon, permanent way-marks of progress.

Chapter XIV.

THE CITY OF PALACES.

> "We are quite at home when we are with Jesus! Jesus is altogether one of us! Surely Jesus is our Jesus."
>
> *Keshab Chandar Sen.*

From the first arrival of The Salvation Army in India, all classes of the Calcutta public assumed a most friendly attitude to our work, and it was from that city that the most emphatic protest against the Bombay prosecutions was sent to the Viceroy. The Meeting for this purpose was held in the Town Hall, and was presided over by Babu Keshab Chandar Sen, who was then popularly regarded as the most eloquent orator in India. The telegram and letter which he addressed to me in Bombay have already been referred to in Chapter II.

The following extract from his address, "India asks, Who is Christ?" will serve to show something as to his opinion regarding what may be termed the Westernization of Christianity:—

"Perhaps you will tell me that this question has been answered already. Look at the flood of Christian literature that has swept over the length and breadth of the country. There are heaps of books and numberless teachers and preachers around you, all endeavouring to give a complete answer to the question before us. Doubtless, from these sources, India has some knowledge of Christ of Nazareth. But such knowledge has not given her complete satisfaction. It is true the people of India have been satisfied in some measure, but they have been disappointed in a much greater measure. For England has sent unto us, after all, a Western Christ.

"This is indeed to be regretted. Our countrymen find

that in this Christ there is something not quite congenial to the native mind, not quite acceptable to the genius of the nation. It seems that the Christ that has come to us is an Englishman, with English manners and customs about Him, and with the temper and spirit of an Englishman in Him. Hence is it that the Hindu people shrink back and say, 'Who is this revolutionary reformer, who is trying to sap the very foundation of native society, and bring about an outlandish faith and civilization quite incompatible with Oriental instincts and ideas? Why must we submit to one who is of a different nationality? Why must we bow before a foreign prophet?'

"It is a fact which cannot be gainsaid, that hundreds upon hundreds, thousands upon thousands, even amongst the most intelligent in the land, stand back in moral recoil from this picture of a foreign Christianity, trying to invade and subvert Hindu society, and this repugnance unquestionably hinders the progress of the true spirit of Christianity in this country. When they feel that Christ means nothing but denationalization, the whole nation must certainly, as one man, stand up to repudiate and banish this acknowledged evil.

"But is not Christ's native land nearer to India than England? Are not Jesus and His apostles and immediate followers more akin to Indian nationality than Englishmen? Are not the scenes enacted in the drama of the Christian dispensation altogether homely to us Indians? When we hear of the lily, and the sparrow, and the well, and a hundred other things of Eastern countries, do we not find we are quite at home in the Holy Land? Why should we then travel to a distant country like England in order to gather truths which are to be found nearer our homes?

"Go to the rising sun in the East, not to the setting sun in the West, if you wish to see Christ in the plenitude of His glory, and in the fulness and freshness of the primitive dispensation.

"Recall to your minds the true Asiatic Christ, divested of all Western appendages, carrying on the work of redemption among His own people. Behold, He cometh to us in His loose flowing garments, His dress and features altogether oriental, a perfect Asiatic in everything. Watch His movements, and you will find genuine Orientalism in all His habits and manners, His uprising and down-sitting, His going forth and His coming in, His preaching and ministry—aye, in His very language, and style, and tone. Indeed, while reading the Gospel, we cannot but feel that we are quite at home when we are with Jesus, and that Jesus is altogether one of us. He is our Christ. Surely, Jesus is our Jesus."

Cordial invitations had been received by us to send representatives to Calcutta, and accordingly Captains Bullard and Gladwin were sent in the latter part of October 1882, to conduct meetings and prepare the way for the future opening of the city. Their visit—though brief—was very successful, and towards the end of the year I was able to visit Calcutta and conduct a series of meetings there, and arrange for the opening of permanent work. At first, a theatre was engaged, and after a time a cheap hall was erected in an excellent position facing Wellington Square.

Amongst the most remarkable of the gatherings held at this time was one in Wilson's Circus on the Esplanade. A telegram sent to the *War Cry* describing this meeting runs as follows :—

"Calcutta, 22nd January, 1883: Yesterday Wilson's Circus crowded, 3,000 people, enormous crowd shut out—people of every section of Calcutta society—lions roaring—Salvation fire—grand time—Captain Bullard."

In connection with this meeting the following letter was received from the Manager, Mr. Wilson :—

"Sir, I am glad to inform you that you can have the use of the tent for next Sunday afternoon *free*.

"Sorry I cannot let you have it in the week afternoons as our rehearsals occupy the arena a good part of the day.

"Your show not requiring rehearsals you will therefore be able to use it without using it beforehand. Of course, you will be responsible for the chairs, damages, etc., as a number of crazy people are expected to attend.

"Yours faithfully,

(Signed) "JOHN WILSON."

To this, I sent the following reply:—

"You are quite right. We require no rehearsals. We have learnt our lesson by *heart*. Our 'Show' is so good that it will last all the year round. It is a Grand Gift Enterprise in which every one is warranted to draw prizes of inestimable value. There are no blanks!

"Wanted! Wanted! for our great Salvation Circus—Lion Tamers who shall not be afraid to face the lion of Hell. Jockeys who can ride the wildest horses and bring them in to the winning-post of Heaven. Clowns who can mend broken hearts and make the sorrowful jump for joy. General Managers who shall talk Salvation, write Salvation, advertise Salvation, and above all, live Salvation, through the eyes and ears, right into the heads and hearts of every soul in India. God grant that we may capture many such at your Circus next Sunday!"

Next door to the new hall in Wellington Square there happened to be a very objectionable liquor shop. Captain Bullard decided to start a campaign against this place. The following description of the siege is culled from the columns of *The Indian Witness*:—

"The Salvationists have been 'bombarding' a liquor shop next door to their barracks in Dharamtolla Street for a week past, much to the amusement and, we may add, satisfaction of the people of the neighbourhood. The method pursued is simple enough, although it involves a great deal of patience and hard labour. The 'soldiers' take turns, each serving on duty for two hours daily. The man who is posted to the guns simply walks up and down the pavement in front of the shop and advises all who come in his way not to drink. The result is that very many customers are turned away from the shop. The proprietor estimates his loss at ten rupees a day, and has expressed his fear that he will have to remove from the neighbourhood. In the evening large crowds assemble to witness the bombardment, and many amusing episodes occur. The people of the neighbourhood wish the most complete success to the besiegers."

Owing, however, to the necessity for the recall of Captain Bullard to Bombay, it was not possible to bring this interesting episode to a successful conclusion.

The following account of his farewell meetings serve to show how, under his energetic leadership, the whole neighbourhood was aroused :—

"'Sin,' 'Blood,' 'Cleansing,' 'Purity,' 'Glory,' Enormous Crowds, Barracks not quarter large enough, Monster meeting Wellington Square.

"'Sin,' 'Blood,' 'Cleansing,' 'Purity' and 'Glory' were to march single file as an advance guard. Many were the enquiries 'What is it? What does it mean?' They could not understand how 'Sin,' 'Blood,' etc. could march in front!

"But the devil understood it, as he saw us during the day in the midst of cloth of various colours, sewing and cutting, and we knew what it meant, when, about half an hour before the time to meet, with aching back and sore fingers we were able to smile upon the last flag finished.

"We were expecting great things, and therefore were not surprised, when we arrived in Dharamtollah Street (the place we had announced to meet), to find a very large crowd filling the end of the street, waiting our arrival, besides a large number in carriages.

"We soon formed into marching order. Lieutenant Vanzyl took the lead, carrying a large deep black flag with the word 'Sin,' in large, conspicuous white letters upon it. Then a large red flag, borne by a Madrassee, with the word 'Blood' upon it. Another Madrassee came next with a White flag and the word 'Cleansing.' Then came a Light Blue flag with 'Purity' upon it, carried as high as possible by one of our recruits. After this came a bright yellow flag with 'Glory' upon it. One of our soldiers carried this and he seemed immensely pleased when some one shouted 'Glory Taylor.'

"The flags were followed by a dozen Bengali Hallelujah Lasses marching two deep, two of whom had tambourines. They sang in splendid style, and above the music could be heard, 'Glory to His name, Here to my heart is the blood applied, Glory to His name.'

"A very popular missionary, one who has been in India many years, said it was the most wonderful and impressive sight that he had ever seen. Only two or three years ago a Bengalee lady was not allowed to go even to church without being veiled, but here they are marching in procession and playing tambourines in the street. Never before our arrival had a Bengali lady spoken in public, but now they not only testify but interpret while others speak, and even go and sell *War Crys* in the streets. Praise God, our Bengali Lasses will be a power in India.

"These were followed by several Madras ladies and Captain Thompson and Lieutenant Cassidy with tambourines and their red and green chadders. They have only been here a week, and many crushed around them anxious to see a real, live Hallelujah lass.

"Then came the band. To be sure it was only a big drum and cornet, but we did the best we could; yet we were not surprised when some one with over-musical ears remarked that we deserved six months in the Presidency Jail for the noise we made. After the band came The Army Flag, the well-known Red and Blue with the Yellow Star and Motto 'Khun aur Ag' (Blood and Fire). Then our Soldiers, Auxiliaries, and Friends followed, a crowd of several thousand people bringing up the rear.

"It was a grand sight. The sun after a burning day was just sinking in the west, casting its last rays upon the bright-coloured flags, which spread out in the beautiful breeze, the Bengali Lasses with their snow-white dresses and fine worked veils thrown over their shoulders and dropping down almost to their feet, and the large crowd lining the way and following us, of almost every nation and costume. The palm trees rose high above the mud huts and flat-roofed houses, and the lovely sky and setting sun gave it an effect far beyond my power to describe. On we march. Every one seemed very much interested, and when we got to the Hall it was with difficulty that we got in. But then we found it impossible to have a meeting, the place was so crowded and a very large crowd outside all anxious to get in. So we determined to go out on the large square opposite, the announcement being received with loud shouts of approval. When we reached the square Dr. Thoburn, who had been preaching, kindly gave us his stand, and our Soldiers and Lasses and flag-bearers got inside the square of benches, while the enormous crowd stood around listening attentively to every word that was spoken.

"Babu Kali Charan Banerjea was the first one to speak, first in Bengali and then in English, followed by myself and others. We then went into the Barracks for a prayer meeting which was crowded to overflowing. Lieutenant Hawthorne sang a solo, and then six souls came forward for Salvation. Thus closed one of the grandest sights I have ever seen."

The following is a description of a personal visit which I paid to the home of Babu Keshab Chander Sen :—

"Major Tucker spent a pleasant evening with the Leader of the Brahmo Somaj. A number of the Babu's family were present, and the Major was tempted to claim his sons and grandson as future Captains in The Salvation Army. The Babu gave an interesting account of his work with its 23 Ministers and 150 branches."

The history of the work in Calcutta has very much resembled that of other Indian cities. In many respects it has been disappointing, owing to a policy of aiming at everybody and hitting nobody in particular. It has been necessary to learn from painful experience that caste distinctions in the city are really as clear-cut and decided as in the villages. There our success has been due to singling out some particular caste of artisans, or workers, known as the depressed classes, and concentrating our whole time and attention upon them. It was not till about 1912 that we decided to steadily pursue the same policy in the cities which we occupied.

We took pains to discover in what particular streets, "mohallas," or "chawls," the people we were after, lived, and opened our halls and schools in their midst, as if they were the only inhabitants of the city. The response was immediate and satisfactory.

We have recently followed the same policy in Calcutta and we have been able in a short time to open nine Corps in these specially selected localities.

At the same time one or two Corps continue to be maintained in the more public thoroughfares for the general public, and as centres where from time to time we can gather our people for special meetings.

CHAPTER XV.

CAMPAIGNS AMONGST THE MARATHAS AND BHILS.

> "You cannot be a saviour of men, and yet save yourselves."
>
> *Catherine Booth.*

Apart from the work in Gujarat, The Salvation Army has also a considerable work in the Marathi country, the pivotal centres being Poona, Satara and Ahmednagar. The tract of country here mentioned is part of the great elevated table-land to the east of the great mountain Ghats, or Ranges, which skirt the Western coast of India. The clouds of the South-west monsoon, on which India so largely depends for her annual rainfall, strike against these mountains, empty their contents on them and on the narrow strip of fertile coast between them and the sea, and then frequently sweep over the arid area of the Deccan, without discharging their precious contents for the benefit of the waterless and parched plains. Only perhaps once in five years will the monsoon be really effective in this region. In other years, it is largely made up of broken promises, which often mean successive sowings with a single stunted crop, or no crop at all.

Scarcity and famine are always staring the Maratha in the face! How he continues to thrive, and keep up a cheerful existence is a mystery. If there were rivers, or a generous underflow as in the alluvial plains of India, these could be harnessed, and the scarcity of rainfall would not matter. But unfortunately he is above, and not beneath, nature's reservoir, the mountains, and there are practically no ranges across the plateau to capture the fleeting clouds, which chase each other above his fields and seem to mock his anxieties and agonies.

Whether an artificial barrier could not be created which would compel the clouds to disgorge their contents is an interesting question which has never been properly dealt with.

In the year 1912, when my wife was recovering from a serious attack of typhoid, and we happened to be on a visit to Europe, we spent some time in Switzerland investigating the system of storm cannon and rain rockets which were utilized by the vineyard proprietors and Insurance Companies for the protection of the vines from the frequent hailstorms which are so destructive. The theory was that by these artificial means the formation of the hail was prevented, and the clouds discharged beneficial rain instead of destructive hail. The effectiveness, or utility, of the method was disputed by many, but the fact remained that they continued to grow in popularity, and had gradually been adopted by Insurance Companies, as well as by vineyard owners, especially since the introduction of the Rain Rocket.

The Storm Cannon was a peculiar weapon, consisting of a funnel-shaped iron tube, from which a bomb was discharged into the midst of a cloud that appeared to be likely to produce hail. The effect of the discharge was to create a kind of cyclone in the cloud, arresting its progress and compelling it to scatter its contents in the form of rain. Naturally these cannon had to be fixed to the ground, and could only protect a limited area. Hence, they were dotted about the great vineyard areas at certain intervals. Quite recently the idea had occurred to some one that rockets could be utilized for exactly the same purpose, and would have the great advantage (1) of cheapness, (2) of being movable, and (3) of being usable in such quantities as each locality might actually require.

We were told that these rockets had been found still more successful than the Storm Cannon, and had been rapidly replacing them. We obtained a small supply for experimental purposes in India and deposited them with a reliable Officer in the United Provinces, for the protection from drought of one of our Settlements for Criminal Tribes. At the time they arrived, we were threatened with a failure of rain in this particular district.

The clouds were there, but had failed to discharge their contents. The atmospheric conditions were favourable, the air being heavily laden with moisture.

The experiment with these rockets was entirely successful, and a welcome supply of rain fell upon our parched fields, while the adjoining region continued to be destitute of rainfall. However, the experiment was only a small one, and our supply of rockets soon gave out, but it was watched with interest by many persons, and we received numerous enquiries. Just at this juncture, however, the European War broke out, and the question naturally dropped out of sight for the time being.

The fact is well known, not only in India, but all over the world, that wherever *rain-bearing* clouds strike some mountain barrier, they invariably discharge their contents upon contact, and it seems to be reasonable and highly probable that a similar result would be obtained if a barrier of rockets should be interposed to their progress.

In this region the distances between the various villages is usually considerable, and the population is more sparse than that of Gujarat. The lack of rainfall and irrigation, and the rocky character of much of the country, make it more difficult to traverse. Our own work is almost entirely restricted—as is that of most Missions—to the Mahars and Mhangs, the depressed classes of the region.

The success of the Boom March* system in Gujarat and Travancore, led to an effort being made in 1893 to apply it to the Marathi country, where the work had hitherto been of a very struggling and discouraging character. Staff Captain Sukh Singh (Blowers) was appointed to superintend the March. As a result, two new districts were formed. Staff Captain Yuddha Bai (Bannister) was placed in charge of one of these districts, and gives the following description of this campaign :—

"Previous to the Boom March* of January, 1893, no definite effort had been made to gain a footing in the Marathi village districts. A few pioneering parties had gone out, it is true, but these only in a desultory way,

* See Chapter XII for explanation.

and not being followed up by the opening of any Corps, it may truly be said that no real Marathi work had been started till the Boom March of January, 1893. Then the party consisted of a few Cadets and Officers of various nationalities gathered out of Gujarat, Bombay and Poona, only five of whom belonged to the Maratha nation. With this mixture of Marathas, Gujaratis, Tamils and Telugus, some of whom could not make themselves understood by the people, the village work was started.

"The result of the March was beyond our most sanguine expectations; for, with the exception of one village, we were received with open arms, and over 600 persons sought salvation and welcomed The Salvation Army."

After this Boom March, which opened the way and gave The Army a footing, came the steady plodding work of looking after the converts and putting in the foundations for a solid work in the future. Writing of this after-glow work, Staff-Captain Yuddha Bai says:—

"Various difficulties arose in the establishment of the work when the march was over; one of the principal being the apparent impossibility of getting even the poorest kind of huts from the people for Officers' Quarters or Halls; in consequence of which the lassie Officers had to put up in tents, where the burning heat of the sun through the hot season was extremely trying, while the lads, less fortunate, had to do the best they could in the public *Chowdi*, or Dharamsala. This was a source of great discouragement and temptation to the Officers, who were all young and untried, and who, especially at times of fever and other sickness, suffered very much from want of a quiet corner to call their own."

However, in spite of all difficulties, we have continued to steadily advance, and have now 247 Corps and Outposts, with 207 Officers, Teachers, and Cadets. A Training Home in Poona, a Boarding School for boys in Ahmednagar, and one for girls in Satara, with 75 Day Schools, enable us to obtain a regular supply of Officers from our own people along the lines already described in the case of Gujarat.

Writing from Bombay, in 1923, Lieut.-Commissioner

Jivanand (Julius Horskins), the Commander of the Western Territory, says:—

"We have just concluded a trip to the Bhil Country and part of the Maharashtra, and wherever we have been the crowds have been larger than on our former visits, and in addition to this, a large number of souls have been converted, and, generally speaking, the outlook for good and profitable work within the Territory is very encouraging.

"Last year we made a net gain of some 3,000 Soldiers. Many of our people move from one place to another, but they always return to the village to which they belong, and it is remarkable how good they keep even though away from Army work and influence. They never forget that they are part and parcel of our Organization."

An interesting feature of the School work in this country has been the production, at our suggestion, by the Government Educational Department, of a Village Arithmetic Book suitable for agriculturists. It is based on a model which I obtained from America, but the examples given are entirely altered and very cleverly adapted to Maratha conditions, showing clearly how improvements could be produced by the application of improved methods in village agriculture, and demonstrating the same by suitable sums in arithmetic. Dr. Mann, the Director of Agriculture for Bombay Presidency, was the means of securing the publication of this valuable little book.

From our Girls' School in Satara, a party of twenty was recently selected, and spent eighteen months in an extensive tour through England and Europe, under the charge of their two Swedish Officer Leaders—Adjutant Khushi (Olsson), and Ensign Kamala (Johanson). Immense crowds gathered, and the largest buildings were packed to overflowing, intense interest being manifested in them, and in the work which they represented, while a considerable sum was raised towards the support of the Indian work.

One of the romances of the Maratha work centres round one of its early leaders, Colonel Yuddha Bai (Bannister). Two sisters, daughters of a London solicitor, left their home, and became Officers in The Salvation

Army. Colonel Yuddha Bai joined one of the early parties that came out to Indaa, while her sister followed some years later.

Mastering the Maratha language till she could speak it with great fluency, the Colonel endeared herself to the poor villagers among whom she established the work, and in whose midst she herself spent most of her time, fearlessly facing the peculiar hardships and difficulties of the country.

After a long period of service in the Western Territory, the two sisters were transferred to the Punjab, where their devoted labours met with equal success. Finally, they reverted to the command among the Marathas, where Colonel Yuddha Bai spent the rest of her life. Even when the fatal disease of cancer had made its appearance, and she knew that her days were numbered, rather than return to England, she begged that she might be allowed to spend her remaining days amongst her beloved Maratha people, whom she had adopted as her own, and where the fragrance of her memory has long survived her death.

Her sister, Brigadier Shanti Bai, with similar devotion and tenacity, though placed on the retired list, preferred to remain for some years in Poona, where her ceaseless toil and unflagging consecration were an inspiration and blessing to all her younger comrades in the Maratha field.

Colonel Dayali (Van de Werken) and Lt.-Colonel Sundri (Gugelmann) from Holland were subsequently appointed to take charge of the Marathi Territory, where they rendered excellent service, and helped to further consolidate and extend the work, being subsequently appointed to the command of the work in the Dutch Indies.

The fertile verdant region of Gujarat is bordered on the North, West and East by large areas where the rainfall is precarious, and famines are frequent. On the East spreads a province known as the Panch Mahals, inhabited principally by an aboriginal race named Bhils. Into this district our Officers penetrated at an early stage of our work in Gujarat. The successive waves of Aryan and Mahommedan invasion had driven this race into the forests and fastnesses of the hills, where it was difficult for the invaders to follow them. It had not prevented the moneylender, however, from following them to their retreats, and they suffered much from his exactions.

They were at first very suspicious of our Officers, and feared lest they might be disguised Government Officials come to take them from their homes and enlist them in some regiment. There was some ground for their fears, as the Bhils make good soldiers, and a special Bhil Corps had been recruited for the Indian Army, and had rendered good service. We were soon able to reassure them, however, and to make them realize that though we were Soldiers, and wished to enlist them in an Army, our warfare was of a very different kind and required no carnal weapons. Nor had we come to take them away, but to ourselves settle in their midst. Gradually their suspicions were allayed, and their confidence gained, though it was some time before our Officers ventured to inscribe their names in a Soldiers' Roll, or create the usual outlines of a definite organization. Indeed, newly-arrived Officers were particularly warned not to produce pen and paper in the presence of their people, and to be careful not to make any lists of their names and addresses, lest a scare should be created.

The work progressed slowly, but steadily. The conversion of one of their petty chiefs, or headmen, created a considerable stir, and some of his relatives proposed that he should be expelled from their community, or required to renounce The Salvation Army. A meeting of the clan was summoned for the purpose of considering what should be done. At this gathering their chieftain made an eloquent appeal, pointing out the advantage of the change that had taken place in his own heart and life. Whereas before this time he had been addicted to drinking and gambling, he had now abandoned these sins. He had often wished to do so before, but it was only when Christ entered his heart and gave him the needed power, that he had been able to forsake his evil habits. Now, not only was his life changed, but his heart was changed. Why then should they expel him from his clan, when such a wonderful change had taken place? Moreover, what God had done for him, He was equally willing and able to do for each one of them. This was the good news that The Salvation Army had brought to them.

The effect produced upon the simple and impressionable listeners was such, that they decided on the spot that they approved the action of their chief, and that any member of the clan who wished to do so could join The Salvation Army. Moreover, it was further decided that the man who had proposed his expulsion should provide a feast for the clan at his own expense. Thus the question was satisfactorily settled, and resulted in a considerable number of others following their chief's example.

The poverty of the people led to the organization of a new and original scheme while Lieut.-Colonel Jang Bahadur (Karl Winge), was in charge of the work. The sum of Rs. 2,000 was borrowed from our Central Bank in Simla, and was invested in the purchase of 100 country cows at an average cost of about Rs. 20 each. These were distributed among our converts on the following simple conditions :—

1. No cash payment to be made by the holders.

2. The cows were to be fed and cared for by the persons to whose charge they were committed.

3. They were to be subject to the inspection from time to time of our Officers.

4. The calves were to be divided equally between the holder and The Salvation Army.

5. There was to be an annual sale of young stock, and repayments of capital and interest were to be made from the same till the debt had been paid off, when the ownership of the remaining stock would vest in the holders.

This arrangement was cordially accepted and faithfully adhered to, the debt being wiped out in the course of a few years, and our people greatly helped by the arrangement.

Our work had made considerable progress, when a serious interruption to it took place. Some Hindu Sadhus suddenly made their appearance in the Panch Mahals, and proclaimed that the old Bhil Raj (kingdom) was about to be re-established. A great Deliverer, about whom their songs and legends had prophesied, was about to make his appearance. They were to prepare for his reception.

It was a period when there was considerable activity among a certain number of political agitators, and plots against British rulers were being hatched in different parts of the country, resulting, in one case, in an attempt upon the life of the Viceroy, Lord Hardinge, when a public Durbar was being held in Delhi, and a procession of elephants was entering the Chandni Chauk. A bomb was thrown from the window of a house, and struck the howdah of the Viceregal elephant, killing the Indian attendant who was holding the royal umbrella over Lord Hardinge, and seriously wounding the Viceroy, though Lady Hardinge, who sat beside him, miraculously escaped without a scratch.

The attempt to stir up trouble among the Bhils appears to have been engineered from a small State adjoining the Panch Mahals, where the agitators had been known to be active.

The Sadhu propaganda spread like wildfire, and the credulous people accepted the story, and gathered in considerable numbers to meet their new Raja, who was accredited with miraculous powers.

They were directed to bring in all their seed-grain to be blessed by the Sadhus, who would return a few handfuls to them with the assurance that it would produce an enormous crop. They were also directed to bring in their brass vessels, which they were told would no longer be needed. In fact, whatever little possessions they owned were to be surrendered to the representatives of the new ruler.

Above all, they were to take a solemn oath that no Bhil should henceforth attend any Christian service. Those of them who had joined The Salvation Army, or any other Christian body, were to be compelled to abandon the same, and in case of failing to do so, were to be expelled forthwith from their community.

Our work was for a time seriously affected, and, terrified by the threats which had been made, hundreds of our converts ceased to take part in our meetings, or to acknowledge us. However, the non-appearance of the new leader began to arouse their suspicions, and the Bhils demanded that he should visit them without further delay.

A day was named when he was to miraculously make his appearance in their midst, but the manifestation was marred by two incidents. The first was the discovery by some Bhils of the individual hiding in an adjoining field, previous to his supposedly miraculous appearance. The second was that when the Sadhus introduced him, to their keen disappointment he appeared as a very ordinary babu, dressed up in English clothes.

Now they felt certain that this babu (clerk) could not be their Deliverer, and that the Sadhus had been deceiving them, and many of them returned to their own homes. It was not, however, till a British force made its appearance in the neighbourhood that the incipient revolt was finally suppressed.

Those of our people who had been forcibly driven from us, or deceived into believing the story of the Sadhus, felt ashamed to return to us and confess the mistake they had made. Moreover, the terrible oath of renunciation, which they had been compelled to make, continued to exercise a great influence upon them. How could they break their word? They had promised solemnly never to attend another Salvation Army meeting. These aboriginal tribes, and especially the Bhils, are remarkable for their truthfulness, and a promise once made is regarded as peculiarly sacred.

Suddenly, one of their leaders, who had been a Sergeant with us and had great influence with them, made up his mind what was to be done. In order to get up his courage, he drank a quantity of native liquor till he was thoroughly intoxicated, and then ran through the tribesmen, waving a flag and crying, "I am going back to the Muktifauj! I am going back to the Muktifauj!" And the people followed him! It is perhaps the solitary instance in our history of drink being utilized for such an admirable purpose as a return to duty!

The work amongst the Bhils has since made steady progress, and we have now in the Panch Mahals 50 Corps, 200 Societies, and 172 Outposts, with 96 Officers, Cadets and Teachers, 36 Day Schools with 846 Scholars, and a Children's Industrial Home with 48 Inmates.

Chapter XVI.

COMMISSIONER RAHIMAN IN INDIA.

> The little-minded ask: Belongs this man
> To our own nation? But the noble-hearted
> Regard the human race as all akin.
>
> *Panchatantra.*

The work of The Salvation Army in India has had the advantage of the ripened experience and devoted efforts of some of our ablest Officers. Prominent amongst them will ever be the name of Commissioner Rahiman, more familiarly known in Army circles as Consul Emma Booth Tucker, the second daughter of our Founder.

It was on April 10th, 1888, that we were married at the Congress Hall, Clapton, London, on the anniversary of the Founder's birthday. Her interest in India had long predated this event. As Principal, or "Mother" of the women's side of the Clapton International Training Garrison, she had, from the first, taken a keen interest in the formation and choice of the various parties of Officers who were sent out after the Policy of Parties had been inaugurated by the Founder to meet the growing needs of the Indian work.

And when the call came for her to enter that field herself, she responded with the same enthusiasm and readiness with which she had inspired the women Officers whom she had trained, and sent into the many countries which had now opened their doors to the Army.

Her departure for India was postponed till the autumn, as it is not wise for Europeans to proceed to India during the hot weather or rainy season, a good start during the cold weather giving time for them to become acclimatized.

The interval was spent, however, in selecting and getting together a large reinforcement of Officers to be

1. Lt.-Col. (Dr.) Andrews, V.C., at time when he began the Hospital work of The Army in India.

2. Emma Booth Tucker—known in India as Commissioner Rahiman—second daughter of the Founder.

3. Colonel Arnolis Weerasooriya.

Officers of a Province in South India. The large proportion of native Officers is an indication of the success of The Army's policy of winning India for Christ by Indians.

known as the Wedding Fifty. The party embarked at Genoa in the SS. "Dominico Balduino." They absorbed the third-class accommodation on that boat, the ship's Officers making us very comfortable and facilitating our arrangements for language lessons, lectures, and meetings during the voyage.

The following account gives an interesting glimpse of what has constituted one of the most remarkable chapters in Missionary history:—

THE VOYAGE OF THE WEDDING FIFTY.

"'Is it hotter than this in India?' was the exclamation that some of the party could not but give vent to, after exchanging the fogs and east winds, and what one might call the summer icicles of old England, for the cloudless skies and sultry sunshine of France and Italy. Those who had spent years in India were able to say that anyhow, if it was not much cooler, it would not be any worse for at least nine months out of the twelve, and in many places infinitely better. 'Oh well, if it's no worse than this, I'm sure we can stand it!' was the cheerful rejoinder of those who came, after having made up their minds for the very worst, and determined to look on the bright side of matters. They reported wonderful times in Paris, where the city was stirred, and nearly all the newspapers contained notices of the meetings, with the result that since their departure greater crowds had been attending the meetings, and the French work had received a real lift.

"All along the route across the Continent, there was no end of excitement, and the refreshment rooms were crowded with interested spectators, whose faces manifested mingled feelings of curiosity, amusement, surprise, interest and (when they knelt to pray) a sort of involuntary awe. Though arriving at Genoa as late as midnight, numbers gathered round to ask questions. The party embarked in the dark, singing 'Victory for me,' and 'No, we never will give in,' as boat-load after boat-load shot from the quay to reach the SS. 'Dominico Balduino,' which was moored in the harbour ready to sail at daybreak.

"The presence of Commissioner Rahiman acted as an

inspiration to the party during the whole voyage, and every Officer on board felt glad and proud to be with her, and determined that not one anxiety on their behalf should occur to make the voyage more difficult. The lasses, from Staff Captain Haswell to the latest Cadet recruit, in spite of sea-sickness, were all happy at the thought of being back again for a time as Cadets in their floating Training Home. From their smiling faces and cheerful songs no one would have guessed that they were leaving behind native country and friends.

"How dreary is the long sea voyage to most people! But to the party the time hurried quickly by. What with language lessons, lectures, meetings, private and public, singly and all together, good use was made of the extra leisure. The Brass Band also made itself heard, though in the hurry of the departure our favourite big drum had been left behind. The evening united meeting was a great attraction to all on board. Officers, sailors, native firemen, stewards, and in fact all hands who could get away, would crowd round, while it was almost amusing to see the first-class passengers forsake the attractions of the quarter-deck to go and listen to the speaking and singing.

"The friendliness of all on board was quite delightful. It seemed as if the entire ship was fairly taken by storm. Not only so, but after reaching Bombay, the Officers of the ship were at the welcome meeting, and gave the party an invitation to return on board in order to hold another meeting, telling them with a laugh that the crew had all turned Salvation Army as they were wearing the topis which had been used on the voyage and left behind by the party!"

From October 9th, 1888, to April, 1889, a very full programme of tours and meetings followed, in which Commissioner Rahiman took a very prominent part, winning the hearts of our own people as well as of the outside public.

A good deal of special time was devoted by her to cheering and guiding the now numerous European Missionary Officers, to whom the Indian work was a strange, and in many respects, a trying field.

The following extracts from one of her special addresses

to them will show how thoroughly she accepted and advocated the Indian lines as then laid down, and urged every European Officer to concentrate their whole time and attention on the vast population of the land, and resist all temptation to be side-tracked into easier and more alluring paths :—

"*Go to the right people!* Of course you will remember that your great call is to the Indians. Do not therefore spend more time than you can help among the Europeans. Your life is on the altar for the natives. No difficulties that stand in the way of your reaching them must cause you to forget this, or to grow weary in going after them. You have made their salvation your first work, and in this God sympathizes with you. He loves them more than ever we can. He counts their number. He recognizes the gulf that separates them from our efforts. He yearns over them every one with a yearning that would pour out His blood again for them if that would help their salvation. We may always know, therefore, that in the battle for their souls He is with us. As we enter their little homes, talk with them on the streets, plead with them in the crowd, or weep over them at the penitent form, He is there, close beside us, loving us *more* because we are sticking to these, humanly speaking, hopeless multitudes whom He believed for on Calvary. Therefore in visiting, mind you go to the *right people.*

"*Go in the right spirit.* I have said, do plenty of fishing—do it in all waters and at all seasons. But after all, unless you do it in the *right spirit* it will profit you little, and still less will it profit those to whom you go.

"*Look out for the milestones!* I am often reminded in this Indian war of a drive I once took with my brother. It was from one village to another. We were in a little trap, and it was raining and blowing very hard. I remember now the difficulty we had in holding up the umbrella, and despite our efforts we got very wet. Indeed everything seemed against us on that journey. The pony was very tiresome, at times shying and starting, and at others hardly inclined to go at all. I was very tired, and it seemed to me that we were making next to no progress. The roads seemed all alike, and the village we were in search of *as far away as ever*. 'Oh,' I said, 'we shall never get there—I don't believe we are any nearer.' Just at that moment we were passing a milestone to which he pointed triumphantly, with a flourish of his whip, saying, 'Don't you see, my dear girl, we have come ten miles? A little more patience and push, and we shall win the day!'

"Now here we are in India. The road often seems long, and the monsoons of difficulty and disappointment sweep down upon us, and the time, 'When saved Indians we shall see, numberless as the sands on the sea-shore,' seems perhaps as far off as ever. But, oh, at such moments, may the Lord have some *tall believers* about, who with a flourish of The Army flag will be able to show us the milestones! I have been seeing some at this council. *We are a long way on*. We are up on the hill! India is looking at us—feeling the influence of our lives and prayers. I want to say to you all, my comrades throughout the Indian field, with a great heart of unwavering faith on your behalf, 'Cheer up! A little more patience and push and we shall win the day.'"

The following incident is culled from one of the public addresses delivered by her at this time:—

"Since I have been in India, I have heard a little story that I don't think I shall ever forget. It was about a Hindu woman. I think I may here say that I am specially devoted to women. I have felt from a very little child a great love for my own sex; the Lord has called me in a very special manner to stand beside and help free them from the fetters of their unfavourable surroundings and of their natural timidity, and bring them on to the platform of God's universal opportunity—to inspire them to do something with their time and their talents, so that the world might be the better for their existence in it. And therefore in laying aside in some measure, and for a time, the work I have been doing in England, I am cheered by the thought that I may be enabled to bless my Indian sisters in a similar manner. Perhaps it was because it was the history of a Hindu woman that this little story sank so deeply into my heart. She was childless, and longed to have a little one. So, bringing her petition to the feet of her god, she vowed that if her prayer were granted she would bring her all to his altar. And the Lord hearkened to her prayer and granted her request, and she was blessed with a child.

"She did not forget her vow, but clothing herself with her most expensive robes, and decked with every jewel and costly adornment that she possessed, she went to the temple, and kneeling there she stripped herself of everything and left before the shrine her all of temporal goods. Then putting on the coarse garb of the poorest class, she went forth with the consciousness that she had performed her vow and kept her faith. Oh! I thought, what a lesson for us! Those of us who have not merely received a child, but *the* Child Jesus."

The news received in April, 1889, regarding the illness of the Consul's Mother, Catherine Booth, was of so serious a character that it was considered necessary for her to proceed to England to assist in nursing her through the malady from which recovery now appeared improbable, and from which a fatal termination was then expected at an early date.

Mother and daughter had been attached to each other with peculiar ties of devotion, and we did not feel justified in holding each other back from what was to us, so soon after our wedding, a severe personal sacrifice. This involved the absence of my wife from the Indian Field from April, 1889, till after the death of her Mother on 4th October, 1890.

The following account of Commissioner Rahiman's farewell meeting is taken from *The Advocate of India*, a Bombay daily paper :—

"The Salvation Army was *en fete* yesterday evening to celebrate the departure of Mrs. Booth Tucker for England. She leaves by the SS. "Singapore," of the Rubattino Company, on Saturday next, and will be, no doubt, very much missed by the whole contingent throughout India. Previous to the meeting there were two large processions. The first one, consisting of a long string of bullock carts, and filled with some seventy or eighty members of the Army, paraded through the native town. At night the Fort was astir with a torchlight foot-march, which attracted great crowds all along the route. The theatre was filled with an expectant audience, and Commissioner and Mrs. Booth Tucker must have been gratified with the reception they met. Those who have heard her gifted mother speak could not but notice the remarkable resemblance as she poured forth her farewell words.

"Commissioner Booth Tucker addressed the meeting, giving some particulars regarding the Indian work. It seems that during the last three years the Officers have increased from 50 to 263, of whom 160 are Europeans and the rest Indians. The Corps have increased from 14 to 57. There is a large circulation of English and vernacular *War Crys*, amounting to more than twenty thousand copies monthly, and printed in five different languages. The total cost of the entire work in India and Ceylon, exclusive of building halls, and bringing out parties, amounts only to £7,000 per annum, of which no less than £5,000 is raised locally in India, showing that the work is not only strictly economical, but almost entirely self-supporting. Some interesting particulars were given in regard to the prison work, which is assisted in Ceylon by a Government grant.

"The meeting terminated with prayer, while all on the platform rose to their feet, being joined by many of the congregation in fresh 'dedication for service.' The scene was certainly a very impressive one."

The coming of her beloved daughter was an unspeakable comfort to Catherine Booth, and helped to brighten the remaining sad and suffering period of her painful and prolonged sickness.

Immediately after the death of Mrs. Booth, a number of Officers were gathered together, known as the Memorial Fifty. This reinforcement sailed for India in November, 1890, and the following account of their tour is gathered from a report written at the time :—

"It was on Christmas Day, 1890, that the largest party ever yet shipped from England, numbering sixty-four Officers, and including Commissioners Fakir Singh and Rahiman and Colonel Ruhani (Lucy Booth), landed amidst great rejoicings on the shores of Ceylon. A day or two later Colombo's largest and most beautiful hall was crowded with an interested audience. Three hundred Officers and Soldiers took their place in the imposing march to the hall.

"On the day after their arrival, 150 Officers were met in council, and in the evening the finest barracks we have in Ceylon was opened: a good, solid, lofty, airy building, seating about 800 people, situated on the main road on Slave Island. It is seated throughout, has a good platform, and is well lighted. It was crowded to excess when, after a long march, the Commissioner and party took possession of it.

"Not less gratifying was the way in which the spacious Audience Hall of the Kandy kings was filled to listen to an address from Commissioner Rahiman, who, though weak and suffering, could not keep away from the front in this glorious season. On the way back from Kandy a great gathering of village troops assembled in a railway shed, and a blessed evidence it was of the extent to which we are striking our roots down into the village life of Ceylon.

"Next to this, an immense demonstration was held at Moratuwa, where Colonel Ruhani laid the foundation-stone of a good substantial barracks for Moratuwa I, and after a brilliant torch-light procession, a packed, enthusiastic, boiling-over meeting and watch-night service was held at Moratuwamulla.

"In Madras the Commissioner and party scored another point of advance by occupying the largest and finest public building (the Victoria Hall) for the first time, where a large crowd of old and new friends gave them a proper reception. This meeting was preceded by a large open-air gathering on the Maidan (Esplanade), and an imposing march led by the Memorial Brass Band and comprising a war chariot, mounted marshals, and about 120 Officers, besides Soldiers, and a vast crowd of interested followers and onlookers. The spacious platform was crowded with red jackets, including quite a number of cadets.

"In Poona, the Lord Harris Theatre was crowded. But surely the crowning time was the brilliant and crowded assemblage which met in Bombay at the Framji Cowasji Institute to consider the Commissioner's proposals for 'Darkest India,' when the chair was taken by the Hon.

Justice Telang. The whole tour was one immense success, a demonstration of extraordinary advance.

"Alas, that such a bright morning should have been so soon clouded! But God's ways are not as our ways; and just when we appeared to be on the eve of a tremendous upheaval of the Social Movement in India, the hand of sickness fell with swift and relentless grip upon Commissioner Rahiman, necessitating her removal, almost at the point of death, to England, and we lost at one sweep both our loved Commissioners. The blow was severe and crushing, but God never fails us."

Unfortunately the long and anxious strain of nursing her mother, had left its mark upon the Consul,* and on reaching Colombo her health was in such poor condition that she was unable to attend many of the reception meetings, and proceeded direct to Bombay, leaving the party, with her sister Colonel Ruhani (afterwards Mrs. Booth Hellberg) and myself to complete the tour through South India.

On reaching Bombay in January, 1891, we found that the Consul, instead of rallying from her illness as we had hoped, had developed serious signs of anæmia, and the doctor considered that the only hope of saving her life was for her to proceed immediately to Europe. After reaching England she began steadily to improve, but medical opinion gave a very decided verdict that it would be impossible for her to return at any time to India.

The Founder therefore appointed us as Foreign Secretaries to supervise the work of The Army in other lands, under the direction of the then Chief of the Staff, the present General. This post we occupied from 1891 to 1896, when the Founder desired us to take charge of the work in the United States. In this position the Consul helped to carry The Salvation Army through a particularly difficult crisis in its history, and endeared herself greatly to the people of America.

It was on October 28th, 1903, when the Consul was returning from a transcontinental tour, that the train in which she was travelling was derailed, and the accident

* A special rank conferred on Mrs. Booth Tucker.

occurred which terminated fatally, her death being universally lamented, not only in America, but throughout The Salvation Army world.

The following year, December, 1904, I returned from America to our Foreign Office in London.

After our departure from India the Consul's sister, Colonel Ruhani, bravely volunteered to fill the gap, and was appointed to the command of India. Shortly afterwards she was married to Commissioner Booth Hellberg, and they jointly directed the work till 1896, when they were transferred to the command of France and Switzerland. Under their leadership the Indian work continued to make steady progress, several new fields being opened up.

A change was now made in the system of supervision. India was divided up into separate commands, and a Resident Indian Secretary was appointed to represent International Headquarters, and to form a link between the different Territories.

The first to occupy this post was Colonel Jai Singh, (now Commissioner Bullard). He was succeeded by the late Commissioner Higgins, the father of the present Chief of the Staff, who held this position for several years, greatly endearing himself to the Officers. He was succeeded by Colonel Jang Singh (Hammond), who occupied the position with success till 1907.

Chapter XVII.

THE FOUNDER TWICE VISITS INDIA IN 1891-2 AND 1895-6.

> "*The Hope of India:* Men and women who will literally lay themselves on the altar, strip themselves of all encumbrances that would hinder them in the war, adopt the Salvation of India as their life work, go forth to practise just as much self-denial and endure just as much suffering as may be found necessary and helpful in learning the language, conforming to the customs, becoming all things lawful and expedient to the people and so ensure their reaching that God-made Christ-like character of *Saviours of India.*"
>
> *William Booth.*

India was twice visited by William Booth, the Founder of The Salvation Army. On the first of these occasions his tour took place in December and January 1891-2, and followed closely on his campaigns in South Africa and Australasia. The Darkest England Scheme had been launched a few months previously and had created a sensation, the effects of which were felt throughout the world. One of the objects of the Founder was to ascertain how far the plans there outlined might be adapted to other lands, and more particularly to search for some possible opening for his proposed Colony Over-the-Seas.

In regard to India, his object was mainly to investigate the possibilities of applying the same principles to the vast social needs of her submerged tenth. When he returned to India four years later, in December and January 1895-6, the Founder was able to present some definite plans in the shape of concrete proposals for "Peasant Settlements" and "Village Banks." The ultimate fruition of these schemes in the shape of Agricultural Colonies and

Industrial Settlements for our own Soldiers and for Criminal Tribes, are referred to elsewhere in these pages.

The general outcome of these proposals, however, had a far-reaching effect which extended beyond our own borders, and resulted in widespread efforts on the part of Government itself as well as of the Indian Community at large to ameliorate the condition of the depressed and suffering classes very much along the lines sketched by our Founder. It may be truly said that all philanthropic India was set a-thinking, and, may we say a-hoping, and may we not say a-helping on a scale of magnitude which had before seemed impossible.

The following account of the Founder's arrival in Colombo after his Australian tour, and of his interesting interview with a press representative, is taken from *The Ceylon Times* :—

"The 'Valetta' bringing General Booth arrived in sight soon after daybreak, at which time rain was steadily falling, and when the vessel rounded the breakwater at 8 o'clock, the downpour was still continuing. At the jetty, which had been specially decorated for the occasion, the arrival of the vessel was the subject of animated conversation amongst the large body of Salvationists and others gathered there ; while out in the harbour, adorned with banners that tried their best to look gay but signally failed, was the 'Ruby' steam launch bearing several Officers of The Salvation Army, who cheered the General when they saw him on the steamer.

"The General, it may be remarked, has altered in appearance but very little since our representative last saw him in England. He is a trifle thinner perhaps ; but this may be due to the great strain he has recently undergone in Australia and Africa in the way of public speaking. He was dressed in the familiar long dark blue coat bearing the 'S' collar badge, and wore his usual red jersey.

"The General is not a man who spends much time over welcomings and handshakings, and he was very soon *au courant* with all he cared to know in the way of preliminaries, so that, in the interval before he came ashore, our reporter had time to get in half an hour's chat with him concerning his travels, and his hopes and anticipations. The General of course is greatest on the scheme that he published to the world a year or more ago, and he is very pleased with the kindly encouragement given to his views in that respect in Africa and in Australia.

"The Governors of all the Colonies visited appear to have treated him very cordially. To the probable invasion of Australia by a band of the unemployed workmen of England, however, the workmen of Australia have strong objections, and this feeling seems to have impressed General Booth a good deal, for he often reverted to it in the course of conversation. 'The principles of Darkest England,' he said, 'are applicable to all countries and with all peoples wherever misery exists, and in Australia they are as much so as anywhere else. Yes, I did notice an apprehension in Australia that my scheme might lead to an overstocking of the colonies with labour. That is always the cry. If you go to the Officers on this ship here, I dare say you will find that many of them have Captain's certificates. "Well," you say to them, "Why are you not a Captain?" And the reply is, "Because there are too many Captains." Isn't that so? Aren't there too many in every profession—except reporters, eh?'

"This last remark was met with the reply that one would have thought that after his experiences The General would not have complained of any scarcity of journalists, to which the General replied that he certainly did think there were too many.

"Continuing his remarks, he asked why there was all this overstocking and crowding, his manner of putting the question indicating that he had all the means at his command for putting a stop to the existing state of things.

"'Yes, I was very pleased with the reception I got everywhere. The novelty of the scheme had not worn off by the publication of my book, and the people assembled in large crowds everywhere to hear me. It was a great strain. I addressed meetings of over 5,000, 6,000 and 7,000 often in Australia, and many a time had to give an unexpected address on a railway platform where crowds, who had come in for miles, had gathered to receive me and to get an address out of me as I was passing through'.

"'However, hard as the work was, I have felt the benefit of it. All change of work is recreation, and change of work and change of scene are good for a man. Still, I assure you I have worked a great deal, and I have been dreading my arrival here in Colombo for fear I should not get my work which I had planned for this voyage done in time. You hear people around say, there is nothing to do on board ship. Well, I have found plenty to do each day, without reading novels!'"

The route taken on each of the Founder's tours, and the character of receptions accorded to him, were so similar that it will be sufficient to select a few incidents to enable the reader to gather a general idea of these important events, which helped to place The Salvation Army on a new and more favourable platform of opportunity before the Indian public.

In the great Presidency cities of Calcutta, Bombay, and Madras, Europeans and Indians alike flocked to see and hear the great author of the "Cab-horse Charter" of humanity, and they were not disappointed. The Viceroy and Governors and other leaders of the people vied with each other in the cordiality of their reception.

The following is an account of the reception of the Founder in Madras:—

"Seldom has Madras witnessed such a scene of animation as that which reigned throughout the city yesterday evening. In and around Egmore station some thousands of people had assembled, and so great was the crowd that the station authorities found it necessary to close the various entrances to the platform, including even the Station Master's, Booking and other offices. The hackney carriage drivers must have reaped a good harvest, for by 6 p.m. not a carriage was procurable, and throughout the afternoon the fares demanded and paid were exorbitant.

"The platform of the Egmore station was prettily decorated with flags and Chinese lanterns, while a *Shamianah* with pink canopy had been erected in the centre.

"Admission to the platform was by ticket only, the railway authorities having issued directions that only a limited number of persons should be admitted; but notwithstanding this restriction there was an enormous gathering on the platform. Outside the building, the shades of evening were turned into the light of day by some hundreds of torches.

"On alighting from the train, General Booth was received by Dewan Bahadur Ragunatha Rao, on behalf of the Indian community in general, and by the Rev. Mr. Satthianadhan on behalf of the Indian Christian community He was then conducted to the *Shamianah*, where he was garlanded, rose water sprinkled over him, and flowers thrown upon him. This preliminary over, addresses were presented to him on behalf of the Indian and Christian communities respectively."

Similar scenes were witnessed at the other cities visited when the largest halls available were crowded with enthusiastic audiences. But we pass on to a description of one of those vast village gatherings when the Founder felt himself to be indeed face to face with the real ***heart of India***.

" We think we were not wrong in surmising that the demonstration at Samarkha would be the most remarkable event in The General's Indian tour.

" Far into the night lanterns were bobbing about here and there on the extensive grounds, and little finishing touches were being put to the arrangements. It was only for a brief hour or two that all settled down into silence, and before the earliest streak of grey had heralded the dawn of this 'day of days,' the shrill notes of the bugle's call woke the sleeping encampment into life and activity. Soon after, troops of soldiers began to arrive, and as the hour of eight approached, we were startled by a salute of seven guns, fired from a cannon posted somewhere on the edge of the encampment and which announced the arrival of the General and his party. The General's tent was approached by an avenue of plantain trees and Indian corn, and so situated as to furnish an admirable view of the ground.

"Gun-fire announced the 8 o'clock assembly, the bugle summoned the band, and the earliest arrivals were soon arranged in the spacious pandal. Oh, what a time we had, as after some lively, happy testimonies, the

General sought to put everybody in tune for the day's engagements and enjoyments by turning our thoughts in upon our own heart's needs, kindling heavenly desires and making it so clear to everyone that from God and God alone these needs could be met.

"By this time the grounds began to assume a most animated appearance. Some thousands had arrived, and streams of new-comers kept steadily pouring in. Full soon the firing of the gun recalled us to duty, and the spacious pandal was filled with Salvationists from end to end. This time the General was to deliver an address especially to his Soldiers.

"It was a wise provision which the Major had made in arranging a sort of signal code of flags for controlling the unrestrained enthusiasm of that happy crowd. White flags waving vigorously hushed it to silence, and again, there was a blue flag which brought us all to prayer. This arrangement was an undoubted success, notwithstanding that now and then the signalmen got a little mixed up, and the wrong flag was used instead of the right one.

"After affording an opportunity for letting off a little of the surplus spirits of that eager crowd by devoting half an hour to testimonies, the General set to work, dealing faithfully with them as to their duties and responsibilities, urging them to become the men and women whom God could use to become the Saviours of their countrymen. As soon as the invitation was given, some fifty or more pressed forward to seek cleansing.

"Soon after one o'clock thousands of Hindus began to arrive on the scene, and preparations were hurried forward for the great March Past, the forces forming up in a lane some distance from the field. A grand stand had been built after the fashion of an Egyptian pyramid with the apex cut off, so as to afford space on the top for a few chairs designed for the General and the most distinguished visitors, with a handsome canopy overhead, as a protection from the sun. It was built of brick and white-washed, as was also the band-stand which was, however, raised on a circular base and surmounted by a flagstaff from which floated our colours.

"Taking a seat on one of the sloping steps leading to the

summit of the grand stand, we had time to survey the grounds, which had become by this time covered with a dense mass of people rapidly increasing in numbers, through which the police were busy trying to preserve a way for the march, when it should arrive. The trees were literally alive with onlookers, and every bit of rising ground was densely packed.

"First, there was the band with those marvellous Indian trumpets about nine feet long. What a sight! They do not march in solemn stateliness and commence on the third beat; it is hard to suppose that they ever did commence, or that they will ever leave off. What a kaleidoscope of motion! Every bandsman is now shifting his position, now twisting round, now here, now there; one moment his trumpet is perpendicular, the next horizontal, and anon at every conceivable angle, facing in turn every point of the compass. The band was, without doubt, one of the most live things we have ever seen.

"On, on, comes the long line of soldiers. Well, it is scarcely a line; it is an elongated mass. Perhaps they started four deep, but ere long they had become so excited that they were a score deep and filled the road, at least what there was left of it, for dense crowds of spectators lined the route. Then clearly discernible came a crowd of Bhils armed with bows and arrows, dancing after their own wild fashion every step of the way. Then came the picturesque camel corps consisting of about 25 camels. Later on came the brass band, followed by cadets and soldiers in somewhat better order than the earlier part of the procession, and then a splendid elephant whose massive proportions and grave demeanour added much to the dignity of the scene.

"The march was continued round the grounds, and the whole was brought up in a dense mass around the grand stand, while the camels careered gaily round the grounds to the delectation of the crowds of onlookers, and then the camels were brought up and made to kneel on the edge of the big crowd. The solemn elephant looked on in silence, the irrepressible trumpeters were quieted, and, by a vigorous use of the white flag, some approach to silence was secured while the General addressed the vast crowd.

"By this time every one was hungry, and very soon there was a rush for the one-anna tickets which entitled the holder to attack what was very literally a *mountain of kichery*, (rice and lentils). Need we say that ere the sun went down that mountain was brought low? In the meantime the General was once more hard at work—this time addressing some 1,500 caste people who had assembled in the pandal, and who were greatly taken hold of by the General's words.

"It is estimated that at least 10,000 Hindus were on the ground during the afternoon, in addition to some 2,500 soldiers. Night, however, was the crowning time. The crowd of hungry soldiers took some time to serve, so that the meeting was somewhat delayed, but once it got into swing it was a wonderful time. After a short run of testimonies led by Major Jivi, the General addressed the meeting, and soon made us all feel that he meant business for eternity. By and by the front of the platform was cleared and such a scene as we had seldom witnessed before presented itself. The front of the platform was soon filled from end to end, men on one side, women on the other, and a second, and third, and fourth, and fifth, and sixth row were prostrate, in one solid mass, one man's shoulder serving as a penitent form for his neighbour, while those who were dealing with the penitents had often to clamber over the others. This blessed work went on until we counted 102 seeking salvation. Then there was a Hallelujah wind-up of that indescribable sort, when it seemed as if earth had got somehow mixed up with the skies, and the multitude on earth mingled with the multitude round about the Throne.

"While this had been transpiring in the pandal, a wonderful transformation had gone forward outside. The grounds had been illuminated with 5,000 lamps, and one of the most startling effects produced. We had seen little patches of lamps strewed about the grounds in the oddest of fashions during the day, some suspended in rows and others placed in irregular patches on the ground. We little dreamed what the combined effect would be. The perspective of the flat fields over which they were spread was completely changed, and it was difficult to imagine that we were not looking out over a vast city brilliantly illuminated, while passing figures looked like giant shadows stalking through its streets. It was a bright and fascinating scene!

"By the time the General and party were seated on the platform, which had been erected conveniently for viewing the evening display, the band had occupied the band-stand, and our Gujarati warriors had commenced one of their famous war dances, while the fantastic group and the living wall of spectators stretching right across the field were alternately lit up with a glow like that some of us remember to have seen round a blacksmith's forge on winter nights at home, and then lost in shadow like the smithy when the roar of the bellows ceases, while ever and anon powerful fountains of fire shot far up into the black night scattering myriads of gleaming stars, or a great blaze of red light made for a brief space every face discernible. Then the General once more gathered his children around him, spoke a few parting words and gave them his blessing. The happy groups started on their homeward march and the camp settled down into silence."

CHAPTER XVIII.

THE VISIT OF GENERAL BRAMWELL BOOTH TO INDIA IN 1922-23.

Twenty-eight years had elapsed since the Founder's second visit to India, when his son and successor, General Bramwell Booth, landed in Colombo, in December 1922. The striking progress which The Salvation Army had made during the interval may be gathered from the following extracts which are taken from the General's Journal. These carry the narrative from the voyage to Ceylon in the P. & O. Steamer "Macedonia," to the time when the General bid good-bye to the Indian Officers and Soldiers in Bombay, the tour lasting from December 18, 1922, to January 27, 1923.

In the case of Ceylon it was not his first visit. Some two years previously he had spent several days in the Island, and had conducted an important and successful series of meetings. He had urged Lieut.-Colonel Dayal Singh, the Territorial Commander, to arrange a special campaign in Moratuwa, promising to assist with the necessary expense. The remarkable awakening that followed, and extended to other districts in Ceylon, is described in Chapter XXVII.

As may be imagined, the tour was a severe physical strain upon the General. Nevertheless, he was able to fulfil his engagements, and bring his visit to a successful conclusion. He was accompanied through the tour by Commissioner Mapp, Major Evan Smith and Ensign Wycliffe Booth, while the various Territorial leaders were with him in their respective commands.

Amongst the leading personages whom the General interviewed were Their Highnesses the Maharaja of Travancore, the Maharaja of Bardwan and the Agha Khan. He was also received by the Viceroy, and the Governors of Madras, Bengal, Punjab and Bombay. All of them expressed their warm sympathy with The Salvation Army, and especial gratitude for the noble and self-sacrificing work which it had carried on among the Criminal Tribes and Depressed Classes.

The extracts from the General's Journal commence with some of the incidents which took place during his voyage from Europe to Colombo:

"*Saturday, 9th December,* 1922, SS. 'MACEDONIA.'

"Lectured in the Saloon last night, Sir Charles Armstrong, one of the railway magnates of the East, in the chair. Very good audience. All seemed very much interested and many impressed.

"*Thursday, 14th December,* 1922.

"Beginning to be weary of the ship!

"Three interesting interviews to-day. An important lawyer of Bombay, a Parsee, very friendly to The Army. Talked freely about the affairs of India. Deeply convinced of the enormous value to the people of the British control, while still ardently wishing for a larger measure of self-government.

"The Parsees are deeply interesting. They are a small but very influential force in Indian life. Smith made the following extracts from one of their books of instruction:

> Who is the most fortunate man in the world?
> He who is most innocent.
> Who is the most innocent man in the world?
> He who walks in the path of God and shuns that of the devil!
> Which is the path of God and which that of the devil?
> Virtue is the path of God and vice that of the devil.
> What constitutes virtue, and what vice?
> Good thoughts, good words, and good deeds constitute virtue, and evil thoughts, evil words, and evil deeds constitute vice.
> What constitutes good thoughts, good words, and good deeds?
> Honesty, charity, and truthfulness constitute the former; and dishonesty, want of charity, and falsehood constitute the latter!

"His Highness the Agha Khan greatly interests me. Mahommedan leader—wealthy, and a very influential man, returning from work with the British Government on the new financial arrangements for India. Very free and warm. Believes in The Salvation Army! Cordially approves our work for the lost of every nation. Has been taking a holiday in Switzerland, and seen The Army among the mountains. 'You have reason, General, to be proud of your people in Switzerland.'

"Concluding a long talk we spoke of his own relations with God, and he seemed pleased, though our views so different. I said, 'Cannot you go so far as to think of Him as a Father?' 'No, I cannot go so far as that.'—Anxious I should speak in India of the importance of getting the best men of every creed into the various governing bodies. I asked him if he thought the new system of government would help the lower castes. 'Not at first, they will suffer, but later, yes! Hope you will speak of this.' An able and large-hearted man.

"*18th December.* COLOMBO.

"Landed at 5 o'clock. Landing-stage very crowded, above and below. Mayor and Mayoress welcomed me in the name of the City, and introduced me to important men on the Council. Mayor speaking a few words led me to open space outside. Huge crowd greeted us with enthusiasm. Spoke of service to God and man. Prema Bala translated. Remarkable scenes; endless colour, life, banners, uniform. Above all the people, the dark faces of all shades, the children of our Schools, the Young People, the Officers. A sense of true human sympathy spread over the great crowd and over me. A really wonderful feeling!

"The Army is a comparatively small force here, and yet how evidently it has impressed the multitude, mind and heart. *A memorable reception.*

"*19th December.*

"The Hon. Mr. De Mel (Member of Legislative Council), old and tried friend, loves Salvation Army 'because it loves the lost.' Talked freely of National Revival in Ceylon. Tide turning towards their own dress, food, and other ancient customs, and away from European ways. Many well-off people giving up Western manners. His firm no longer employs clerks who do not dress as the people."

"*December 20th.* HEWADIWILLA.

"Outside the village met by Salvationists, songs, and dancing and flowers. Procession formed, fully a thousand persons marching, led by converted devil-dancers, whose wonderful energy was the despair of some of us! Three elephants and streams of fine, upstanding and attractive men and women.

"Meeting followed in special pandal, a frame of bamboo covered with leaves and branches of trees; open sides. The children sang, and then came garlands! Congregational singing disappointed me, but the praying was good. The attention of the outside crowds very impressive. They joined with the Salvationists in tense interest in the affair, laughed and cheered, and then as suddenly grew serious and solemn; everything so natural. Prema Bala translated me in part, and Samaraveera (Colonel). About sixty at the penitent form. One giant of a man deeply interested me. He was so broken down about his sin. A woman with her baby made another wonderful picture; her countenance was literally illuminated. The *intensity* of everything was greatly to my liking."

"*December 24th.* TRIVANDRUM.

"First meeting at 4 o'clock. Fully 5,000 people chiefly our own Soldiers, a few visiting Syrian Christians having come, mostly on foot, a hundred miles to be present. Some of our Soldiers, I understand, have been walking four days to be here.

"The scene a remarkable one indeed. People seated for the most part on the ground, proper formation preserved, aisles marked out, men and women quite separate, thousands of Salvationists carrying small flags of our three colours, which they raise every now and again to emphasize some point of song, or to show special approval of something said. The freedom, the shouts of praise, the songs, the music, the flags, the evident joy of all, or nearly all, combined to produce an extraordinary effect. *I can never forget it.*

"The platform a small raised stage covered by a slight roof of branches and leaves afforded the speakers protection from the sun, the ground rising from its front, and the whole scene spreading out like a fan. Spoke through interpreters. Magnavox a complete success. We were well heard without shouting or straining, and, in fact, the

1. General Bramwell Booth examining the women's needlework in Travancore.
2. Portion of one of the monster gatherings during the General's Campaign (1923) in South India.

1. Boys of The Salvation Army Home in Trivandrum (South India).

2. Staff Officers of the Indian Field gathered at Bombay for Councils with the General (1923). It is significant that nearly one-third of the number are native born.

ease with which the people could hear helped the deep silence so favourable to a Meeting in the open.

"An invitation to the Mercy-Seat was followed by a steady stream of men, and then later women. They prayed aloud as they rose to their feet, and their praying could never be forgotten by anyone who heard them."

"*December 27th.*

"After a fair night up at 6, and at 6.40 to Palace with Sukh Singh to see His Highness the Maharaja by his appointment. His palace is within what is called 'The Fort,' a large enclosure containing several royal and other houses, also barracks for soldiers. Arrived at a few moments before 7; was met at the door of the Receiving Hall by His Highness himself, who greeted me with a stately courtesy, and we were soon in deep conversation. His Highness, a man of about my own age, tall and slim, with exceedingly expressive eyes; was simply dressed in a kind of black surtout buttoned up to the neck; dignified and useful. He is full of interest in The Salvation Army, especially in the Hospital at Nagercoil, and anxious that that work should be extended. Talked with him freely about his people; evidently deeply sympathetic with—perhaps a little puzzled by—The Army. Among the points mentioned were our need of land, help for Schools, for wells, and for roads to our villages now without them. The Maharaja came with me to the door at parting, and, taking my hand as I left, said most earnestly, 'May God bless you and guide you.' He is a strict Hindu, and the Ruler of about five millions of people."

"*December 28th.* NAGERCOIL, TRAVANCORE.

"A restless night, but full of gratitude. At 8.30 meeting of Local Officers of the two Divisions represented here. Six hundred men and a few women. A magnificent sight. All men of splendid physique. With few exceptions, recovered from heathendom. The singing was really wonderful and the praying equally so. The penitent-form also a wonderful scene with some glorious confessions and consecrations. The whole thing was out-and-out Salvation Army, so significant for the future.

"In the evening an enormous gathering—certainly

between 15,000 and 20,000 people. The attention wonderful. Greatly impressed by the Band here; am told the best Band we shall meet.

"In the Prayer Meeting, the singing in so vast a gathering difficult to control. We counted fifty drums scattered about, most of them the centre of a singing group. But we managed to unite them by playing Daniel's cornet through the magnavox—a great hit!

"The Prayer Meeting and penitent-form scenes indescribable. Dealt personally with one or two people. One woman with child in her arms greatly stirred, me and truly as I looked upon the scene deep called to deep in my soul."

"*4th January.*

"Arrived at Bapatla in the Telugu country about 9 a.m. Food, and away to Criminal Tribe Settlement at Stuartpuram, about two miles. A most hopeful effort—about two thousand souls. The Cabinet Minister overlooking this department told me in Madras that before we took them, this tribe had an average of one policeman to one family. *Now they have none.* The Settlement is organized in eight villages—each choosing its head man. Some of these are Salvationists, some not—all uniting in the election of one of their number as a judge to settle internal disputes, who is a local Officer in our ranks.

"My visit evidently a great event. A high day. The procession with its contrasts remarkable. The flags—the native music—the clothes and lack of clothes. The simply wonderful difference in appearance and demeanour of the settlers lately arrived, with those already here—the women—the charming children—the singing—the evident progress of many. All quite captivating.

"The Meeting followed—500—mostly men. First came some offerings by Local Officers for the Work—gifts of the Salvationist part of the community. Then three or four most telling testimonies—quite easy to see the speakers thoroughly believed in.

"Exhibit of work followed—industries—of Schools—the old thread and rope making in which toes as well as fingers work—cooking, the germ of the present-day 'baker's oven'—the grass-weaving—the sewing—the mats—the puddling of mud for a mud house—the potter—the trial of an assumed drunk—the singing of the children! The uplifting influences very evident. After food at the Governor's quarters went with Adjutant and Mrs. Robilliard to one of the village centres—entered one or two of the settlers' huts. These are provided by Government and well made, but ought to be better. Poultry everywhere, *and babies*! Next to no furniture. Wardrobes not necessary! Cooking goes on—savoury though primitive!

"The happiness of many of the Settlers a kind of *contentment*. How far they have already come from the conditions in which we found them! Government grant only a few hundred pounds a year for this place, mainly spent in the improvement of the land—the most trifling sum when compared with the former cost of police and prison.

"Returned to Bapatla. Public Reception—enormous crowd—streets, housetops, market, trees, all full and the people glad—a sense of true sympathy. Spoke of The Army and its revelation from God for all men. Attention riveted. Immense juggernaut wheel here—glad to notice much out of repair!

"After business, Meeting in enclosure—three thousand people, mostly our own. Fire and enthusiasm and glow in everything. More easily stirred than in the south. Shouting and singing responses very striking. The after Meeting presented an extraordinary scene—rows and rows of weeping and praying men—a few women. Officers who know them well speak of their serious and earnest sincerity. Closed at 9.20. Over three hundred names taken."

"*January 9th*, 1923. CALCUTTA.

"At one o'clock lunch with Lord and Lady Lytton. Rather a disappointment, as I wanted a quiet talk, and we had rather a formal military kind of ceremony with twenty guests. Fine, upstanding men with beards, and in gorgeous uniform, to wait upon us. I drank my tea and listened to Lord Lytton, who said some good things. We spoke of Education. I prophesy an army of educated unemployed more difficult than the uneducated. What is the use of education here or anywhere *which unfits people for life*?

"At three o'clock, interesting interview with three newspapers. They catechized me!

"At four to see the Maharajah of Burdwan, one of the two or three largest land-owners in India. Fine house. Encouraged me to hope about our Settlements and the grant. 'I am a Hindu, orthodox—but I don't care what you do for my people—if everything is voluntary, and you do not press or bribe them.'

"This is the centre of the Brahmo Samaj, a very interesting branch of Hinduism. Their paper of to-day's date speaks of me in very warm terms.

> You (that is, The Army) have come to present Christ to us in an Oriental garb and with devotional enthusiasm, humility, meekness, and poverty, which are truly Oriental, therefore will the Lord God of India bless you and your message. . . After a reference to the Founder—General Booth is no ordinary man. He is a man of God inspired for the great work He has given him to do, and as such we revere him and love him, and we regard the entire organization of The Salvation Army as the work of the Holy God.

"*January 19th*. ANAND, GUJARAT

"Travelling all yesterday. Arrived Anand, fifty miles from Ahmedabad, at 8.20 a.m. to-day. Great crowd to meet us; many Salvationists. Shouts and songs and music united to make a strange melody of beautiful sounds. Many strangers in the crowd, including some wearing the white boat-shaped Ghandi cap.

"Afternoon Meeting in enclosure; four thousand people, perhaps more. Talked with some freedom. The Magnavox again a wonderful help. The crowds very solemn and earnest. Some camels broke into the enclosure, but nobody moved. Another mighty penitent-form scene—with the exception of a handful, all men, pathetic incidents. Such prayer, such confessions, such humbling—*literally to the dust*! 247 names registered.

"*January 20th*. ANAND.

"Midday, great March past. A wonderful scene. The enthusiasm of our people, the wondrous manifestations of Eastern life, the deep sympathetic interest of the crowds looking on, the children, the weird music, the camels—chiefly belonging to the Local Officers, who rode on them—the colour, the banners, all very moving. Not an unkin word from the astonished onlookers. Took a baby into my arms to bless, to the immense delight of all. More and more the people draw me. Allowing for some excitement and a natural desire to please me, this was still a very wonderful scene. The procession was two hours in marching past. The Bhils gave us an 'extra,' a most extraordinary native dance. The singing of our people was good in parts, the music defective. The Cadets, both men and women, looked most hopeful.

"At four o'clock, Local Officers and Field Officers. Fewer of the former than expected; some mistake about the day. Some hard hitting and a good Meeting.

"A wealthy Hindu, landowner, came thirty miles to greet me; very cordial. Has been reading some of my writings translated into the newspapers here. I spoke with him. God make my words words of life! How wonderful the feeling towards us appears to be. And more and more I see that it is the spirit of Jesus which is the real attraction."

"*January 21st.*

"This is the last Sunday of my present visit. Wakened at 3 a.m. by two policemen set to guard us. They suspected robbers and desired to search my room! Called Smith, who did it for them.

"Officers at ten o'clock. A fine lot of men. More responsive—perhaps a little more emotional—than the north. Talked to them with some freedom. Continued at 3.30 and at 6.30. Very good. Excellent singing. A wonderful scene at the finish. Surely God spoke to His servants bowed before Him and we had a bright light in the gloaming.

"Walked through the Hospital with Staff-Captain (Dr.) Draper. *Pleased.* The new wing for the Blind will cost us about two thousand pounds but will be worth it. The Doctor wants an X-ray outfit and I half promised. In course of conversation he said that The Salvation Army people of the rank and file are undoubtedly better patients than others—stronger physique. The Hospital has seventy beds and dealt with thirteen thousand out-patients last year. Many get saved."

"*22nd January*. BOMBAY.

"Arrived at eleven o'clock after an improved night in the train. Met by Sir Narayan Chandarvarkar, President of Legislative Council, accompanied by a group of important men with a fine and happy crowd. Sir N. spoke in very appreciative terms both of The Army and me, and garlanded me amidst applause. I replied briefly.

"To billet—Taj Mahal Hotel, rather a swell place, but I was thankful. Cheering Press here. It seems as if my visit has shown some things in a true light and done a little on behalf of the forgotten and the friendless of the people. The *Times of India* at 12.20. Interesting talk with their representative—knew The Army in Aberdeen.

"Lectured at six o'clock in the Cowasjee Jehangir Hall. Met Governor of the Bombay Presidency, Sir George Lloyd, at the door, and walked through with him to the platform. Very cordial. He and others told me that we had the most representative and influential audience ever gathered in this city, except perhaps for Royal visitors. All classes and nationalities here. Place too full, every avenue crowded, and fully fifteen hundred left outside.

"Lecture went fairly well. Had been warned that the Hall was bad for speaking but I found it good! I got in a very definite testimony for my Lord and Master. Sir Narayan Chandarvarkar moved the vote. He is one of the most well-known and influential Hindus in India. He made a clever speech. Sir Norman McLeod, Chief Justice, seconded, and spoke delightfully of The Army's work, making a happy reference to the Founder and also to Tucker. The whole audience rose on my reading the King's Message and loudly cheered at its conclusion. Walked out with the Governor amidst another striking demonstration of enthusiastic goodwill. Our own dear folks very pleased and cheered.

"At the outer door we found the Chief Justice waving his hat and calling upon the crowd for three cheers for General Booth! A former door-keeper at International Headquarters took my hand.

"This is the end of my public work on this visit. How thankful I am that God has helped me and above all that He has been glorified. Here is the King's Message read at all my Lecture Meetings amid signs of deep respect and many indications of loyalty and regard :

> You may tell your people that I have watched with the greatest interest the advance of The Salvation Army in India, and what you have been able to accomplish on behalf of many of the people of that great land leads me to expect still more important achievements in the near future—particularly on behalf of the depressed and suffering classes.
>
> I should be especially pleased to hear that you found it possible to extend your Medical Work so as to do something for Lepers there just as I understand you have in some other Eastern Countries.
>
> I cordially wish you every success in all branches of your great undertaking, and you may, on my behalf, assure all sections of my Indian subjects that their happiness and well-being are very near to my heart.

" It was at Buckingham Palace where I was received by The King a few days before leaving for India that His Majesty gave me this kind message."

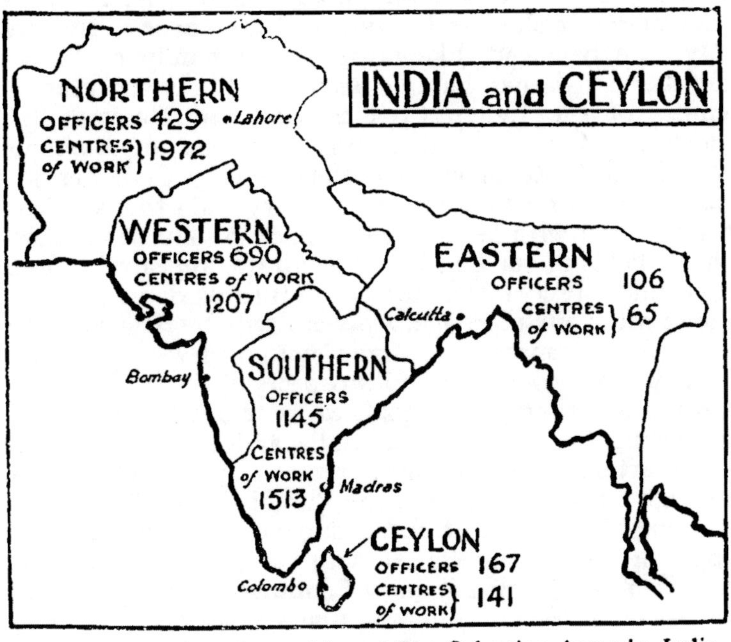

This diagram gives the position of The Salvation Army in India and Ceylon—in each territory—in 1923.

Chapter XIX.

FAKIR SINGH AND DUTINI IN INDIA.
1906-7—1919.

"Go straight for souls, and go for the worst."
William Booth.

In June, 1906, I was married to Lieut.-Colonel Minnie Reid, who had for about twenty years been an Officer, most of this period being spent in European Continental warfare. The fields had included Belgium, France, Germany, Switzerland, and Italy. In the last of these for nearly five years she was in command. At the time of our marriage she was Provincial Commander of Ireland.

My wife belonged, like myself, to a family of Indian Officials, her father having been for thirty-six years a member of the Indian Civil Service, and, towards the conclusion of his career, Acting Governor of Bombay. Two of her brothers were in the Bombay Civil Service, while several others were in the Military and other services. This, together with her long experience in some of the most difficult fields of our Continental warfare, appeared to be a providential preparation for her future work in India.

Soon after our marriage, we were sent by The Founder on a visit of inspection to India, with a view to reporting on the present condition and prospects of the work.

In the following year (1907), we were appointed to take the oversight of the work in India and Ceylon, with our Headquarters in Simla, the Summer Capital of both the Government of India and of the Punjab.

During this period of our command in India, we were happy in having associated with us in the position of Chief Secretary, Colonels (now Commissioners) Sena Singh and Sena Bai (Sowton) for the first six years. Their long experience in many lands made them accept Indian conditions with a readiness which we had seldom witnessed, and it was with great regret that we bid them farewell on their transfer to other lands.

Fortunately the vacant position was filled by the appointment of Colonels Sukh Singh and Mithri (now Commissioners of the Southern Territory). They had grown up with the Indian work from its early days, had shared in its privations and taken part in its Boom Marches, besides commanding in turn its various Territories. In season and out of season they cordially co-operated in every advance.

Up to the year 1911, when the King and Queen visited India, Calcutta had been the Winter Capital of the Government of India, but it was decided at this time to transfer the Winter Capital to Delhi, which had originally been the Imperial Capital of the Mahommedan Emperors. Not only was it more centrally situated for all parts of India, East, West, North and South, with many railway lines converging at this point, but it was near Simla, so that the cost of transfer for winter and summer would be considerably reduced, and the two Capitals could at all times maintain closer touch with each other.

The fact that Simla, owing to its position amongst simple and loyal hill tribes, in the great mountain range of the Himalayas, was practically free from elements of political unrest and disturbance, led to the stay of the Imperial Government being prolonged, till most of the offices remained there from seven to eight months out of the twelve, and some of them for the whole year. Quite recently the Government of India has decided to make Simla its Capital for the whole year.*

During the five cold-weather months, the Viceroy and the principal officials of the Imperial Government spend much of their time in travelling all over the Indian States and British India, getting into close personal touch with the leading Princes, Provinces and Peoples.

* It is a little remarkable that the policy inaugurated by George Washington, and adopted by all the various States in the United States, has been to locate their Capitals and Legislatures in the smaller Provincial towns, where they would be free from intimidation by mob violence at times of popular excitement. It is a policy which might wisely be followed in other lands.

During the summer period, nearly all the Princes, and Provincial Governors in the country, visit Simla with a view to discussing the various questions of principle and policy which constantly arise, and the fact that all the heads of departments are then within reach of one another, and not absent on tour, tends to the prompt dispatch of business.

Although after we left India in 1919 it was considered by the General that Simla had served its purpose as a central Headquarters for India, the country being reorganized as separate commands, directly responsible to International Headquarters in London, there can be no doubt that the establishment of our central Headquarters in Simla during the twelve years we were there was very helpful to us in bringing The Salvation Army into close personal touch with the rulers of India. Hitherto they had only been able to judge of it by mere hearsay, or newspaper reports, and these frequently of a very unfavourable character. Now they were able to see it for themselves, and as is often said, seeing is believing.

For instance during the three week-ends preceding the incoming of the monsoon, they would see crowds of from 3,000 to 5,000 Hindus and Mahommedans congregate on the Ridge, the principal, and indeed only, public review and open-air meeting-place in the city. By the kindness of the Municipal Authorities we were permitted to occupy the entire Ridge from 9 p.m. till nearly midnight, while the bazaar emptied itself to attend the great open-air services of the Muktifauj conducted by my wife and myself, with our Headquarters Staff, together with the Officers convalescing in our Home of Rest. Not only men, but hundreds of women attended, a special enclosure being arranged for their benefit, a large proportion of them being parda (veiled) and wearing the boorka.

So large were the crowds, extending far up the hill-side of Mount Jakko, that we used megaphones for the speakers. These consisted of gramophone horns furnished with a mouth-piece. As they were of the largest size and their weight was considerable, a post was fixed in the ground in front of the platform and the horns were suspended from it, with a chain that could be shortened or lengthened to suit the tallest or shortest speakers. Friends living half-way up Jakko assured us that they could sit in their verandahs and hear every word of the service.

Perfect order prevailed, and it was an impressive sight to see these huge congregations gathering for the meetings and remaining to the end. It was impossible, however, to continue them after the rains had set in, or at other seasons of the year, when the cold at night was too intense, though day-time open-airs are held both on the Ridge and in the bazaar throughout the year as well as in a small Hall near the Ridge, where an Indian Corps has been organized.

If the Founder's motto "*Get into their skins!*" exercised a supreme influence over the earliest period of our work in India, his later motto "Go straight for souls, and go for the worst!" may be said to have supplemented the first, though in no sense being a substitute for it, during the years that followed our appointment to India. The motto hung on the wall of our office at Headquarters, and in the little "den" at home, where our tours were planned, subject-notes for meetings and Officers' Councils prepared, and articles and letters written, during the brief intervals between our constant wanderings.

It was during this period (1907-1919) that our work among the Criminal Tribes, and our agricultural and industrial operations for their support, were introduced. It was a surprise to us to find that there were Tribes who, while not inferior, and sometimes superior in caste to the depressed classes amongst whom we mostly worked, were steeped in criminality, drunkenness, gambling, vice and wickedness of all sorts, thus enabling us to carry out our Founder's injunction to "*Go for the worst!*" The story of this interesting work in the various Territories will be found in Chapters xxiv. to xxvi.

Simla proved also to be an excellent market for the goods produced all over India by our Industrial Homes and Criminal Tribes Settlements. A shop was opened on the Mall, where our goods were always on view, while an Annual Sale was arranged which was usually opened by Her Excellency the Vicereine, and attended by many of the leading Officials and visitors in Simla. A totally new conception of the practicality and vastness of The Army's operations in India was thus given to its rulers, the benefits of which were quickly felt by us in all parts of the country.

The first to recognize our industrial work was Sir Louis Dane, the Lieutenant-Governor of the Punjab, and Sir James Wilson, the Financial Commissioner. They saw The Salvation Army Hand-loom, invented by Staff Captain Maxwell, in actual operation, and with their knowledge of the crude implements employed by the Punjab weavers they formed the idea of establishing a Hand-loom Weaving School, where improved methods could be taught and up-to-date implements introduced.

A part of the large fortress in Ludhiana was placed at our disposal, and was formally opened as the Sir Louis Dane Weaving School of the Punjab. Not many months had passed before the whole of the Fort was made over to us for much needed extension. The school has now become the most important institution of its kind in North India. Under the able and energetic management first of Brigadier Gnana Dasen (Barnett) and then of Major Yisu Chandra, a Maratha Officer, its operations were greatly extended, and it was in a few years placed on a thoroughly self-supporting basis.

Although Simla became our Central Headquarters, it must be remembered that each Territory had its own Headquarters, with its Territorial Leader (as at present). With a view to developing these Territories and placing each one on an independent footing, it was considered desirable that our Headquarters should not be in any of these centres, but that they should be visited in turn by us, not less than once or twice every year. Hence, we were constantly on the wing, and used often to describe our real Headquarters as being in the train, somewhere between Simla and Colombo, or Bombay and Burma.

On the other hand, Simla was a very convenient centre for the great annual Councils, when, in accordance with Salvation Army principle and practice, our Staff, Field or Social Officers were gathered together for periodical re-inspiration and refreshment of body and soul. This was greatly appreciated by the Officers themselves. To the

European Officers it had become an imperative necessity, with the increase of their families, that there should be a good and healthful climatic " City of Refuge," where they could recuperate in case of illness, and escape for a brief period from the oppressive heat of the plains. And it was a great advantage to them that when they came to Simla they found a purely Indian work in full swing, with a goodly band of soldiers, and with the Ridge meetings above described drawing such crowds, The Army congregations on these occasions being by far the largest of any in the town. Moreover, the fact that the Supreme Government of India and that of the Punjab were so extremely friendly to us, and that the leading Officials attended our annual Exhibition, was very helpful to our Officers all over India in securing recognition and assistance for their work, and in settling any difficulties and differences that might have arisen with Officials in their various commands.

At a later period the annual Congress and Councils in Simla were duplicated and extended by the establishment of a similar centre in connection with our Home of Rest in the Nilgiri Mountains in South India, this being more convenient for those Officers who were working in the Southern, Western and Ceylon Commands.

In connection with the Simla Corps, there were some interesting incidents. The Soldiers consist mostly of Chuhras (Sweepers), the caste amongst whom we are largely working in the Punjab. The Sweeper is an essential member of every European household in Simla, and there are several thousands of this class in the town during the summer, though most of them migrate to the plains during the winter months with their employers. They are wonderfully faithful, however, and turn up year after year with great regularity at the meetings. We had for some time about forty adult Soldiers on our roll, and did not seem able to get beyond this point. The Officer in charge one day called upon his people to pledge themselves each individually to secure one recruit during the next three months. He made a list of those willing to make the promise, and as few of them could read or write, he asked them to affix their thumb-marks to their names, a common method of signing documents in India. They gladly responded, one of them undertaking to enlist at least five new adherents.

Amongst our regular attendants was a man named Tatu. He could not be enrolled as a soldier, as he periodically gave way to drink. But he asked that his name should also be added to the list as he felt sure he could add someone to our rolls.

A few days later he was in the meeting, but kept near the door. Pressed to come inside, he replied he was waiting for his recruit, and when he did not arrive, Tatu set off to fetch him, and soon brought him into the meeting. He was a cook, and had to return shortly to prepare his master's meal, so Tatu asked that the Captain should suspend his address till the man had come forward to be prayed with. He had been attending our open-airs for some time. Tatu had seen him, and though himself such a weak brother, had undertaken to further explain to him the way of salvation. The new convert proved to be thoroughly sincere.

Another of our soldiers, a woman, was known amongst us as the Duchess, on account of her dignified manner and appearance. She came to one of the meetings bringing with her three women, to whom she had been explaining the way of salvation. Seating them in front of her, she watched over them with prayerful interest, and when the invitation was given, she went forward with them to the penitent form. "Tauba karo! Tauba karo!" (Repent of your sins!) she earnestly insisted, and then urged them "Iman lao! Iman lao!" (Believe, believe, i.e., that Jesus saves you here and now). When the meeting was over she accompanied them to their homes, further explaining things as they walked along the road, and tenderly shepherding these newborn souls. Great was her joy when, a few weeks later, they were duly enrolled as soldiers under The Army Flag.

So successfully did the soldiers work, that within a few months the roll had increased from 40 to more than 150.

It must not be supposed, however, that the Congresses held in India were confined to Simla and Coonoor. While these were convenient for our European Officers, they could not, of course, meet the needs of our Indian Field Officers, teachers and soldiers, or of the increasingly vast numbers of non-Christians who had now contracted a habit of attending our great annual gatherings.

India is the land of "*Melas*," or periodical Congresses. Indeed, those conducted by the Indian religions in some places far exceed for vastness anything that exists in other lands, the pilgrims being often numbered by lakhs (hundreds of thousands) rather than thousands.

The Salvation Army has not yet reached the "lakh" stage; but we have come well up into the tens of thousands, and the tendency has been for these, where properly fostered and encouraged, to increase year by year.

The period 1907 to 1923 may be said to be specially distinguished from those that preceded it by the careful development of the "*Mela Policy.*" Hitherto we had been obliged to run after our congregations, now the congregations had begun to run after us. Who can estimate the enormous advantage this has given to our Officers, both Indian and European? To the Indian Officer in particular, often stationed at some lonely outpost, this revolution in public sentiment has meant untold cheer and encouragement. Not only did he and his Soldiers look forward year by year to going up to their own particular Jerusalem to worship, but the sight of enormous and increasing crowds of Hindus and Mahommedans, who had come up to witness The Salvation Army Mela could only mean one thing. They were getting ready for the time when they could throw off the shackles and prejudices of centuries which had hitherto bound them, and would become part and parcel of The Salvation Army in its worship and service of Jehovah.

What a vast difference did those outside hungering and thirsting crowds now discover between their jatras (pilgrim resorts) and "tiraths" (bathing places), and those of The Salvation Army! One of our Officers, who was in charge of a Girls' Industrial Home, was located on a high road which led to two of the most famous Hindu resorts—one at Allahabad (the City of God), where the Ganges and Jumna unite—the other at Benares. The ceaseless tramp of tens of thousands could be heard passing her doors day and night during these seasons. Most of them had come from great distances. They went to the resort with bright, hopeful faces. They returned dejected, miserable, downcast.

The Major would turn out with her girls in relays to hold constant open-air meetings amongst these soul-hungry and disappointed crowds, and tell them of a Saviour who was " Mighty to Save " then and there.

A woman, who had measured her length along the road for more than 100 miles to visit some particularly sacred shrine for a darshan (vision) of the deity, was asked on her return how she had prospered. She replied sadly, " Mere dil ke liye bas nahin tha ! " (" *For my heart it was not enough !* ")

Alas, what multitudes could echo her words! An Indian poet has said :—

" Tirath gae tin jan,
  Chit khhota man daur ;
Ek hi pap na kathiyan—
  Das man lade aur ! "

Three men went on pilgrimage to get rid of their wickedness ; they did not cut off a single sin ; they added ten maunds (800 lbs) more.

Such is the sad verdict of one of their own sages. It may be easily imagined how great is the contrast to those who have vainly sought relief in visiting these resorts, when they witness our Melas, and see the joyful faces of thousands of Salvationists and listen to their heartfelt testimonies and songs. There is a ring of reality about it all which must needs carry conviction to the hearts of the onlookers. But most impressive of all is the sight at these gatherings of hundreds of seekers pressing forward to the Mercy Seat to confess and forsake their sins and seek Salvation.

We were visiting one of these great Melas one year, when a message came from a certain village, inviting us to take over their temple, and destroy their idols and shrines. For twenty years they had been watching the changed lives of a Salvationist village in their neighbourhood. Their testimonies, and in particular the earnest appeals of one of their Jemadars, had made them decide that they too would seek Salvation. It was a heart-stirring scene next day when our party travelled over in bullock carts to the village, and took part in demolishing the shrines, and in welcoming the villagers under The Flag of The Salvation Army.

Congresses, or Melas, of this character were conducted by us at regular intervals at the following among other centres :—Bombay, Calcutta, Madras, Lahore, Gurdaspur, Batala, Bareilly, Moradabad, Gorakhpur, Bapatla, Nellore, Trivandrum, Nagercoil, Mavelakarai, Tiruvellar, Satara, Ahmednagar, Ahmedabad, Anand, Dohad, Colombo, Moratuwa, and other places.

During the Melas held at various centres during the last year of our command, more than 3,000 persons came publicly forward to seek Salvation, or to consecrate themselves for service, or to seek cleansing.

In some of these gatherings, the Prayer Meetings were of a truly remarkable character. At times all the Salvationists would simultaneously burst out in earnest and audible prayer, which could indeed be compared to "the sound of many waters."

> Time is awake, while mortals are asleep!
> None can elude his grasp, or curb his course—
> He passes unrestrained o'er all alike.
>
> *Ramayana.*

CHAPTER XX.

PEASANT SETTLEMENTS.

> **Place the waste Labour upon the waste Land by means of waste Capital, and convert the Trinity of Waste into a Unity of Production. . . The Landless Man to the Manless Land.**

One of the main planks in the Founder's Social Platform for India during his second tour was a proposal for Peasant Settlements, which would place the Landless Man upon the Manless Land. Congestion of population in India applies rather to the fertile country districts than to the towns. As mentioned elsewhere, 90 per cent. of the population live in villages, and the possession of a piece of land, however small, is greatly valued by all classes. Hence our efforts have been directed towards securing for our converts on favourable terms tracts of land which they could own and cultivate.

An early experiment was made in this direction in Gujarat, where a few hundred acres of land were obtained from Government for the purpose of settling our Dher converts.

Muktipur, as the Colony is called, has gradually emerged from a long series of disappointments and difficulties, and now constitutes a bright and prosperous little community of some three hundred souls—all Salvationists.

Our two chief difficulties were as follows :—

1. The land was situated in the dry belt of Gujarat. Droughts were frequent, and the water in the first underflow was brackish at a depth of twenty or thirty feet. Beneath this, however, there was in most places an abundant supply of pure water at a further depth of some fifty feet.

The development of this settlement has been mainly along pastoral lines, and they possess remarkably fine herds of the draught cattle and milk buffaloes for which Gujarat is famous.

The recent introduction by Government of irrigation in this area has also greatly improved the prospects of our settlers.

2. The Dhers are essentially Weavers, and not cultivators, and it was a long time before they got gradually accustomed to purely agricultural pursuits. Time and patience have, however, completely overcome this obstacle, and our colonists now compare favourably with the best farmers in their neighbourhood.

Our most remarkable and successful Colony is, however, located in the Punjab, and started with the great advantage that there was an abundant supply of water for irrigation, and the settlers were expert farmers.

And here we may pause to explain the general scheme so successfully inaugurated by the Punjab Government during the last thirty or forty years for the irrigation and colonization of the extensive areas of fertile lands which had hitherto remained arid and unoccupied, owing to deficiency of rainfall and lack of irrigation.

This vast and beneficial scheme, so statesmanlike and noble in its inception and execution, has been little known and appreciated by the British public, perhaps largely because its creators and administrators, instead of seeking to enrich themselves, have lavished the benefits of the scheme upon the toiling masses of the people, and have themselves been willing to remain in the background, unknown, unthanked and to a very large extent unrecognized.

The vast prairie lands of the West had always constituted a parched desert where the smallness of the rainfall and the burning heat had made cultivation impossible, except in the immediate neighbourhood of the rivers which flowed through it, and which were liable to change their course from year to year. The daring plan was conceived of harnessing the five rivers (Panj-Ab) after which the Province is named, and of distributing their waters in regular channels, the main arteries of which should resemble stately rivers. The scheme was worked out in all its details, and it was clearly shown that while a heavy expenditure of capital would be necessary, Government might fairly expect a clear profit of ten to twenty per cent., while the dense agricultural population in the bordering districts would make excellent colonists, well-skilled in agriculture by irrigation.

At first the land was given away to suitable colonists, on the sole condition that it should not be sold, or mortgaged, and thus fall into the hands of the non-agricultural money-lending class.

The colonists were carefully chosen, the villages were well planned, and the water charges and land taxes were very reasonable. Government not only made and supervised the canals and placed in charge of them expert irrigation engineers, but also planned the necessary railways and public roads for getting the produce to market.

From the first the scheme proved to be a great success, far exceeding the most sanguine expectations of its originators. Ultimately Government modified its policy, and decided to sell the newly irrigable land by auction to the highest bidder, withdrawing at the same time the restrictions on sale and mortgage. A very large additional revenue was thus secured.

The Salvation Army had long been promised a grant of land for the purpose of settling its converts. These promises did not materialize, and we did not ourselves press very strongly for their fulfilment, as we had some knowledge of the difficulties involved in such schemes. However, as we gained experience we gained confidence, and in 1915 we applied for a grant of land.

We were informed by Government that, if we wanted land, we would have to buy it at the ordinary market price. Through the kind offices of Sir Michael Fenton, the Financial Commissioner, a plan was finally agreed upon that Government should sell us a tract of 2,000 acres at the market rate, but that we should be allowed thirty years in which to make our payments.

The plan followed by us was to allow our future Salvationist colonists an opportunity of seeing and choosing the tract. They were skilled agriculturists and well acquainted with the irrigation system. Some of the best of them were chosen to visit the land which Government had offered to us. They turned it down. It was reasonably cheap and much of it was very good, but it was more or less patchy, and there were signs of alkali which might cause difficulty. They were willing to pay the highest price for the best land, rather than get inferior land at a cheaper price. It was the voice of the practical farmer, who knew that out of really good land the same labour would secure such harvests as would quickly make up the difference in the price.

The Canal authorities then pointed us out a tract which fully answered this description, but the estimated value was Rs. 240 per acre, instead of Rs. 130, that of the tract previously offered. The moment our Salvationist experts saw this land, they unanimously and enthusiastically agreed to it, saying that the price was quite reasonable for such land. The main canal half encircled the land, and the supply of water was sufficient and secure.

The total cost of the land was close upon five lakhs of rupees, say £32,000 at the usual rate of exchange of 1s. 4d. to the rupee, and for this amount The Salvation Army became responsible. The Rs. 240 per acre, distributed over a period of thirty years, only meant an annual payment of Rs. 8 per acre, which the colonist was easily able to make. Each settler was given a lease, by which, subject to regular payment of his instalments, he would own the freehold of his land at the end of thirty years. The payments have been regularly made. The land has meanwhile more than doubled in value. There are two harvests, and the crops are easily disposed of for cash. The settlers are prosperous and contented. Nearly 2,000 Salvationists (men, women and children) are settled in the colony. They support their own Officers, schools and hospital, and contribute generously to The Army funds. The success of the colony may be said to be due,

1. To its God-recognizing, God-honouring character. The religious standard is high.

2. The land is of the best.

3. The water supply is adequate.

4. The colonists were chosen with care. They were skilled agriculturists, well acquainted with irrigation and local crops and conditions.

5. They are granted the ultimate ownership of the land. This has proved to be a great encouragement to thrift and careful cultivation.

The following particulars regarding the colony are from the pen of its first manager, Adjutant Wafadar (Hackett).

"The colony was officially opened by a Flag-hoisting ceremony on May 28th, 1916, and to quote the words of an eye-witness, there was then 'nothing to see but jungle.' The whole of the land was brought under cultivation within eighteen months.

"The village is situated in the centre of the colony, one hundred acres of land being reserved for that purpose. The village site actually stands on forty acres, and the remainder is left for extension. Each colonist has built his own house, and enclosed his compound with a boundary wall. The size of a full square-holder's compound is 99 ft. by 110 ft., so he has ample room, both for his family and his livestock. There have also been built the Manager's bungalow, hall, Officers' Quarters, and dispensary, while an excellent well has been sunk in the centre of the village with eight push-taps—an unusual innovation for a village community. The testimony of the Governor of the Punjab when visiting the colony was, that our people had done exceptionally well. Also many other Government Officials have been surprised and delighted at the progress made.

"Water we have in plenty. The colony has a frontage of three miles on one of the main distributaries of the Lower Bari Doab Canal, and I might say in passing that the land in our neighbourhood is now worth three times the amount of money it was worth when the colony was founded.

"Our main crops are cotton (American), sugar-cane, and wheat. Our cotton crop last harvest amounted to about 5,500 maunds and was worth close on Rs. 100,000. The sugar-cane harvested this year was worth Rs. 15,000, and the 1,000 acres of wheat which is now being harvested I estimate will be worth Rs. 70,000 in grain alone, with an average out-turn of from 17 to 18 maunds per acre. Do not imagine, however, that this is all income to the colonists. The Government dues for water and revenue amount to Rs. 17,000 per year, and the holders' purchase money instalments amount to Rs. 16,000 per year. But I must say that there is great cause for gratitude to God for the bountiful harvests we have reaped in the past.

"We do not allow our colonists to go to law with one another. I have heard that in some parts of the Punjab, cultivators put aside the proceeds from one acre of land for court cases, and if they don't spend it in that way they are disappointed. But this is not so on the colony. All difficulties and grievances are settled as far as possible by the Manager, and in the majority of cases the people say 'Well, you and The Salvation Army are our mother and father, and we accept your decision.' Some do not do this at once, but they invariably come back and ask forgiveness. Of course, if they do not like the Manager's decision, they can appeal to the Territorial Commander, whose ruling is final. But we try to get along without troubling the Commissioner.

"I estimate our population at 1,800, including 1,200 adult Soldiers. Our hall only seats about 500, so you will understand that it is impossible to have the men and women together. All work is suspended on Sundays, apart from works of necessity, and all our colonists are expected to attend the services on Sundays. Sunday morning is allotted to the men, and I can tell you it is a sight to see five or six hundred men assembled together every Sunday morning for worship. They sing well, pray, testify and listen very attentively to the Word of God, and we talk to them of Salvation and Holiness.

"In the afternoon the hall is again packed with women, and babies in arms. My wife usually conducts this service, and the improvement in the women during the past twelve months is great—both from the standpoint of cleanliness and godliness.

"The collection in the women's service is unique, and it is interesting to see the women going around with baskets, gathering up the wheat, flour, cotton, pice, etc. But what is more important than the large gatherings in the hall, are the small meetings in the compounds and houses of the people, and we have three meetings going at the same time, in different parts of the village, for four evenings each week, where the people are taught the value of family worship.

"I am also pleased to say that the Colonists give towards the self-support of the spiritual work. We started at the beginning of 1919 to pay the Corps Officers' salary, and we are now paying the salary of three day-school teachers. Our Self-Denial Appeal this year yielded Rs. 700; the Harvest Festival over Rs. 400. We have also built a small dispensary at a cost of Rs. 900, the whole of the amount being subscribed by the land-holders, and I have also Rs. 400 in hand towards fitting up the dispensary, also given by the colonists. So you will see that we include in our teaching the principle of giving.

"I would say in closing, that the Colony is only in its infancy. When we consider that what is now known as 'Shantinagar' was all waste land and jungle seven years ago, we do truly say, God has been with us and to Him be all the Glory! The land is excellent, the water is plentiful, and humanly speaking there is no danger in the future of failure of crops as there is in so many parts of India. But not only from an agricultural standpoint is the prospect of the future for the colony bright, but I believe with careful teaching and training, there is a bright spiritual future before us."

The above account of the Colony, written in 1919, may here be supplemented by a recent sketch written in April 1923:—

"It has to be remembered that the men who have come as tenants on the colony are from a class of age-long servitude, and, considering this, the measure of self-control, hard work, and management which they show augurs well for the future. Moses found it no light task to evolve a nation out of the slaves of Egypt, and we can hardly expect that our task will be much easier.

"From a financial standpoint the colony is prosperous, but what rejoices us most of all is that from a Salvation Army standpoint also there is a very great deal to thank God for, as was evidenced quite recently on the occasion of the farewell of Lieut.-Commissioners Hira Singh and Amrita Bai (Hoe).

"The Young People's Annual is easily the first in interest and popularity of all the annual festivals at Shantinagar, and the Manager, Major Jiwan Singh

(Tyldesley), with pardonable gratification mentions the fact that there are well over a thousand Young People under the age of eighteen years connected with the Corps, this number of course including the Cradle Roll.

"The first item of the week-end was a Young People's Demonstration, with seventeen items on the programme, and the Coming Army acquitted themselves with credit. The closing moments made a strong appeal as twenty boys, each with a lighted candle, stood behind a Cross, from which streamed a bright light, and sang in Punjabi, 'Jesus, keep me near the Cross.'

"On Sunday morning a meeting for men only was led by the Commissioner, and this was followed by a Dedication Service—on a large scale. The scene will surely long be remembered as sixty-eight mothers, each carrying her babe, came to the platform. The fathers stood in front, with The Salvation Army Flags of the Corps and various Wards waving overhead. It surely was a sight rarely seen in any Salvation Army Corps in any part of the world.

"At night, the air of Shantinagar was filled with the spirit and sound of worship and praise. This Corps is divided into eight Wards, each Ward having about two hundred Salvationists, and Sunday night is given up to the holding of the Ward meetings."

During the week-end, twenty-six Corps Cadets received their certificates for the Third Grade Course. Eighty Junior Soldiers were sworn in beneath the Flag. There was a swearing-in of sixty transfers from the Junior Roll to the Senior, also the swearing-in of thirty-five new Senior Soldiers. The prize distribution was the occasion of tremendous interest and excitement, and a very happy crowd dispersed to their homes shortly before midnight.

CHAPTER XXI.

COTTAGE INDUSTRIES.

Back to the Home, away from the Factory.

The choice of Industries which would be suitable to our people, and which would enable them to self-support, as well as the marketing of the goods when produced and the training of expert foremen, have constituted problems which have not been easy to solve.

We have found it best to concentrate our attention mainly upon Weaving, Silk, Needlework, and Mat-making, and each of these branches has been developed with a thoroughness and attention to detail that leave little to be desired.

India possesses eleven million Handloom Weavers, once among the most prosperous members of the community, now reduced to poverty and destitution. To throw away their wonderful technical skill seemed a poor policy. After a careful examination of existing conditions, The Salvation Army decided to try to improve their crude looms and warping machines, as well as the quality of cloth they could produce. Some sixteen years ago, a skilled mechanic-Officer, Staff-Captain Prem Das (Maxwell), was appointed to live among the weavers, study their art, and improve their apparatus. God's special blessing rested upon the plan. A new and fast loom was invented, which could produce four or five times the quantity of cloth woven on the old hand-loom.

But this raised a new difficulty. The warping was done by the women and children, and they could not possibly keep pace with the new loom. Oh, the patience of those women! To produce a single warp of fifty feet length, they would have to walk backwards and forwards about fourteen miles! Oh the weariness! But the Staff-Captain soon solved the new problem and produced a simple machine which would prepare warps of 500 feet and upwards, and would supply from ten to twenty looms, with the labour of two or three people, and the simple turning of a wheel! The day of miracles was not past. The factories were taking work away from the home and the village to the city; the Muktifauj was bringing it back. There was a bright sparkle in the eyes of many a weaver when he came to understand what we were after.

Of course, this did not mean that the wife and children of the weaver would have nothing to do. On the contrary, they would be kept busy helping at the loom, which was so simple and easy to handle that it could be operated alike by men, women and children. Thus the unpaid labour and skill of the entire family could be utilized to the full.

We found out also that for quality, and for hard wear and tear, our hand-made stuff was far better than what the mills produced. Our cotton was cotton, and not fifty per cent. sizing. "Why," said our lady customers, "your jharans (house cloths) simply defy the 'dhobi' (washerman). They don't and won't wear out. They seem almost everlasting." They recommended us to their friends.

How to sell our goods when made was a serious problem. We organized annual sales. Then we opened shops, where we could supply our customers. We studied the requirements of the market, and found out what the people wanted, and passed on the information to our Officer Managers and Weaving Masters and they again to the Weavers.

We owe much to our Officers and Weaving Masters. We have a splendid staff now, and they have rendered us invaluable service. But we had to train them ourselves. It was in vain that we went to the Government Weaving Schools. We would ask how many hand-loom weavers they had? The answer would usually be one or two, or perhaps none out of from fifty to one hundred students. What were they being trained for? To take positions in factories, with salaries ranging from fifty to five hundred rupees a month. Did they know anything about hand-loom weaving ? Oh, no, it was a *dead* industry, at any rate, *dying*, and the sooner it died the better for the mills !

So we gave it up as hopeless to attempt to obtain our weaving masters from such schools, and had to start our own schools, and train our own Weaving Masters and Weavers. It was a tedious business and took us several years, but it was abundantly worth while.

However, nearly every Settlement for the Criminal Tribes became in process of time a Weaving School, as we found this to be an industry which was popular with the tribesmen. Moreover, they were less conservative than the weavers, and took readily to the new and improved methods and machines which we had introduced.

While studying conditions and the market, we were not long in discovering that Silk weaving was a much more paying industry than cotton. But then it required far greater skill. The secrets of the business were more jealously guarded, and unless we could produce our own silkworms and cocoons, we could not secure the best results or profits.

Again, a careful survey was made of this industry, and information collected from all sources. France, Italy, China, Japan and Kashmir were the principal countries where Silk was being successfully produced on a vast commercial scale. These countries were personally visited by my wife and myself, their experts were consulted and their best books collected. Then our Officers and Weaving Masters set to work to solve the problem of Silk.

Our Weaving Schools made excellent centres for studying and developing the question, and when the celebrated Tata Company made over to us their Silk Farm in Bangalore, this proved to be an admirable centre for training our Silk staff.

The connection and friendship of the well-known and eminent Parsee family of Tatas constitutes an interesting chapter in our Indian history. The late Mr. Jamsetji N. Tata, the head and founder of the firm, and father of Sir Dorabji and Sir Ratan, was one of the first and most generous of our Indian friends to rally to our assistance. Between him and myself a warm personal friendship sprang up which lasted to the end of his distinguished career, and while I, with Commissioner Rahiman, was in charge of The Salvation Army work in America, it was a great joy to us to introduce our friend to the Steel Magnates of that country as the great Indian Philanthropist, who might be regarded as the Rockefeller of India.

It was in connection with the mammoth scheme for Steel works since established in Sakchi in Eastern India, that the visit was paid, and when in later years we visited those works, now employing some 60,000 hands, it was a great satisfaction to know that the vision had attained so remarkable a fulfilment.

After the death of his father, Sir Dorabji Tata suggested that The Salvation Army should take up, and seek to bring to fruition, another of that great dreamer's schemes, which had not so far met with the success which he had anticipated.

Mr. Tata, after visiting Japan, had felt satisfied that India offered at least an equally good field for the Silk Industry. He obtained the services of an expert Japanese, under whose management a small model farm of seventeen acres was organized, and a filature of ten basins established for reeling silk. Altogether some Rs. 50,000 had been spent in starting this venture, but it had not achieved the results which their father had anticipated. Sir Dorabji therefore suggested that we should take it over and see what we could do with it. He thought that with our organization behind it, the scheme might still be made a success. If that were so, they would gladly make over the whole property to The Salvation Army as a gift—a generous offer which has since been carried into effect.

We took up the proposition and organized a Silk School, which soon had about one hundred pupils and workers, studying Silk in all its branches, from the growing of silk-worms and mulberry, and the reeling of silk, to the production of the most delicate fabrics. A demand quickly sprang up for our silk goods, and orders were booked six months in advance of our capacity to produce, enabling us gradually to increase our reeling basins and looms.

The School is situated at Bangalore, in the centre of a district which is the home of the famous Mysore multi-voltine silk-worm, which practically produces cocoons all the year round. The silk is of the finest quality and commands a ready sale.

We were able, in this way, to train expert Silk foremen and weavers, who could take charge of our Silk centres in other parts of India, besides supplying the Mysore and other Governments with silk supervisors.

India is the home, not only of the Mysore, but of the Muga, Tussore, Bengal and Eri silk-worms. The commercial value of these has been attested over and over by British and French experts, but the "*laissez faire*" policy pursued, and the half-hearted and unskilful attempts occasionally made to encourage the industry have only resulted in its continued decadence.

Contrasting strongly with these is the vigorous policy of the Kashmir Government, under the wise and skilful guidance of the late Sir Thomas Wardle. Following his expert advice the Industry, which had dwindled to nothing, was rapidly re-established, until it has become one of the most flourishing in the East, and a source of revenue to the Government, and of income to the ryot (peasant).

The examples of Japan and France also furnish admirable models on which the necessary legislation could be based for the recovery of this important industry from the low stage which, purely through ignorance and gross neglect, it has been permitted to reach.

We have now got the best and most up-to-date Silk School in India, where the various branches of the art are studied and taught, and such is the demand for the woven material we produce that we have been unable to keep pace with the orders we have received.

We cull the following particulars from a report written by Brigadier Diriyam (Jackson), who, with the able assistance of his wife, brought the Institution to a successful position during the seven years that he was in command:—

"I am writing this report for the encouragement of those who are thinking of starting the Silk Industry. This is an industry in which all the family can take part. If a man has land, he can supplement his income from it by rearing silk-worms. The system of rearing is very simple, and can be done by all the members of the family. Even the children can help.

"Our Market for raw silk was extensive, including Switzerland, America and England. A bale of our silk was shown in the Silk Exhibition, in London, in 1912, after which the President wrote, saying: 'Your Silk attracted the attention of many visitors, including the King and Queen and other members of the Royal Family.'

"Our chief work has been to train others. To the student we give a one year's course, or more if he cares to stay longer. We charge a small fee to cover any waste caused by his work in learning. Apprentices stay with us four or five years. We prefer the latter, as they ultimately become experts in the industry in all its branches. The Superintendent, or one of his staff, gives lectures every week, taking each branch of the work in its turn. We have trained about twenty Europeans, and two hundred and eighty Indians of all castes. Some of these are now inspectors in Government Service, others managers, reeling masters, and weaving masters in our own institutions, while others have started on their own in various States in India and Ceylon. The Farm is open to take in and train students and apprentices at any time.

"We are making about twenty different kinds of silk cloth, both plain and fancy materials—some in the latest style. There is a great demand for Indian silks."

Our Bangalore Silk School was visited by Lady Hardinge, who took a deep interest in all that concerned India's welfare, and whose premature death was sincerely mourned by the people. The following record of her visit will be read with interest :—

"Her Excellency, Lady Hardinge, the Vicereine, visited the Bangalore Silk Farm to-day. The whole process of silkworm culture, and the spinning and weaving of silk were shown by Commissioner Booth Tucker and the staff of the Farm and Factory. Her Excellency was exceedingly pleased with all she saw, and realized how great is the future of this industry."

Sir J. R. ROBERTS, C.I.E., M.B., F.R.C.S.,
(Lieut.-Colonel, I.M.S., for Her Excellency).

There is a great deal of cheating in Silk. Purchasers may have palmed off upon them "artificial" silk, which is not silk at all, or "mercerised" cotton, which has a bright appearance and is not silk, or a mixture of cotton and silk, where cotton greatly predominates, or fabrics made of "waste" silk—none of these of course equalling the wonderful fabrics produced from pure "raw" silk, or the unbroken thread of the silkworm. As long as people know what they are buying, and pay accordingly, no objection can be raised to the production of these inferior fabrics. But too often this is not the case, and very few people have the skill to detect the difference between the make-believes and the pure silk. Purchasers soon found that with us they could rely on knowing exactly what they were buying. If they wanted a cheap mixed fabric, we could produce it for them. If, on the other hand, as was often the case, they wanted to get the best and purest silk, we could supply it.

Another interesting Industry which we have developed has been Lace, Drawn-thread and Needlework. We have organized this industry for the benefit of our Industrial Schools, and Village Soldiers. In South India, the women are taught the work in Nagercoil, and are then supplied with materials, and are paid for their work, which we sell to our friends and customers. More than three thousand women are thus found profitable employment, without having to leave their homes, or go to city factories. This movement *back to the home*—and *away from the factory*—is well worthy of consideration on the part of employers of labour. It could often be done with advantage to both employer and worker, as it saves the employer the expense of costly buildings, while the workers fix their own hours, preserve the sanctity of home life, and are not liable to suffer nearly so seriously if bad times should come for the trade which they follow, as they have their garden produce, poultry, or crops to fall back upon.

CHAPTER XXII.

OUR MEDICAL WORK.

Sickness, thou Antechamber
  To Heaven—approach to God—
Ladder by which we clamber
  From earth—our Father's rod!
Welcome, since thou dost bring me
  Abassadors of love,
Angelic songs to sing me,
  New from my Home above.

The problem of disease has been earnestly and sympathetically studied by the Indian Government, and much has been done to alleviate suffering and to introduce the best Hospitals, Medicines and Training. But it is difficult to realize how vast are the problems requiring to be dealt with.

The epidemics of India are both numerous and terrible in their ravages. It is moreover very difficult to enforce the most ordinary precautions. Cholera, Plague, Smallpox and Malaria claim millions of victims every year. Travelling, as we did, over the whole country, it was a common experience to find ourselves surrounded with sufferers from one or more of these scourges. During one year The Salvation Army lost in a few weeks about 2,500 Salvationists, and 25 of our Indian Officers in a single district from a severe outbreak of Pneumonic Influenza, when the Official returns for India showed that some six million persons had succumbed. Two or three months later Plague ravaged the country, and we lost about 3,000 more of our people in the same district.

The great pilgrimages which take place at certain seasons help to scatter the disease germs, especially in the case of Cholera, although elaborate precautions are taken by the authorities. At times it becomes necessary to prohibit these gatherings altogether, though Government is very unwilling to adopt such an extreme measure.

It may be thought by some who are well acquainted with India, that the Medical Department and Institutions organized by Government are sufficient for the needs of the country. But this is far from being the case. To supply the medical needs of 320 million people, and this in a country saturated, so to speak, with Malaria, Plague, Typhoid, Smallpox, Cholera, Eye diseases, Leprosy and other maladies, is a gigantic task.

Moreover, the Civil Surgeon of a district has to divide his time between the Government Hospitals and his private practice among European Officials and leading Indians.

Hence there is ample scope for The Salvation Army Hospitals and Dispensaries which we have established in different parts of India. Indeed, "scope" is a poor word. There is pressing need for them, and they are deeply appreciated by the people.

Moreover, there can be no doubt that in addition to the spiritual meetings which are regularly conducted in our Hospitals and Dispensaries for the benefit of the patients, a great influence is exercised among all classes of the adjoining population, and the barriers are minimized, even where they may not be altogether removed. Christ the Healer of the Body introduces them to Christ the Healer of the Soul.

Our special wards for women are now arranged upon the system introduced in India by Sir James Roberts, revolutionizing the plan on which Zenana Hospitals are generally worked. The Indian woman, when taken to a Hospital, is usually cut off from the male members of her family, except during visiting hours. This she feels very keenly. While shy of strangers, she longs in her sickness to have the members of her family, including her husband, father, or son, about her, to see to her various needs. Hence she will usually prefer to suffer and die at home than go to a Hospital.

The new system arranges a back entrance, with a small courtyard and verandah, where the members of the family, both male and female, can wait upon the patient and attend to her food arrangements. A small charge for suhc private accommodation more than covers the little extra expense, and the arrangement ensures the popularity and success of the Hospital, and is an unspeakable comfort to the sufferer. Probably there are other countries where similar privileges would be equally appreciated.

Our Indian Medical Work was started by Lieut.-Colonel Sikundar (Dr. Andrews), M.D., V.C. As a youth of fifteen, he went out to India with Commissioner Rahiman. Our older Officers well remember fair-haired Harry. For about thirty-three years he laboured in India, starting our three principal Hospitals at Nagercoil in Travancore, at Anand in Gujarat, and at Moradabad, in the United Provinces. Of the last he was himself the architect, and the builder, and the plans were considered so admirably suited to Indian conditions that they were adopted by Government as a model. The beginnings of this medical work were primitive and romantic in the extreme.

As Adjutant Sikundar (Andrews), of the Nagercoil Headquarters Staff, he started in a tiny bath-room a small, amateur dispensary, the first insignificant seed of The Salvation Army medical tree in India. He had at this time received no medical training, but he was what might be truly called " a born Doctor," and he studied diligently to fit himself for his task. As the work grew, and the crowds that came for assistance increased, he felt the need of someone with more skilled medical knowledge. His home furlough being due, he left for London, where he had heard that there was a Field Officer, Captain Turner, who was a qualified Doctor, and feeling that here was the answer to his prayers, he sought this comrade out. Long these two consecrated young men sat and talked together; vivid were the pictures the pioneer Officer drew of the sufferings and need of the crowds that daily thronged to the diminutive dispensary, nestling amongst the graceful palm trees of Southern India, until listening the Captain felt the half-formed desires and aspirations in his mind grow to a certainty.

On parting it was understood that the Adjutant would bring the matter before the then Chief of the Staff, our present General. The result of these negotiations was that

Captain Turner was asked if he were willing to go to India? Willing! Had not the vision of India's needs already pressed upon his heart, and had he not laid himself upon the altar of service for that land? But even in those far-away days Dr. Turner was a cautious man, and did not allow his zeal to outrun his discretion. His qualifications were those of an ordinary practitioner, and with some foreshadowing of the great responsibilities that were to come upon him in the future, it seemed best to him that he should also take a University degree. He laid his proposal before the Founder, and was given a furlough to take up a further course of study at his own expense. The Founder's comment was characteristic—"I have no inspiration on the subject, but if you think it best, go ahead and do it!"

Obtaining a medical appointment, the future Missionary Officer took up the necessary extra courses with an examination each six months till he attained his desired aim.

During this time Adjutant Sikundar had returned to India, having obtained a grant from the International Headquarters in London, to enable him to establish the "Catherine Booth" dispensary at Nagercoil. It was an immediate success, partly because of the need, and partly because of his intense enthusiasm. Often he spent half the night studying for the work which awaited him on the morrow. More and more the burden of the work pressed upon him, and almost every Home mail carried letters to Dr. Turner saying how much he was looking forward to his coming. But the latter still tarried; he had attained the desired medical degree, and now with God-given intuition of the peculiar work that awaited him, felt he had better have some special experience in eye work. Again the Founder agreed to the proposal, and Dr. Turner took an appointment as Resident Medical Officer in an Ophthalmic Hospital.

It was in 1900 that Doctor Turner left England, and for the next twenty-one years he was engaged in the superintendence and development of the "Catherine Booth" Hospital at Nagercoil.

During this period, in addition to establishing four Branch Hospitals in needy localities in Travancore, a

Medical School was started, which was recognized by the State, graduates of this School being accepted as Medical Practitioners, and empowered to take charge of Grant-in-Aid Hospitals, or to practise medicine, surgery, and midwifery.

This Hospital received the personal recognition, and support of His Highness the Maharaja of Travancore, who, in the course of one of his personal visits in August, 1921, spoke as follows :—

" Dr. and Mrs. Turner, Ladies and Gentlemen : It affords me very great pleasure to re-visit the 'Catherine Booth' Hospital of Vadaseri, after a long interval of nine years, and to see for myself the vast advance that this institution has made in its career of public usefulness since I visited it last. I appreciate the valuable humanitarian work that is being carried on within the walls of this Hospital, the self-sacrificing labours undertaken by you, Dr. Turner, and the members of your staff in the different branches of the medical profession here, in the noble cause of the alleviation of human suffering. As the Patron of the Institution for the past twenty years, it is particularly gratifying to me to hear of its success and prosperity, and I am happy to learn that the new Hospital for Women, opened under the presidency of Her Excellency, Lady Willingdon, during Her Excellency's visit to Travancore in October last, is becoming increasingly popular. I may assure you that your Institution will continue to receive my sincere sympathy."

His Highness the Maharaja of Cochin, a State North of Travancore, also visited the Hospital, and recorded his opinion in the following terms :—

" One of the pleasantest recollections of my tour through Travancore will be the memory of my visit to the 'Catherine Booth' Hospital at Nagercoil. The well-planned buildings, the pleasant surroundings, the kindly faces of the members of the Medical and Nursing Staff, and the happy looks of the patients leave an impression not easily effaced."

(Signed) RAMA VARMAH,
Maharaja of Cochin.

February 9th, 1922.

The extensive relief work carried on by this Hospital may be judged by the following figures :—

1921 Out-patients Attendances (1 year)	23,688
1901 to 1921 (21 years) Out-patients Attendances	487,519
1921 In-patients (1 year)	1,046
1901 to 1921 (21 years) In-patients	14,114
1921 Operations performed (1 year)	1,722
1908 to 1921 (14 years) Operations performed	15,295

On the arrival of Dr. Daya Nasen (Turner) in Travancore, Adjutant Sikundar was transferred at his own request to our ordinary operations in Gujarat. But the medical instinct in him was too strong to be thus extinguished. Again he found himself surrounded with a mass of human suffering which appealed to his heart. The experience he had gained in Travancore was once more called into requisition, and before long another Dispensary sprang into existence which quickly developed into a hospital.

The Hospital is centrally situated in Anand, an important railway junction, and is well known and very popular throughout the district. It confers an immense boon upon our own people. The great prevalence of eye diseases has led to a motor ambulance being attached of recent years to this Hospital from which visits are paid to surrounding villages. Those who cannot be treated locally are brought to the Hospital for further treatment.

During the last six months of 1922, the Hospital dealt with 747 In-patients, and 7,401 Out-patients. The staff consists of seventeen Officers and fourteen Employees. The motor ambulance dealt with more than eight hundred cases during the first two months that it was in operation.

After organizing the Gujarat Hospital, the Adjutant suggested that to obviate the possibility of trouble arising, owing to the fact that he had no proper qualifications as a medical man, arrangements should be made for him to go through a medical course. Headquarters in London agreed to the proposal, and the Adjutant spent several years in Chicago, where he obtained his medical degree of M.D.

On his return to India, it was arranged that he should

organize a third Hospital in North India, to be known as the "Thomas Emery" Hospital, a sum of £3,000 being donated for the purpose by the late Miss Emery, in memory of her father.

Through the warm interest taken in the scheme by Sir John Hewett, then Lieutenant-Governor of the United Provinces, we were able to secure a grant of twenty-five acres of land for this Hospital in the neighbourhood of Moradabad, a city with a population of about 100,000 persons, where we had one of our principal Settlements for Criminal Tribes, and also a considerable work in the surrounding district.

While the legacy was only sufficient to erect a Hospital with about thirty beds, the Doctor, with wise forethought, prepared plans for a much larger institution with at least one hundred beds, and with suitable accommodation for the staff. He had the satisfaction of seeing his hopes realized, and when the war was taxing to the utmost the accommodation of existing military hospitals for Indian troops, we were able to place at the disposal of Government one of the best and most perfectly equipped hospitals in the country, together with Dr. Sikundar and his staff.

The Hospital became so popular with the Indian Soldiers that they complained that they "got well too quickly," and were full of sorrow when the time came for their discharge.

At the conclusion of the war, the Hospital reverted to its ordinary purposes, and is now carrying on an excellent work under Major (Dr.) Johanson.

The services of Dr. Sikundar himself were requisitioned by the Military Authorities after the conclusion of the war, for the North-West Frontier, where military operations were in progress against some of the war-like and troublesome frontier tribes. It was here that he met his death, under circumstances which are described in the following extract from the *London Gazette* :—

"Captain Andrews was senior medical officer in charge of the Khajuri post. Hearing that the convoy had been attacked, he immediately took out an aid post under heavy fire and established it, affording some protection to the wounded, but none to himself. Subsequently he was compelled to remove it, but continued most devotedly to attend the wounded. Finally, when an ambulance was available, he showed the utmost disregard for danger in collecting the wounded under fire and placing them in the ambulance. Eventually he was killed on the completion of his task."

From the Commander-in-Chief in India, General Sir Charles Monro, the following letter was received:—

"SIMLA, 30*th October*, 1919.

"DEAR SIR,

"It is with great regret that I have to announce to you that Captain H. J. Andrews, M.B.E., I.M.S., V.C., was killed in action on the 22nd instant in the Tochi Valley.

"I wish to convey my sincere appreciation of the very valuable services rendered by the late Captain Andrews, who in 1916 was responsible for the establishment and administration of the War Hospital located in the hospital buildings belonging to The Salvation Army at Moradabad, which were so generously placed at my disposal by your predecessor, Commissioner F. Booth Tucker, and who after the closing of that Hospital served with a Field Medical Unit on active service on the Frontier.

Yours sincerely,.

(Signed) C. C. MONRO,
Commander-in-Chief.

To the Commissioner-in-Charge,
Salvation Army, Simla.

Major General Sir Patrick Hehir, I.M.S. (retired), writes as follows to the *British Medical Journal*:—

"I should be glad of an opportunity of making a few remarks about the late Dr. Henry John Andrews, V.C., M.B.E., I.M.S., Salvation Army, whose posthumous award of the Victoria Cross has been announced (*British Medical Journal*, September 18th, 1920, p. 456). He was killed in action in Afghanistan on October 22nd, 1919. The brave deed that merited this high distinction has been described in despatches. He met his death in the way

I believe he would have chosen, in service to others, doing his duty—the ideal way for an army doctor.

"It was my pleasure and privilege to know Andrews fairly well, as we worked together in the Northern Command in India when I was A.D.M.S. there. On several occasions he asked to be transferred to the front, but he was doing such excellent work as Commandant of the Moradabad War Hospital that his services could not be spared. Eventually he was employed at the front in the Afghan campaign, where he met his glorious death. He was energetic, brimful of vitality, extremely modest, quiet, thorough and reliable, completely unselfish, and his devotion to duty was most inspiring to others. Whilst serving on the military side I know that he gave the Government the best that was in him. His goodness infected all those around him, and one feels confident that his influence will continue for many a day in the neighbourhood in which he worked.

"He was a man with broad human sympathies, and a splendid type of the medical missionary in India. He was loved by the poor, and their care, comfort and treatment were meticulously attended to in his Hospital. He was a good operator, and crowds of people flocked from various parts of the Moradabad district to be treated by him. He designed and supervised the construction of The Salvation Army Hospital at Moradabad. It is a model of what a district hospital should be in India. It is one of the few hospitals in Oudh that has its own tube well. I was particularly struck with the admirable way in which the various departments of the hospital were arranged. It was well organized and administered. The hospital was made over to Government as a War Hospital in a whole-hearted manner by The Salvation Army, and did most laudable work for our sick and wounded Indian Soldiers. For such a man the future life could have no cause for apprehension, and we may be certain that he was welcomed into the other world with the words, 'Well done, thou good and faithful servant.'"

Chapter XXIII.

THE BEGGAR OF THE EAST.

Think not by shaven face and head
To prove your appetites are dead;
Who shaves his head and not his heart,
Is only a fakir in part.
But he his head has rightly shaved,
Whose heart from wickedness is saved.
Mrichakatika.

The Medical Body in Colombo deserve credit as being the pioneers in one of the greatest and most urgently needed sanitary reforms in Eastern lands, namely the dealing systematically, and sympathetically, from a health standpoint with the beggar population, which swarm in the streets of every Eastern city.

Ceylon may take the credit for being the first country, and Colombo for being the first Eastern City, which has attempted to grapple seriously with what appears to be a gigantic and costly undertaking.

A discussion had for some time been occupying the attention of the papers as to the causes of the unhealthiness of Colombo, when a doctor of that city brought to the notice of the public the large number of beggars in the streets, and the loathsome diseases from which they suffered. He pointed out that the flies which settled on their sores infested and infected the food sold in the boutiques (bazaar shops), and expressed the opinion that while this evil was allowed to exist unchecked, they could not expect Colombo to be a healthy city. He suggested that a census should be taken of the beggar population, and of their death-rate.

The proposal was immediately taken up, and the inquiry

covered a considerable period. It revealed the fact that there was an average beggar population in Colombo of 1,200; that more than 100 dead beggars were picked up off the streets every year, and that about five hundred were carried to the hospitals, mostly in a moribund condition. The beggar death-rate was nearly five hundred per thousand, whereas the ordinary total death-rate was in the neighbourhood of thirty-five per thousand. And yet there was never any diminution in the total beggar population, the gaps in the ranks being speedily filled up by new arrivals.

The figures startled and thoroughly aroused the public, and Government was urged by the Press to take immediate action. It so happened that my wife and I were visiting Colombo at that time, and our attention was called to the matter by our Commanding Officer there.

Some of the papers suggested that the best agency for dealing practically with the question would be The Salvation Army, and that seeing that the leaders for India and Ceylon were visiting the Island, it would be well for the Ceylon Government and the Colombo Municipality to consult them, and see whether some definite arrangement could be arrived at. Some interesting negotiations of a prolonged character ensued.

We suggested that it would probably be found on inquiry that the beggars who really belonged to Colombo and were properly chargeable to that city were few in number, and could easily be handled by the Municipality without incurring any serious burden. It was the wholesale and unrestricted admission of beggars from all over the Island, and even from India, that constituted the real costliness of the scheme. If each city, district, and country could be made to "consume its own smoke," and care for its own beggar population, this difficulty would disappear.

Again we pointed out that while many of the beggars were really sick and incapable, a large proportion would be found to be vigorous and able-bodied, and should be compelled to return to the ordinary channels of labour. Even the sick could in many cases, by proper treatment and suitable nourishment, be restored to health, and then found employment.

In the year 1907 the Ordinances regarding Vagrancy had been amended and brought up to date, and Government had been empowered to establish Houses of Detention to which Vagrants could be committed for observation and detention. Until such a place, or places, had been established the law was practically a dead letter. It was not till 1913 that this improvement was finally effected. The Ceylon Administration report for 1921 contains the following interesting particulars :—

"Eight hundred and seventy vagrants were admitted to the House of Detention during the year. Of these, 553 were admitted from Colombo, 281 from Kandy, 14 from Nuwara Eliya, 12 from Karunegala, 6 from Anuradhapura, 2 from Hatton, and 1 each from Moratuwa and Galle. Of the 870 dealt with, 710 were Tamils, 123 Singhalese, 16 Ceylon Moors, 15 Coast Moors, 2 Burghers, 2 Malays, 1 Maratha and 1 Bengali.

"Employment was found for 84 vagrants; 674 natives of India who were unfit for work were deported to India, and 128 were sent to the Home for Vagrants.

"There was a slight decrease in the number of vagrants admitted to the House of Detention, 870 as against 926 in 1920.

"Since the House of Detention was opened in 1913, 5,260 vagrants have been dealt with. In 1921, fifty vagrants were found dead in the streets, and 185 removed to hospital, as compared with 109 vagrants found dead in the streets, and 513 removed to hospital in 1913. The provision of the House of Detention has rid the streets of vagrants to a great extent."

The Ordinances deal with the difficulty in what appears to be a wise and business-like manner :—

1. They empower the Magistrates and Police to clear the streets of the beggar population ;

2. They authorize the Ceylon Government to deport to India the large number of incapables, who properly belong to that country ;

3. They also enable the Authorities to send back others to their own town and district, unless the latter should be willing to pay for the cost of their support in Colombo ;

4. Able-bodied vagrants are dealt with summarily,
   (a) by sending them to the tea gardens, where their labour is required;
   (b) by making it a punishable offence for them to relapse to vagrancy.

The House of Detention here referred to has two branches. One is entirely under Police control for receiving, sorting and classifying the Vagrants. The other, for the care of the residuum of bona fide sick, or helpless vagrants, is under the charge of The Salvation Army.

Some considerable delay was caused by the difficulty of deciding what proportion of the expense should be borne respectively by the Ceylon Government and the Colombo Municipality. But a satisfactory arrangement was finally made by which it was agreed that they should jointly bear the expense, and that they should use the agency of The Salvation Army for the repulsive task of taking charge of the hopelessly diseased, and permanently, or temporarily, incapable. A large disused jail was placed at our disposal for the purpose.

This Home has now been under our charge for the last nine years, and there can be little doubt that it has filled a real need, and has indicated to other Eastern cities the possibility of dealing with this problem along the sensible, and at the same time merciful, lines laid down by the Ceylon Government.

According to the latest figures to hand for 1923, we have now in our Home 101 inmates. Of these 58 are men, 42 women, and 1 child. These include 14 blind, 4 deaf and dumb, 12 cripples, 9 mentally deficient, and 11 abnormal.

The Bombay Government and Municipality, after considering the Ceylon system, could not see their way to adopt their plan of compulsory segregation. But a movement was set on foot for dealing with the difficulty on purely voluntary lines, the agency of The Salvation Army being chosen for putting the plan into operation. We cannot do better than quote the report for January 1923, of the Helpless Beggars' Relief Committee to the Bombay Corporation :—

"*How it was started.* In May, 1920, Mr. W. B. Manley,

who was then Deputy Commissioner of Police, Bombay, having learned from the statistics collected from the Police Department that a large number of beggars were dying of starvation on the streets, convened a meeting of the citizens of Bombay with the object of forming an organization to help such people. A Committee was formed and the work was commenced. A party of voluntary workers systematically swept the streets, and the human sweepings were deposited in the Bombay Benevolent Society's Home at Byculla, day by day. This was the only place at that time available for the reception of these helpless people.

"In about three weeks' time, the Home absorbed about one hundred helpless beggars, and then the accommodation gave out. Some weeks later, through the good offices of the Bombay Improvement Trust and the Military Authorities, a Military Camp was handed over to the Committee for a short period only.

"The Salvation Army undertook the management of this new settlement, for which funds were provided by a Mahommedan gentleman. Street collection of beggars was at once resumed by the members of the Committee and the Officers of The Salvation Army. By December, 1920, this temporary refuge was housing 130 helpless beggars.

"*The Camp at Rowli Hill.* Knowing that the period for which the Military authorities had loaned the Camp to the Committee was very short, the Committee had to consider measures for more permanent accommodation, and for this purpose a Committee was formed under the Chairmanship of Sir N. G. Chandavarker, and the Bombay Improvement Trust was again approached and a site was secured at Rowli Hill. By May, 1921, the Camp was in working order, and there were sixty-eight persons in residence.

"Since this time, the camp has steadily been fulfilling the purpose for which it was brought into being, and the following statistics will convince all of the need of such an asylum, and also that it is a work that is worthy of their liberal support.

"*Some Statistics.* The total admissions to the Camp

number 1,174; Mahommedans 298, Hindus 816, Christians 60. Forty-nine different castes are represented here. Mahommedan 298, Maratha 222, Mahar 145, Bhaya 81, Hindu 81, Christian 60, Wagri 35, Madrassi 32, Mang 18, Thakur 16, Telugu 15, Brahmin 15, Ahir 14, Chamar 13, Pardesi 12, Koli 11, Pathan 9, Garthi 8. There are thirty-one other castes represented by small numbers.

"It will be seen that those from the Marathi country predominate. This was probably a result of the scarcity in that part in 1921, and with the influx into this City of those seeking work, came also those who were lame, halt and blind, etc. Whole families came, in some cases the parents both blind, with five or six little children.

"Many of the Mahommedans come to Bombay from the North of India, but in many cases they have been plying their trade in Bombay for a long period.

"*All Starving or Helpless.* All who are admitted to the Camp are in a helpless condition at the time of admission, as the following statistics of the total admitted will show: 237 were blind, 188 were lame, 390 sick, 30 mentally deficient, 5 were deaf and dumb, 324 were children under sixteen years of age.

"*Sickness.* Most of the sickness is a result of lack of nourishment, and exposure. Fifty per cent. of these soon recover, and are able to proceed to friends in Bombay, or go back to their country. The majority, as will be seen, are permanently disabled, either blind, paralysed, mentally deficient, lame, minus limbs, deaf and dumb, or infirm through old age.

"*Collecting the Beggars.* Many of the beggars are sent to the Camp by the Police, but the majority are collected from the streets by volunteer workers, comprised of members of the Committee, and Officers of The Salvation Army under the control of the Social Secretary, Salvation Army. The method of collecting beggars is as follows: The volunteer workers fix upon a centre, where the beggars are known to congregate, and two by two they scour the streets and lanes, picking up any who are willing to go. Let it be understood that no pressure is in any way brought to bear on these people to come to the Camp; they all come of their own free will.

" Very often the workers have arrived just too late on their errand of mercy, for death has overtaken the poor creatures before the workers could reach them. There have been many such cases noticed by the Officers of The Salvation Army as they have gone round.

" The Municipal Health Department has very kindly given the Committee the loan of horse and motor ambulances for the purpose of conveying the beggars from the streets to the Camp.

" *Life in the Beggars' Camp.* The Camp is situated at Rowli Hill, Matunga, on some new-made ground, on one of the Bombay Improvement Trust Development Schemes. It is about fifteen minutes' walk from the main road, a little beyond Matunga Station. The location of the Camp is healthy, as is seen by the improvement made by the beggars soon after their arrival. Many who come to us in an almost dying condition, after a few weeks' residence are quite well and hearty. The whole population of the Camp look well.

" When a new batch arrives at the Camp, after their particulars have been taken and a record made, they must all see the Doctor, who very carefully examines the case and gives treatment where necessary. After this is over, each has to take a bath, and this presents quite a problem, for some have not bathed for months, and they very much resent the idea of taking to water after such a long time. Bathing is followed by a good substantial meal, which all appear to enjoy.

" *Food.* The food times at the Camp, are as follows :— Morning, 7 a.m., tea ; 11 a.m., rice and curry ; 6 p.m., rice, dhal and chappatties. Mutton is given to those who wish to have it twice a week. As far as they are able to do so, the inmates of the Camp assist with the cooking, and the cook needs all the assistance he can get, when he has to make and bake something like 450 chappatties daily, in addition to rice and vegetables for such a large family.

" The Camp is divided into ten different wards ; two are specially reserved for women, and eight for men. The total accommodation is sufficient for about 250 people.

" *Medical Attendance.* Every morning a Doctor from the Municipal Health Department attends to the sick, and when the new arrivals first come, he has his hands quite full and his work is not to be envied, for some of the cases he has to deal with are beyond description,—sores which have been neglected for weeks; disease which, had it been treated at the proper time, could have been arrested, but now, owing to neglect, is beyond medical skill.

"*Industries.* It must be borne in mind that this Camp is for helpless beggars only, and only such are admitted. This being so, there is not much hope of successfully carrying on any industry. However, an attempt has been made and quite a number of the beggars have been employed on cane work. Those who have had an opportunity of doing this work appear to take to it well, especially the caning of chairs, but unfortunately it is not easy to get much of this kind of work, as the Camp is so far from the City. The young people learn weaving. Two special hand-looms have been installed, and it is intended to have more looms as funds permit. The object is to induce the beggars to make their own clothing, and also that of those incapable of any form of work.

"The inmates are also very interested in gardening, and almost every available foot of spare ground has been utilized to grow something or other. This is the kind of industry which should be encouraged. The inmates will not only be employed, but the employment will be of a healthy kind and they will be helping to provide themselves with food.

"*Supervision of The Salvation Army.* The Salvation Army, under whose direction the Camp has been so successfully run, have put in good service. The present Chief Officer, Lieut.-Commissioner J. Horskins takes a keen and active interest in this, as in all other work where the poor and helpless are concerned.

"The Salvation Army have a resident Manager, Adjutant Anand Rao, and he with his good wife attend to all the daily needs of the inmates. The Manager's wife is in charge of the sick ward, and daily attends to feeding those who are too feeble to feed themselves.

"*The Future.* Very fully does the Committee realize that their work touches only the fringe of the great problem of vagrancy in Bombay, but it is the only institution of its kind that seeks to succour starving humanity. There is a pressing need for the extension of the Rowli Hill Camp.

"The maintenance of each beggar at Rowli Hill costs roughly ten rupees a month. The Bombay Helpless Beggars' Relief Committee aim at accommodating 500 beggars, and it is to achieve this object that the Committee, through the Joint Honorary Secretaries, appeal for an increased grant.

"It will be seen by this Memorandum that the work is purely humanitarian, conducted strictly on non-denominational lines. The Commissioner of Police in Bombay certified its urgent necessity, and it enjoys the cordial sympathy of His Excellency the Governor of Bombay. The Municipal Corporation of Bombay generously sanctioned a monthly grant of Rs. 1,500 for one year, which expired on the 31st December, 1922. If the Corporation is satisfied that this grant has been faithfully applied and has really helped to relieve suffering, feed the starving and mitigate the dire distress of a large number of helpless beggars in the City of Bombay, then the Committee not only appeal for a renewal of that grant, but hope it will be increased to Rs. 2,000 per mensem, so that the Committee's work can be extended and the Beggars' Camp enlarged."

Here, as in all our Homes, Settlements, and Institutions, we have our regular meetings with music and singing. These afford a welcome relief and cheer to the sufferers, and serve to lighten the monotony of their lives, and to bring in a new element of hope and gladness. In passing through Colombo,* on our way from Australia to England, my wife and I held a meeting at the Beggars' Home, when some twenty of them came forward to give themselves to God, and one felt glad to realize that there was a place in the great Shepherd's Heart and Fold for those who had been hitherto the despair alike of the Legislator and the Philanthropist! Instead of being left to perish miserably in the streets, they are now surrounded with an atmosphere of love and sympathy which must indeed contrast strangely with their miserable past!

* July, 1923.

CHAPTER XXIV.

THE CRIMINAL TRIBES.

"The most gratifying feature in the history of criminal tribes in the year has been the success of The Salvation Army Settlements in Gorakhpur and Moradabad. . . They are on the way to turn them from hopeless enemies of mankind into useful citizens. . . . The Lieutenant-Governor wishes to place on record his appreciation of what has been done by that Organization. In his opinion it is not too much to say that their efforts show the way to the solution of a hitherto unsolved problem."

Government Resolution by Sir John P. Hewett, M.P., when Lieutenant-Governor, United Provinces.

Much of the work described in the previous pages was in operation when we arrived to take the oversight of India and Ceylon as the General's representatives.

Both the Founder and the present General felt that what was needed was the strengthening of the existing work, rather than spreading out to new fields. In this we were able to co-operate with the various Territorial Commanders.

There occurred, however, at this time another of those marvellous and unexpected interpositions of Providence in which one could but recognize again with gratitude the hand of God opening before us a new and remarkable door of opportunity.

India presents many perplexing problems, but few if any are more difficult to deal with or more urgent than the vast network, or what we may appropriately call the conspiracy of crime which overspreads the entire country in the form of Criminal Tribes whose whole and sole occupation consists in the commission of crime, from the proceeds of which they not only support themselves, but bribe the subordinate representatives of law and order to grant them a certain amount of toleration and immunity from punishment.

In other lands criminals are individuals who may be described as the "rogue elephants" of society. They are branded, boycotted and segregated from the decent law-abiding members of the human race. In India they consist of entire Tribes, Villages, Clans, and Families, all the members of which are devoted from the cradle to the grave to a life of crime. Nor are they ashamed of their profession. Rather do they glory in it, and regard themselves with all the pride of ancestry of warriors engaged in a perfectly legitimate war against society.

The origin of this dates back to the age-long condition of society in India. While certain portions of the country are rich in agricultural resources, others on their borders have a precarious struggle for existence. Their mountain homes or waterless deserts yield them a scanty and uncertain subsistence, which they have from time immemorial supplemented by periodical raids on their more prosperous, but often less warlike, neighbours.

It is only necessary to refer to the history of the Marathas, Rajputs and Afghans to illustrate the condition of things which has existed for centuries, and which has taxed for the last hundred years the utmost skill and patience of India's rulers to overcome.

Gradually the turbulent tribes have been restrained and their raidings brought under control. Extensive schemes of irrigation, industrial employment, and emigration have legitimately relieved the pressure of population, and the strong arm of the law has gradually made itself felt, till the Pax Britannica in India has become one of the great marvels of the age.

But there has remained a vast and widespread residuum of crime and criminals which has baffled the best efforts of the British Ruler. Tribes, numbering at the lowest calculation one million men, women and children, have parcelled out, so to speak, the entire country between themselves as a happy hunting ground, where they could gain a comparatively comfortable and easy subsistence by preying on society at large.

The fact that apart from British Territory there are some 500 Indian Princes, each with their own self-governed territory, laws and police, and that these regions are interlaced with one another, has served to make the task of the police particularly difficult. Not only so, but in many of the 220 Districts into which British India is subdivided, a friendly policy is frequently adopted towards these Tribes, who, when thus treated, grant such areas a large measure of immunity from raids, while they direct their special attention against those who are the most active in restraining and punishing them. Frequently the boundaries of three or four States and Districts converge at a particular point. This will be a favourite haunt for one or more Tribes, as they can pass swiftly from one jurisdiction to another, and thus evade the Police.

It must not be imagined for a moment that Government has been inactive in dealing with the matter. Efforts have been made alike at controlling, punishing and reforming them.

1. A special Act has been passed. But its provisions are more or less permissive, and in the case of independent Territories few of the Indian Princes have availed themselves of its provisions. In regard to British Territory, while some Provinces have enforced it, others have failed to do so, while some have only put forth very half-hearted efforts to carry out its provisions.

While I was in India I suggested the holding of a regular annual Conference, to be summoned by the Government of India, at which all States and Provinces should be represented, when those who were experts at this class of work should be invited to read papers and state their views. One or two such Conferences were held with good effect, but it was not adopted as a regular annual event, several Provinces objecting, I believe, on the ground that it was an undue interference with their independent liberty of action, and others on the score of expense.

2. Several British District Officials, and one or two Indian States have made efforts at reforming these Tribes by giving them land and inducing them to settle down to

gain an honest livelihood. Almost without exception these Governmental efforts failed as soon as the particular official interested in them was transferred, or left India, the Tribe relapsing into crime.

3. The District or Police official dealing with these Tribes, and seeking to reform them, finds himself seriously handicapped by the fact that this kind of crime is very lucrative, and he has often to deal with the secret obstruction of vested interests which frequently include his own subordinates. In a single year in one Province 3,500,000 rupees' worth of property had been officially reported as stolen, of which less than half a million had been recovered. The unrecovered balance had been divided between the thieves and those whose duty it was to detect and punish them.

4. Again, his official position prevents the District Officer from making any use of religious influences to persuade the people in whom he is interested to turn from their evil ways.

5. Nor is his wife as a rule capable or desirous of bringing her reformatory influence to bear on the women and children of the tribe, as is the case with the wives of our Officers. This is really the key to the position in any reformatory effort that may be made.

6. Some Police Officers have made sincere, earnest and partially successful efforts to reform particular tribes, but when the time came for their promotion or transfer, there was seldom anybody willing to step into their shoes, or devote any considerable portion of their career to such distasteful and inconspicuous work, which was practically a blind alley position where their future prospects of advancement would be marred.

Otherwise they had a great advantage in that they were able to check and control their subordinates. These, however, knew that sooner or later the time would come for the transfer of the official, and that they would then be able to renew their strangle-hold upon the Tribe.

It was in 1908 when we were conducting one of our annual Congress Campaigns throughout India that we visited Bareilly. Amongst the audience at one of our meetings was the Hon. Mr. Tweedy, then Commissioner of

Rohilkhand, and a member of the Government of the United Provinces. He spoke to us about the Criminal Tribes, in whose welfare he was keenly interested, and asked whether we could undertake reformatory work among them. He felt sure that the Lieutenant-Governor, Sir John P. Hewett, would be glad to consider any proposals we might submit, and to afford us every possible co-operation and assistance. We gladly agreed to the proposal, and the matter was then submitted to the Lieutenant-Governor and met with his cordial approval. Sir John Hewett suggested that we should make an experiment with one Tribe and promised that if this should be successful other Tribes should be committed to our charge.

We were invited to visit Gorakhpur, where the Government proposed to make over to us some 300 Doms, who had been for some time under charge of the Police.

The people were confined at night in what were known as Dom Khanas, a kind of walled prison enclosure, where men, women and children were locked in. During the day they were allowed to go into the city, where many of them were employed and paid as city scavengers and road-sweepers. They also begged food from the people for whom they did odd jobs. It was well known that they added largely to their income by robbery and other crime. They were further notorious for drink, gambling and immorality. If any of them absconded—as they frequently did—when captured by the police, their captor received a reward of Rs. 5. This led to a system on the part of the subordinate police of leading some of them out into the country and bringing them back as captives in order to claim the reward. It was a common saying among the Doms that no one need be captured provided he had in his possession Rs. 6—one rupee more than the reward—to offer to the policeman as a peace-offering.

My wife and I visited the tribe in their principal Dom Khana to talk matters over with them. The police offered to accompany us, saying that it would not be safe for us to go without an escort. We declined their assistance with thanks.

There is little doubt that they had been warned by the police not to accept our proffered help, for the first question they asked us was whether if we came they would be required to give up drink and gambling. This information they had undoubtedly received from the police, who did not view our coming with favour, as the Doms had shared with them the proceeds of their thefts and robberies in order to secure immunity from punishment.

They assured us that it was hopeless for us to expect them ever to give up drink or gambling. It was impossible. Still, The Salvation Army could not be any worse than the police, and they might possibly be a little better, so that we could come if we liked.

They appeared very unpromising material, but we determined to make the attempt. They were such inveterate gamblers, that when a Dom died they would put a few pice into the hand of the dead man with which to commence gambling in the world to come. Their idea of Paradise was a land where they could gamble to their hearts' content, with no police to check them.

Government placed at our disposal some extensive Police Lines, and to this soon afterwards was added a large vacant Jail. These were in every way convenient, and were a great improvement on the old Dom Khanas. Brigadiers Bahadur and Ratna Bai (Hunter) were appointed to take charge of the Settlement, and threw themselves heart and soul into the task.

A change was soon visible in the lives and appearance of the people. At first the suggestion that they should wash their clothes was met with the indignant declaration, "We are not Dhobis (Washerman caste)!"

"Why not get your wives to do it?" was suggested, to which the reply was made, "It would spoil the taste of our food!"

But by degrees they fell into line in this as in other ways, and in place of their dishevelled, dirty appearance and ragged clothing, they gradually became neat and clean.

Among other privileges, the Brigadiers were allowed to visit the many Doms who were serving sentences in the Gorakhpur Jail, and to hold meetings among them. On one of these occasions five of the prisoners requested Brigadier Ratna Bai (Mrs. Hunter) to take a message to their wives who were in the Settlement. "Tell our Mem

Sahibs," they said, "not to marry anybody else while we are in prison, but to wait for us till we are released."

The message was delivered that night, when the Brigadier called upon the five women to stand up, and then told them what their husbands had said. "Bahut achcha"—very good—they replied, not a little flattered at the honourable title of "Mem Sahib" which their husbands had conferred on them. It was only too common a cause of feud and possible bloodshed, when the women, whose husbands had been imprisoned, married someone else as their sole means of support. Now that the Settlement had been established this was no longer necessary.

The faith of the Brigadiers in the people who were committed to their care was beautiful to witness. For years they toiled among them with increasing devotion, and had the joy of leading many of them to the Saviour. And when they left the Settlement and proceeded on their well-earned furlough, they were able to leave behind them blessed evidences of their success.

It was when they were returning to their post of duty in 1914, while travelling from Canada with a large number of Officers who were proceeding to the International Congress in London, that the SS. "Empress of Ireland" met with the disaster which resulted in the loss of many lives including no less than 140 Salvationists. Brigadiers Bahadur and Ratna Bai, and their two children were amongst those who received their tragic Home Call. Their work among the Doms survives them as their eternal monument.

Government were so well satisfied with the success of our efforts to reform the Doms, that other Settlements were soon afterwards organized. Among the buildings placed at our disposal was the large fortress of Aligarh, surrounded by a wall and moat.

The following description was written soon after its opening by the Officer in charge regarding the first party that was sent in by the police:—

"The first settlers to arrive were a set of criminals called Beriahs from Akrabad, who were brought in by the police. A motley crew indeed, consisting of sixteen women, and thirty-one children, with hardly a rag to cover them. Men there were none, for the simple reason that every man belonging to them was in jail for different degrees of dacoity (robbery) and theft.

"To the gates this crowd was brought, but further they refused to go. Here they sat and wailed, the children joining their mothers in the outcry. They called upon their dead mothers to see their misery, and how they would die. At last, however, they came in, but alas, they only sat on the ground, and moaned, and wailed day and night, refusing to be comforted. After four days they made a rough bamboo ladder, by means of which they escaped during the night, and paddled through the moat into the jungle, and, as they thought, to liberty.

"They were, however, found and brought back to the Fort in two parties on different days, and before long they discovered that their fears were unfounded, and that we were really their friends and had come to help them.

"Already some progress has been made. They now call themselves Salvation people."

Perhaps the best tribute to our success was the increasing eagerness of these Tribes to avail themselves of our help. In one case a gang sent us word that they were marching from a distant point to one of our settlements, hiding in the jungles by day and travelling by night. As soon as they arrived they intended to place themselves under our direction and do whatever we might say.

Another tribe wrote to us as follows, on a one-rupee stamped paper:—

"Your good name has come to us, and we long to place ourselves under your care and control. We are in great distress!"

In one settlement a band was formed and they bought their own instruments for twelve annas. Those who were short of instruments placed their shoes on their hands and clapped them. It was primitive but successful. The official hangman acted as Band-master.

Another of our settlements was in Bareilly, where Government assisted us in acquiring and fitting up a large Brewery. The rapid progress of the Temperance cause amongst the British Soldiers in India, more than half of the Army having gone "dry," had led to the closing of these extensive and solidly constructed buildings, costing originally about Rs. 150,000, but sold to us for Rs. 40,000.

One of our latest settlements was in Moradabad, where 200 acres of land were made over to us by Government for the double purpose of a settlement and a hospital. The land was poor, and had been formerly used for a rifle range. But it had two great advantages; (1) the immediate vicinity of a city of 100,000 inhabitants enabled us to find a variety of work for many of our settlers, and a good market for our produce. (2) There was a considerable underflow about thirty feet below the surface of the land.

The respectable inhabitants were greatly disturbed when they heard of the proposed settlement, and petitioned Government against our coming. They were so far successful, that the original settlers were composed of Haburahs, and the more turbulent Bhatus were dealt with elsewhere.

The Haburahs were not looked upon as dangerous criminals. They were clever thieves, but seldom resorted to violence. They had been for a long time located near a small town called Kanth, about twenty miles from Moradabad. But there was neither work, nor land sufficient for their support. At the invitation of Government we visited their camp. Their appearance was miserable in the extreme. The scanty scraps of clothing they possessed were ragged and dirty, and they themselves were little more than skin and bones. In the middle of the night, about 2 a.m., they would get up, and fill the air with their lamentations and howls. They had a theory that one of their ancestors had incurred the wrath of a certain demon by killing a rabbit to appease his hunger. They might eat jackals, lizards and serpents—almost anything—but a rabbit they must never touch. Now they were suffering for their ancestor's disobedience. And so every night for about an hour they would howl their regrets and beg forgiveness. Surely the God, whom they knew not, heard their cry, and sent The Salvation Army in answer to their prayer!

They had never heard of us, but were glad to welcome deliverance from any source. A quadrangular enclosure was put up for them on the chandmari (rifle range), and to this they were transferred. Agriculture, weaving and outside employment constituted their means of support. Soon after their arrival the police reported that all the jackals in the neighbourhood had disappeared, for they were expert hunters and looked upon jackal flesh as quite a delicacy. But they had not been many months in their new location when regular work and good food had made a revolution in their tastes as well as in their appearance, and the jackals began to reappear! Being the principal scavengers, their loss had been regarded with some alarm.

The Haburahs never made any objection to our religion. They enjoyed the meetings, though occasionally incidents would occur. Of course the women had to bring their babies with them, and the meetings were not always as orderly as we ourselves might desire. My wife and I were conducting the service one Sunday morning. A baby was fractious. One of the women turned to the mother and scolded her. The latter retaliated. Then the two sprang at each other and there was a scene, which would have horrified the worshippers in St. Paul's Cathedral. The husbands intervened and there was peace till the meeting was over, when the controversy was renewed. The husband of one of them seized his wife, swung her across his back and carried her off struggling, screaming, vociferating and shaking her fist at the owner of the baby, which had been the innocent cause of the trouble. That was in the early days.

How different was the scene a few years later when we visited the same settlement! The numbers of the settlers had increased from 200 to 800. The people were well dressed, tidy, well fed, bright and intelligent. One of the most touching scenes was when several of the young girls sang together a new song of their own composition, describing the work that was being carried on in the Settlement. The chorus was :—

> " We are Nekmashes, you must know!
> If you doubt it, you can see our Certificates ! "

There were clear and definite testimonies of Salvation, and the entire character of the people had undergone a radical change. Under the management of an Indian Officer, the land itself had been brought into perfect cultivation by the sinking of wells, with the addition of an oil engine and pumping plant. The industries had also been extended, and during the war the women were engaged in making uniforms for the Military Department. The whole Settlement became a hive of industry.

One of the most picturesque of our settlements in the United Provinces, is the one which is located at Najibabad in an old Mahommedan Fortress. Here the more dangerous classes of tribesmen had been sent, as the high thick walls gave a better chance of controlling their movements. The settlers are supported mostly by industry, though some crops are also grown on the forty acres of land inside the walls.

The bad past of these settlers made them always fear that the police would use the settlement as a trap to catch them.

On one occasion the police had succeeded in capturing an outside tribesman who had eluded them. The evidence of one of our settlers was required. He agreed to attend the Court, and paid the penalty with his life. On the way he was attacked by other members of the gang, hacked to pieces and cast into a well.

Another of our settlers, who knew the facts, refused to give evidence, and was therefore sentenced to several years' imprisonment, preferring this to the probability that he would share the fate of the first witness.

It can readily be imagined how difficult is the work of reforming such characters. While Government is willing as far as possible to allow bygones to be bygones, it is impossible for them to altogether ignore the more serious crimes of the past. However, time serves to obliterate many of these blood-stained footprints in its sands, and as individuals give obvious evidence of their reformation they are passed on to other settlements where the restrictions are less rigid.

It will be readily understood that the action of Government in asking The Salvation Army to undertake the reformation of these Tribes exposed them to considerable criticism from some Indian members of the Local Government. Referring to this in a meeting at the Royal Society of Arts in London, on the 15th December, 1922, Sir John P. Hewett gave the following interesting account of what occurred :—

"Very shortly after certain tribes in the United Provinces were made over to The Salvation Army, some Hindu members of the Local Council raised a debate on the question. They contended that it was unfair to employ a Christian agency in preference to Hindu agencies. But these opponents were in a minority. The Indian members, with few exceptions, were firmly of opinion that no Hindu or Indian agency was so fit to have control of the criminal tribes as The Salvation Army. Every Mahommedan member voted in favour of the Government's decision, and a Brahmin, now one of the leading non-co-operators, made a speech on the same side. The majority was something over forty to about seven against."

A touching story is told of one of our settlers, who absconded to escape arrest. A few handfuls of stolen maize which another settler had brought in had been traced to his home. He could not face the pending enquiry and disappeared, leaving his wife and baby in the settlement. We hoped he would return, and in all probability a warning would have been all that he would have had to face. But he did not come, and his wife, taking the baby, set off to find him and bring him back.

A short time after, the settlers came to tell our Officer that Girdhari had come back to the settlement to die. He was very ill, and seemed near death, but had felt he could not die away from the settlement. The Captain hurried to his side to see what could be done. The man was beyond the reach of human remedies, but expressed his joy at being back under The Army Flag and his trust in his Saviour for the pardon of his sins. Some days after his wife returned. She had failed in her search, and now she heard that her husband had returned, but only to die. "And our Jitli too is dead!" she moaned sadly. The little one's life had been sacrificed in her efforts to find its father. Full of pathos and tragedy are the stories which these criminals pour into our ears. It has been a new experience to them to find sympathetic listeners ever willing to guide and to help.

In another of our settlements the Officer was aroused one night by sounds of a disturbance. He hurried out to see what was the matter. It proved to be a quarrel among some passers-by. Everything in the settlement was quiet. As he returned to his quarters he heard the voice of someone reading, and looking in the direction saw one of our settlers sitting on the ground reading to his wife, who was lying beside him on a charpoy.

"I had no idea, Roshan, you could read so well. What are you reading?" asked the Officer.

"It is the story of Jesus and His death," replied the man. "Every night after supper I sit and read to my wife." His Bible was spread before him, and he was reading by the dim light of an Indian diwa—clay lamp—with a rag as wick in a little oil. They were two of his best and most reliable settlers, hard workers, an example to their people, and a stand-by to their Officers.

CHAPTER XXV.

MORE ABOUT THE CRIM.

"We have been enormously interested in seeing the Silk factory, conducted by The Salvation Army. The young members of the Criminal Tribes were working away merrily. The experiment, first tried under Sir John Hewett's Government, of placing the Criminal Tribes in charge of The Salvation Army, is evidently proving a great success, and is proving a solution of one of the most troublesome problems with which Government has to deal. The greatest credit is due to The Salvation Army for the success now being achieved."

The Rt. Honourable Earl of Ronaldshay,
(Former Governor of Bengal).
Royal Commission on the Public Services in India.

The full story of the work among the Criminal Tribes deserves to be separately written. In this volume we can only give a few passing glimpses, and cannot pretend to do justice to what is certainly one of the most interesting chapters in the romance of Missions.

The example set by the Government of the United Provinces was quickly followed in succession by the Punjab, Madras, Bengal, and Bihar and Orissa Governments.

Our latest figures regarding this entire field of effort are as follows :—

Province.	Name of Settlement.	No. of Settlers.
I. *United Provinces.*	1. Gorakhpur	386
	2. Moradabad	813
	3. Kanth	140
	4. Bareilly	215
	5. Sahibgunj	172
	6. Najibabad	256
	7. Boys' Home	58
	8. Girls' Home	50
	9. Young Children	40
	Total ..	2,130

Province.	Name of Settlement.	No. of Settlers.
II. *Punjab.*	1. Kot Adhian	601
	2. Changa Manga	222
	3. Kassowal	419
	Total ..	1,242
III. *Bengal.*	1. Saidpur	318
IV. *Bihar and Orissa.*	1. Chautarwa..	305
	2. Angul	101
	3. Children's Home	37
	Total ..	443
V. *Madras.*	1. Sainyapuram	1,107
	2. Stuartpuram	1,783
	3. Guntur	219
	4. Perambur	217
	5. Pallavaram	231
	6. Boys' Home	58
	7. Girls' Home	50
	8. Children	42
	Total ..	3,707

Thus the present population of the Settlements amount to :—

United Provinces	2,130
Punjab	1,242
Bengal..	318
Bihar and Orissa	443
Madras	3,707
Total ..	7,840

There are now twenty-four institutions with a total population of 7,840.

The Tribes dealt with include the following :—

Sansias, Bhatus, Haburahs, Nats, Karwals, Doms, Maghaya Doms, Yerikulas, Veppur Parias, and Korachas.

In addition to the above there are Day Schools in all the Settlements. In one case, no less than sixteen teachers are required, and nine of these come from the Settlers themselves.

The earnings of the settlers vary very much according to the location and character of work, ranging from Rs. 5 to Rs. 30 per month, per family. They now realize the full benefit of being able to keep what they have earned instead of having to share it with the subordinate police.

In the Punjab the earnings of the settlers amounted in the year ending 30th June, 1922, to Rs. 23,018. In the United Provinces Rs. 91,748 were earned. In Madras the figures in one Settlement (Stuartpuram) amounted to Rs. 90,301, and in two others Rs. 20,416.

Of all the Settlements it may now be said that the settlers support themselves by their own labour, and Government assistance is limited to Schools, Buildings, Supervision, and grants for the old and infirm.

The problem of making the settlers self-supporting was one of the most serious that faced us when we commenced this work, seeing that few of them had ever done an honest day's labour, while all objected to hard work, and few knew any handicraft, or had any inclination for agriculture. The rapidity with which this change has taken place has surprised the most experienced Government Officials, who were well acquainted with their thriftless habits, and their propensity to drunkenness and gambling as well as robbery.

The work amongst the Maghaya Doms of Bihar was of a very difficult character. They were related to the Doms of the adjoining District of Gorakhpur, and were of a very criminal and troublesome type. An agricultural settlement had been established at Chauterwa, in the Motihari district, by Sir Edward Henry, afterwards in charge of the London Metropolitan Police, when he was a young civilian, some thirty years previously. Later on the same settlement was for some time under the direction of Mr. W. R. Gourlay, afterwards Private Secretary to successive Governors of Bengal.

Much had been done for them, but there had been little or no sign of reformation. They were a positive nuisance and danger to their neighbours, and a constant anxiety to the Police. Neither punishment nor clemency seemed to cure their predatory habits, nor would they work the land which had been obtained for them.

The Times of India, dated 9th September, 1921, gives the following interesting particulars of the way in which these difficulties were overcome :—

" Application was made to Government for 25 bullocks which were sent. These the Doms refused to have anything to do with, and the Commandant and his assistants had to feed and tend them themselves.

" The Commandant studied the nature of his people to see how he could make it seem to them to be worth while to take up work on the land. He commenced himself by cultivating a model holding. He arranged it that the bullocks could become the personal property of individual selected families on condition of easy payments. On similar conditions he parcelled the land out. He offered to guide their unaccustomed hands in the rudiments of preparing the ground and ploughing, and he offered to do all the actual sowing himself.

" Now and for some time, to quote the Commandant, his people 'are mad' to take up cultivation. They are on their own and will not stop. The weaving has to be confined to children whose parents have no land. The Commandant has a fat rent roll, and prosperity abounds. The fields as I saw them were good to see, but in September, I was told, they are veritable gardens. These statements were confirmed by Mr. Amman, of Kharpokhra, a planter.

" The assistants and some of the Doms own highly cultivated gardens adjoining their houses. These houses are well built of bricks and tiles and are surrounded by high walls.

" There are practically no cases of bad behaviour on the Settlement and no complaints from outside. This is remarkable to those who know the Dom and what he was. But here the desire to prosper, to be respectable and at peace seems to have crushed out former propensities. Their racial bump of acquisitiveness has been shown a more convenient way of development.

" There is moral and spiritual development also ; but not enough to please the manager. When he took me round the day school in my short visit, I thought I saw some evidences of it, particularly in the teacher of the younger children's class. She is a Dom girl in her teens, a pure product of the Settlement, who has prospered in appearance and mental and spiritual equipment, whilst her parents have been hard at it prospering materially. But the dominating fact of the Settlement seemed to me to be the personality of Commandant Corneliussen himself. Unassuming, practical, and pious, he is a type not uncommon in The Salvation Army."

In the year 1914, we were invited by Government to undertake work among the Pans of Orissa, commencing operations in the Angul district, where some 28,000 of them were to be found. They resembled in general characteristics the Bhils and other aboriginal tribes, and had retired before the advance of civilization to the mountain fastnesses and jungles, where they gained a precarious living, which was supplemented more or less by raiding their more prosperous neighbours. By the Hindus they were regarded as belonging to the Untouchables, whose presence, or very shadow, meant pollution.

The Government did not think it wise to compel them to enter Settlements such as we had established in other Provinces, but preferred that we should send Officers who would get in touch with them, visit them in their remotest haunts, and gradually wean them from their evil ways. The Pans, like the Bhils, were exceedingly shy and suspicious, and it was believed that our adoption of Indian dress and names and customs would help to gain their confidence.

Some thirty-five Village Day Schools had recently been started among them by the District Officer, Mr. Taylor, and the supervision of these was placed under our charge, thus putting us in touch with the villagers.

In Angul itself thirty acres of land were assigned to us, where quarters were erected for the married European Officer in charge of the work, and an Industrial Home for Orphans and children of Pans who were serving sentences in prison.

Two tracts of land were placed at our disposal in the interior, and tanks for irrigation were repaired. At each of these about fourteen to eighteen families were settled, numbering in all about one hundred men, women and children. Residence in these locations was voluntary, but more would have come had it not been for the breaking of the dams which conserved the water owing to torrential floods.

One of our pioneer veterans, Lieut.-Colonel Jeya Kodi (Johnston) was sent to inaugurate the work, and was able to report soon after that one of the District Officials had said to him :—

> "The Pans in the District last year shewed the lowest record of crime of any caste. You will have to go easy, or there will be no need for The Salvation Army!"

Closely connected with our work among the Criminal Tribes was a new development in regard to the ordinary Jail population. At an early date we obtained permission to visit members of the Tribes who were in prison, and in some cases to hold meetings among them.

The rules concerning non-interference with the religious beliefs of prisoners were very strictly interpreted by the Indian Government. Christians could be visited and meetings held with them, but as most jails had no Christian prisoners, and others only a few, this permission was of no practical value.

The Ceylon Government took a much broader view of the subject. Permission was granted by them to all teachers of religion, whether Buddhist, Hindu, Mahommedan, or Christian, to visit the jails on Sunday, and conduct meetings. The prisoners were allowed to choose for themselves which service they preferred to attend, regardless of the particular religion to which they belonged. As a result, for the past twenty years, or more, our services have been well attended in the Welikada Central Jail in Colombo, and numerous conversions have taken place. The Jail staff have testified to the fact that great improvement has taken place in the conduct of the prisoners who attend our meetings, and that their own task of keeping order has been greatly facilitated.

As an illustration, one of the more recent converts had been a Buddhist Priest, who had received a long sentence for an attempt to murder a Government Official. His conversion created a very favourable impression, and he was looking forward, on his release, to devoting his life to Christ under The Army Flag, but passed away recently before his term had expired.

On the occasion of a visit to this Jail my wife and I conducted an hour's service among about three hundred short-sentence men—after which we had a meeting among about the same number of long-sentence men, finishing up with a season of prayer and personal conversations with about a dozen men who were in the condemned cells awaiting their execution.

About thirty of the short-service men came forward to seek salvation. The long-sentence men were not permitted to leave their seats, but more than twenty hands were raised to ask for prayer, and to express their determination to seek salvation and live a new life.

In connection with this prison, we have a Home for Released Prisoners, who are found employment and assisted to make a new start.

During the Lieutenant-Governorship of Sir Louis Dane, in the Punjab, and while Sir Harold Stuart was in Madras, we succeeded in arranging for a new departure of a very promising character. Two special Homes were set apart for the reception of prisoners who were released to us on parole for the last six months to two years of their sentence.

We pointed out that the main reason why Habitualism was so steadily on the increase was, because the prisoners on their release were sent back to their homes with the hall-mark of crime and the jail stamped upon them. This had the double effect of making employers of labour afraid to give them work, and indeed making all respectable persons afraid of associating with them, and furthermore, whenever any crime was committed in their neighbourhood, however innocent they might be, suspicion usually attached to them. If brought before the Court, there was reference made to their previous conviction, and they usually received a severe sentence.

"Take care of my clothes for me, I shall soon be back again," was frequently the farewell message of a released prisoner to the Jail Darogha (Manager) on his release. He felt his position to be a hopeless one. His associates in crime, or those who were similarly circumstanced, would be the only ones to welcome him.

If on the other hand he could spend the last few years, or even months, of his term with us, he could return to his home without the stigma of crime attaching to him, and in possession of a certificate of good conduct from us, which would enable him to get employment among his own people. Failing this, we would continue to look after him.

Moreover, previous to his return, he could get in touch with his people, and out of his earnings while with us he could send money for the support of his family, and thus ensure a hearty welcome when his sentence had expired.

There was to be no compulsion about the matter. His coming to us would be purely voluntary, and his stay with us would be equally so. If he preferred to complete his sentence in jail, he could always do so. While he was with us he would have the advantage of wearing no prison dress, and we would undertake to find him remunerative work.

It must not be supposed that the prisoners themselves were eager to fall in with the proposal. They were inclined to be suspicious. And it was not until we had explained to them, by means of a lantern lecture, who we were and what we proposed that they availed themselves of our proposal.

I can never forget that lantern meeting. The Jail authorities said that on no account could they consent to its being held after dark. Hence doors and windows had to be closed to shut out the light. This meant that air too was excluded! The atmosphere was oppressive, and before the lecture was over, one after another of the jail staff had slipped out, and those of us who remained inside were on the point of fainting. But we were amply rewarded when, as they streamed past us at the opening of the doors, scores of them said, "May we come? Do let us come!"

After that there was no further difficulty. There were always eager candidates ready to fill up every vacancy, and their behaviour with us was exemplary.

We experienced no difficulty with them. They made no attempt to escape. They worked willingly and their conduct was good. The Jail Authorities reported that hardly any of them reverted to crime, or came back to prison, after returning to their homes.

Unfortunately, our success led the next Lieutenant-Governor to decide that Government would itself undertake similar work on a still larger scale. We earnestly begged that our supply of youths should not be discontinued, but that we should be allowed to compete with Government in the worthy effort to reform these young men. A deaf ear was turned to our entreaties, on the ground that we were a religious organization.

A camp was established by Government in the neighbourhood of some large mills, in which the youths were given employment. After a sufficient period had elapsed, I went with my wife to visit the Camp in order to see how the experiment was progressing. To our surprise we found the youths not only manacled, but fettered, with a guard of more than seventy police. When with us there had been no necessity for restrictions, and yet there had been no attempt or desire to escape.

I asked the Darogha (Superintendent) of the Camp why such severe restrictions had been introduced, remarking that it was far worse than prison, where inside the walls they were perfectly free. He replied, "We tried your plan, but had to give it up, as they all ran away, and it is only in this manner that we can prevent them from doing so now."

The underlying cause of dissatisfaction probably lay in the excessive strain of factory labour. We had already had considerable experience in dealing with factory officials in connection with the employment of our settlers. While the European Directors and Proprietors were usually affable and reasonable, many of their foremen were perfect slave-drivers, and the tendency in all was to exact exceedingly long hours and heavy tasks from their employees.

It had been necessary for us, in another Province, as guardians of the Crims, to call upon Government more than once to come to our aid. The Mill-owners had argued that they could make no difference between Crim and ordinary labour, and that the same tasks which were undertaken by the latter, together with the same hours, must be accepted by our settlers.

To this I had replied that the Free Labour of their employees was on a totally different footing from the Forced Labour of our Crims. It was a notorious fact that their Free Labour was what might be called extremely volatile and unreliable. It was true that they would work full hours for a few weeks, or even months, and earn full wages, but they would make up for it by taking a long holiday to recuperate. On the plea of health, marriage, funerals or other domestic causes, they would simply go off to their native village, or disappear, and perhaps take up for a time some lighter employment. Why? Because the severe physical strain of these long hours, frequently without any Sunday, or other interval for rest, was more than the strongest constitutions could endure.

The case was widely different with the Forced Labour of our settlers. They could only relieve the strain by absconding, which was a punishable offence. They would come back from their day's work absolutely exhausted, and yet if some of them were excused by us from going, and a letter of explanation sent to their foreman by our European Officer, an urgent demand would be received saying that they must attend. It was the fact that they could not get away like the Free Labour that made this class of workman appear so desirable to the Mill Manager.

Government took a sympathetic view of the situation, and adopted our suggestion that our settlers should have their Sunday free, and that the hours of labour should never exceed from eight to eleven per day, with suitable intervals in case of illness.

I pointed out that in the Government Jails, the work hours were strictly limited to a maximum of eight, and with a full Sunday's rest. Apart altogether from the consideration of the Prisoners, Government were unable to exact longer hours from their Staff. Nor could Government venture, nor had it ever ventured, to demand from the Forced Labour of their Prisoners, longer hours. Moreover, every prisoner was weighed at regular intervals to see if he were losing flesh, and should such be the case, a lighter task was assigned.

These contentions were accepted by the Government of the United Provinces, largely through the energetic representations of Mr. A. W. Richardson, the Special Police Officer who had been appointed by Government to supervise our Settlements. He also acted as a very efficient go-between with the Mill Companies.

I have little doubt that in the case of the Punjab mills, the real reason for the youths absconding was the excessive tasks that were exacted from them, and their inability to stand the continued strain.

In the Madras Presidency, a still more interesting and successful work for Released Prisoners was established by us in Guntur at the invitation of Sir Harold Stuart. While the Home in Lahore was exclusively for the benefit of Borstal youths, that in South India was for Released Prisoners generally. Here again there was at first some hesitation on the part of the prisoners themselves to take advantage of the Government's offer for them to spend the latter portion of their sentence in our Home.

However, we were authorised to visit the various Jails, and to confer with their Staff and explain matters to the prisoners themselves. As a result a number of men accepted the opportunity, and before long there were more applicants than we could accommodate. Moreover the friends and relatives of prisoners heard about the Home and began to make application to Government for the transfer of those in whom they were interested to our care.

In many cases the wives and children of the men thus released were allowed to join them, and it was a very happy community of some 200 souls who were thus cared for by us.

Unfortunately, after the retirement of Sir Harold, this promising and interesting work was brought to an end. We understood at the time that, as in the Punjab, Government had decided to undertake the work themselves, but I am not aware that this was ever done. However, greatly to our regret the supply of released prisoners was stopped, and the Settlement was utilised by us for a certain class of Criminal Tribesmen who could not be easily dealt with in an open Settlement.

CHAPTER XXVI.

CRIMINOCUROLOGY.

"The subject is an enormous one, and the fringe has only just been touched. I am, however, convinced that in time The Salvation Army will succeed in the object it has in view, namely the absorption of the Criminal Tribes into the ordinary population. When that has been done, Commissioner Booth Tucker and those who work with him, will have combined to achieve one of the greatest moral reformations the world has ever seen."

Sir John Hewett, M.P.
(Former Lieut.-Governor of the United Provinces, at a meeting of the Royal Society of Arts, London.)

"I agree with what Sir John Hewett has said . . . and I do not think that Government could be too grateful to The Salvation Army for the admirable work it is doing in that and other respects."

Lord Pentland.
(Former Governor of Madras.)

An interesting development of our work has taken place amongst the Criminal Tribes of the Madras Presidency. At the invitation of Sir Harold Stuart, we were asked to see what we could do for the Yerikulas, who had given the Police much trouble for many years. Hovering along the border-line of British Territory, they would make their escape, when pursued, into the Dominions of the Nizam of Haidarabad, a Mahommedan State, when they could only be dealt with by the State Authorities. On being ejected by the latter, they would cross back to British Territory. Their lightning movements were difficult to follow, nor were the Magistrates willing to consign entire clans to prison.

After consulting the Authorities of the United Provinces and the Punjab, as to our success in this kind of work, Sir Harold had come to the conclusion that the agency of The Salvation Army would be more effective in reforming the Tribes than that of the Police. It was proposed, therefore, to gather together and intern about 1,000 of these tribesmen in the neighbourhood of Bezwada, on the bank of the river Krishna. A deserted railway settlement, previously known as Sitanagaram, and renamed by us Sainyapuram, or Armytown, with several bungalows, and about one hundred acres of land, was placed at our disposal in December 1912. In the neighbourhood were extensive stone quarries where the men, women and children could all be employed, the stone being required by the railway which ran through the Settlement, and for numerous district roads. Several canals converged at this point, supplying barge-transportation, and Bezwada was a junction for many railways, and could ultimately absorb much of their labour as they became reformed.

We encountered many difficulties. The tribe was nomadic, and resented internment, nor did they like the work in the quarries, their chief objection being that it was not nearly so remunerative as their hereditary employment of theft and robbery. Moreover, the work was undoubtedly hard, and they were paid by results, the amount quarried being measured. In fact, they objected to everything. Even the six hundred donkeys which they brought with them entered into the spirit of their non-co-operating masters. They had been accustomed to carry heavy loads of salt, which served as a blind when their masters were on their raids, but to carry stone was distinctly beneath their dignity, and when so loaded they would simply lie down and rid themselves of their burdens. Nor could the donkeys see any reason for refraining from browsing along the railway line. When a train came in sight, they would simply turn their backs to it and kick, a proceeding which, needless to say, resulted in numerous fatalities.

The settlers objected most strongly of all to The Salvation Army religious services. They complained to Government that we were trying to make them change

Top and Bottom. Types of Criminal Tribes people of whom many thousands are under The Salvation Army's care; the former represent large numbers who, giving evidence of transformation in character, have been released from Government surveillance.

Centre. A village gathering of Salvationists for the purpose of publicly destroying idols surrendered by converts.

Types of beggars in India and Ceylon who are being cared for by The Salvation Army; many have been won for Christ.

their religion! Like most of these tribes they were demonolaters, and their religion restricted itself to efforts to appease offended spirits by sacrifices and devil worship of the crudest character.

Major (now Brigadier) Anandham (Mackenzie), an Officer from the United States, was in charge of the Settlement, and lived amongst these trying tribesmen for several years. His patience was simply inexhaustible. He had a heart which entered into their sorrows. The following touching verses, which were written by him at the time, will serve to show how sympathetically he entered into their conditions :—

THE CRIM.

I've oft been to prison and tasted their fare,
For I am a Crim, yes, I am a Crim!
Learned more of my business profession while there,
Seeing mine is a criminal mind.

And when I get out into freedom again,
I, who am a Crim, I, who am a Crim!
I fool the Police, with their cleverest men—
Oh, I'm of the criminal kind!

The longer I follow, the more I delight
In this life of a Crim, this life of a Crim!
To rob and to plunder, by day and by night—
This life of a criminal kind.

There *have* been occasions, but that long ago,
Though I was a Crim—yes, I was a Crim—
I would have done better, and tried it, but no—
They'd marked me the criminal kind.

They hunted me, haunted me, hounded me ever,
For I was a Crim—yes, I was a Crim!
My honest intentions accepted they? Never!
I was branded the criminal kind.

So I gave up the struggle and threw in my lot,
For I was a Crim—yes, I was a Crim!
With the worst of my fellows, 'gainst "justice" we fought,
Being classed as the criminal kind.

When I go to prison to serve a few years—
For I am a Crim—yes, I am a Crim!
I leave, as a rule, wife and children in tears—
That's the way with the criminal kind.

I know what it means, she falls straight into debt,
She, the wife of a Crim, the wife of a Crim !
The time will hang heavily on her, but yet
It's the way with the criminal kind.

So when my long sentence is filled to the lip—
I, who am a Crim, I, who am a Crim !
I out thro' the door into liberty slip—
A man of the criminal kind.

So off to the jungles—away to the fair—
I'm only a Crim ; I'm only a Crim !
There's booty, and plenty awaiting me there,
I belong to the criminal kind.

* * * * *

The Salvation Army now comes to our aid,
With work for the Crim—yes, work for the Crim !
And for us a pathway to Heaven has made
For Tribes of the criminal kind.

Now this is our watchword, from day unto day,
There's hope for the Crim ; there's hope for the Crim ;
We wipe from our minds our sad record away—
We Tribes of the criminal kind.

They give us an offer of work we accept—
'Tis *work* for the Crim—yes, *work* for the Crim ;
And soon at our task we become quite adept,
We Tribes of the criminal kind.

They make our life happy with labour and song,
This life of the Crim, this life of the Crim ;
And make us all feel that to God we belong,
We Tribes of the criminal kind.

At last we wake up to the fact, and the thought,
"I'm no longer a Crim ! I'm no longer a Crim ! !
I'm living by industry, honestly wrought,
And have changed from the criminal mind !"

The thought makes a man of him worthy and true—
He who was a Crim, he who was a Crim—
Inspires him with courage his course to pursue—
Who was known as the criminal kind.

With a chance in the world, and a friend to stand by
Not so bad is the Crim, not so bad is the Crim !
He'll respond to the message of kindness and why !
Love's the key to the criminal mind.

So all hands to the work, through the storm, or the calm—
We will rescue the Crim, we will rescue the Crim—
And rid this fair land from a menace and harm,
In the Tribes of the criminal kind.

We'll tell them of Jesus, the Mighty to save,
We'll rescue the Crim! We'll rescue the Crim!
Till over each Tribe Calv'ry's Banner doth wave—
These Tribes of the criminal kind!

The efforts of the Major and of the other Officers who succeeded him were ultimately crowned with success. The tribes came to recognize them as their true friends. One day the news flew round the Settlement that their Major had been assaulted by some caste people from Bezwada. The whole tribe, men, women and children, rushed to the rescue, and it would have gone hard with the caste people but for the prompt intervention of one of the European Officers' wives. She was nursing her baby at the time, but seeing that trouble was brewing, she laid her baby in its cot and rushed between the tribesmen and the objects of their wrath in time to prevent bloodshed. She was afterwards awarded a police medal for her plucky action.

It was amongst the boys of the tribe that the first rift in the clouds appeared. A young lad went to one of the Officers, and asked to be prayed with, saying that he would like to be saved. The Officer gladly responded. A few days later, the boy brought six others who desired to follow his example. Soon there was a prosperous work among the children, and their parents were not long in following their example.

It was in this settlement that a tribesman, dying of cholera, asked for a Bible to be placed under his head, and resting peacefully upon its promises passed away.

The chief difficulty afterwards experienced was when the Police brought us raw and rebellious gangs of tribesmen, who upset the peace of the settlement and created a new element of disorder and difficulty.

"What are the Government thinking about?" remarked a reformed woman settler, as she gazed at one of these gangs when they were brought in. "How can they ask respectable people like us to mix with these ruffians?"

The results of years of patient toil were in danger of being lost. Ultimately Government saw the necessity of strictly limiting the numbers committed to each settlement, and of regulating the influx of new-comers.

A second settlement of a widely different character was soon afterwards established in the neighbourhood of Bapatla. Here Agriculture was to be the main means of support for the settlers. Some 500 acres of sandy land, and about 1,000 of swamp land—the former suitable for "ragi" (a kind of millet), and the latter for rice—were made over to us. It was to serve as a reward for those of the Yerikulas who were willing to reform and settle down. Each family could have its own tract of land as a reward for good behaviour, and subject to forfeiture in case of a relapse to crime.

This proposal to make these tribesmen into land-owners was not viewed with favour by the high caste people of the neighbourhood. As in other parts of India, so here, the proprietorship of land was looked upon as a great privilege, which belonged exclusively to the high-born—some of them self-styled Heaven-born—"squires" of the parish. The rice-land in particular was greatly coveted. All over India this is the case. Rice-land, suitably irrigated, will seldom sell for less than Rs. 1,000 per acre, and often commands two or three times that price.

Numerous were the petitions that flooded Government protesting against the proposal, and also objecting to the establishment of a criminal settlement in their neighbourhood.

Sir Harold Stuart personally visited the district to meet the petitioners and inquire into their complaint. The road from the settlement to Bapatla, a distance of about five miles, was placarded with bills hanging from the trees, demanding the immediate removal of the settlement from the neighbourhood. In Bapatla itself a large crowd of protestors, numbering several thousands, had been gathered to meet Sir Harold. Fortunately for the future of this now prosperous settlement, then only in its infancy, Sir Harold was a strong administrator, and pointed out to the objectors the unreasonableness of their demands, informing them that Government had no intention of changing their policy, but would rely upon them to give these tribesmen, who had so long been a pest to the entire countryside, a chance of reforming. He reminded them that these European Sanyasis, The Salvation Army Officers, were following the best traditions of their own Indian Swamis (religious reformers), and expressed his surprise that they, the leading representatives of orthodox Hinduism, should lend their influence to demands so diametrically opposed to their own scriptures.

The appeal was not in vain. From Sir Harold's timely visit and speech onwards little further difficulty was experienced.

The manager of this settlement was Adjutant Raja Veeran (Robilliard), whose agricultural experience, first in the Channel Islands, and afterwards as a Planter in the Straits Settlements, made up for the agricultural ignorance of the settlers themselves.

The site of the settlement was particularly well chosen for the purpose in view. A few feet beneath the surface of the sandy soil was an abundant supply of pure spring water. Each settler had only to dig down a short distance to obtain all the water he required, both for household and garden purposes. A long narrow strip of such land extends for some distance parallel with the coast. On either side the water is salt, or brackish, and in order to reach fresh water wells require to be sunk to a great depth. The value of this land with its water supply was not realized when first it was made over to us. It was then estimated at some two annas per acre. We had not been there long before its value had risen to more than Rs. 100 per acre, as we were able to demonstrate that it was not only well suited for monkey-nuts and ragi, but that potatoes, tomatoes, coconut palms, eucalyptus and mulberry would flourish in the soil, owing to the nearness and abundance of the water supply.

The settlement quickly became one of the most prosperous that we have in India. It was named after Sir Harold, "Stuartpuram," and has now its own railway station and schools. Its police are chosen from among the settlers. It has a little court of its own, in which petty offences are disposed of in accordance with clan customs.

For instance, a mother was charged with accepting marriage fees for her daughter from two different families. The case was brought before the Court and suitably settled. Infringements of settlement rules are similarly dealt with by the people themselves.

The settlement numbers about 1,800 souls (men, women, and children), grouped in seven little hamlets, the settlers building their own houses. Originally these were simply of palm-leaf and posts, for which a few rupees were allowed. Now comfortable cottages are springing up.

A strong religious element, which has from the first prevailed, has laid a solid foundation of real reform. At daybreak, before commencing work, all the villagers assemble in two centres for prayer and Bible reading, together with a brief exhortation regarding the duties of the day.

One day the manager told the settlers he had brought thirty Telugu Testaments, as he thought many of them would like to possess their own copy for their family. It was true that few of the adults could read, but their children were learning and could read to them at home, when their day's work was over. They would cost six annas each. Sixty hands were immediately raised, and it became necessary to double the supply.

What a change has taken place in the appearance of the settlers since their first arrival! The women's hair was dishevelled, their clothing ragged, and their general appearance untidy and dirty, until the manager announced one day that no woman would be granted a pass to go to the bazaar to do her marketing unless she presented a neat appearance. He could not allow them to disgrace the settlement by going about like so many vagrants. The effect was magic. Each woman vied with the others in presenting a respectable appearance.

When we paid one of our first visits to the Colony, my wife was called upon to present a prize of one rupee each to the ten most neatly dressed women. More than 200 candidates presented themselves, and it was difficult to decide which should be the prize-winners.

The love for the Bible among the Criminal Tribes extended even to the children. A little girl had been for some months in one of our Homes, and had learned to love to listen to the Bible stories, though she had not been long enough with us to be able to read. One day an order came from Government that she was to be sent to her parents who had been released from prison and sent to another settlement conducted by the police, where there was no Salvation Army. The poor child was in tears. It was a heart-rending business, nor by any means the only time when a reformed child was sent back to its wicked parents in spite of our earnest protests. She had one last favour to ask. She wanted to have a Bible to take with her. When the Officer reminded her that she could not read, she replied that she had a brother who could, and she would get him to read it to her till she had learned to read it herself.

In our Madras Industrial Home for Boys of these Tribes, when an Officer once asked the boys to tell him who was the best Tamil boy among them, they immediately pointed out the one they regarded as being the best. He then asked the Telugu boys to point out their champion " best boy." They too at once responded. The Officer then told the two lads that on behalf of the General he would like to give them each a prize. What would they prefer to have? Both without the least hesitation asked for a Bible of their very own. To these Tribes, who have never before seen it, the Bible is indeed a wonder Book, not to be placed on the shelf and produced at intervals for a few brief moments, but to read and re-read and pore over, with a simple faith and reverence that are beautiful to behold, producing a rich harvest of spiritual results.

" I never miss anything in my kitchen," said the wife of our Manager to a youth who was helping her. " How is it?" He replied, " I have had a vision of Jesus in the kitchen, while I was praying there. How could I steal?" " This is life eternal, that they might know Thee, the only true God and Jesus Christ, whom Thou hast sent!" Unflinchingly he had faced his own father, who had threatened, knife in hand, to kill him, when the other settlers intervened and rescued him.

The following vivid pen-sketches of early experiences in a Criminal Tribes' Settlement are from the pen of

Brigadier Ratna Bai (Mrs. Hunter), to whom reference has been made in Chapter XXIV.

"One day when visiting the back row of our settlement I found Jagia very much upset. She was scolding a screaming child, and at the same time endeavouring to pacify it, whilst her husband, a poor sick old man, kept up a continual stream of complaint. To my enquiry, 'Kya hua?' (What's the matter?) she answered through her tears, 'Dekho, Mem Sahib, I am out nearly all day long, working hard to support the three of us, and when I come home to cook the food my husband grumbles and scolds me all the time and I am so tired.' Then, taking the child up in her arms, she exclaimed, 'There, I will leave him: I will go back to the Dom Khana.' 'All right,' I said, 'if you are so bad as to even speak about leaving your poor old husband, especially when he is sick, then go!' The man who was quite old enough to be the woman's father, now began to cry as I talked to him of his sins and ingratitude to God and to his wife. He acknowledged his sins, but blamed his aches and pains for his bad temper.

"Returning with some medicine for the sufferer, I found Jagia standing round the corner wiping her eyes. 'Well, have you not gone to the Dom Khana?' I asked. 'Not yet,' she sobbed.

"'Have you forgotten,' I continued, 'that it is said in God's word that whatever we do to others the same shall be done to us? Some day you too may be old and sick, then you will need some one to attend to you. But if you desert your sick husband, depend upon it, you too will be deserted.' A feeling of intense pity came over my heart for this poor woman who had been, until recently, the ringleader of many a Dom brawl. As she stood there weeping, the woman in her appeared, and laying my hand upon her arm, I said, 'Go back, sister, and do your duty; pray to God and He will give you patience and love to look after your husband, even if he does grumble.'

"A look of relief passed over her face, and she replied, 'Bahut Achcha,' and 'Bahut Salaam.' Then she retraced her steps and went cheerfully back to her house.

"There were no more complaints of either neglect or

bad temper from either of them after that. The old man, however, steadily grew worse, and not many weeks had elapsed when a messenger brought word that he was dead. When we went round, preparations were being made for his burial. The poor widow had laid out her last pice on buying a decent cloth to bury him in. She sat at the head of the corpse, not beating her breast or exhibiting any unseemly show of sorrow, as we see so often in India, but quietly weeping tears of real sorrow.

"After the Brigadier had finished a very nice Funeral Service, to which the settlers had given their most respectful attention, I knelt beside the widow and tried to comfort her, leaving her with the words, 'Thank God, you did not leave him to die alone!'

"'Han, han,' she answered, 'Khuda ka shukr karti hun' (Yes, yes, I thank God!)

"Altered in appearance, sadder and wiser, she really looked a new woman, and her loud, rough voice not only softened, but was seldom heard. Truly Jagia had not been chastened in vain.

"Time sped on. One evening, in the dusk, as we sat outside and talked over the events of the day now far spent, Jagia suddenly appeared, and with the usual profound salaam, she addressed the Brigadier in similar words to these: 'Hazur! Dania says he would like to marry me; he has no wife and I have no husband, but what does your honour say? If you say yes, then I will marry him, but if you say no, then I will remain alone as I am.'

"Now Dania was a man about Jagia's own age, and had proved himself anxious to do well. 'Go, and bring Dania here,' said the Brigadier, and off she went, returning in a very short time with her young man.

"On questioning Dania, the Brigadier found him very anxious to marry Jagia. Then addressing them both he asked them if they were willing to have a Christian wedding.

"'Yes, yes,' they both said eagerly, 'give us a Christian wedding, for we also believe in Jesus.'

"So in due course intimation was given, time and place announced, and finally the Brigadier performed the wedding ceremony in the presence and to the evident satisfaction of a goodly number of spectators. When the sentence, 'Till death us do part,' was translated into Hindustani, the men and women nodded their heads vigorously, saying 'Han, han, yih bat bahut achchi hai' (Yes, yes, that is very good). So far as we have heard the bride and bridegroom have lived happily ever since."

* * * *

"Harpala is a fine, stalwart fellow; you may generally find him at the drum during meetings. If he is denied this pleasure, he will be foremost in the singing, and if there is a chance at all he will be sure to pray. No vain repetition of words is Harpala's prayer, but a real confession of weakness and failure to a great, merciful Father, with earnest cravings for more grace, wisdom and love.

"He first came out for Salvation on the occasion of Colonel Sena Singh's (Commissioner Sowton's) first visit some time ago. It would be nice if I could report that he had been saved and happy ever since, but that would be far from true, for Harpala has had his ups and downs, but he has one redeeming feature—he confesses to God and again seeks forgiveness.

"When Harpala and his wife became the proud possessors of a little son their joy was unbounded, and they besought us to give him a Christian name, which we did, dedicating him to God and calling him David Harpala. Things went on smoothly for a few months, then one evening Harpala, with a very long face, walked up to our house with his baby.

"Startled at seeing the baby without its mother, I asked, 'What's the matter?' whereupon Harpala burst into tears, saying, 'My son will die, my son will die,' and great, scalding tears fell on the sleeping babe's face.

"I was frightened at the man's intense grief as he had now squatted down on the ground, and with the child pressed to his bosom he rocked himself backwards and forwards. I laid my hand on the child's forehead and was still more puzzled by the fact that the child had no fever and seemed in a very healthy condition.

"'There is nothing the matter with the child,' I said, 'he is quite well and having a good sleep.'

"'Yes, yes, he is well, but he will die,' said Harpala, still rocking in his anguish.

"Feeling greatly puzzled, but assuming a stern voice, I said, 'Come, how can the child die when he is in perfect health? Get up and take him to his mother.'

"'His mother,' repeated Harpala bitterly, 'she won't feed him any more. She has left me and the baby too, and what can I do for such a very small child?'

"Beginning dimly to realize that a family quarrel had taken place, I rose to go with him, saying, 'Come, I will see your wife; where is she?'

"'At her mother's,' was the reply, so to the mother's we went, where we found the young wife and mother not looking very happy.

"'What is this? Is it true that you want to leave your husband and the dear little baby God has given you?'

"A fiery explanation from the young wife followed, blaming the husband, of course, and finishing with the words, 'He told me to go, so I gave him the baby and went.'

"'Very well,' I said, 'now that is all past and you must now forgive him, and go back to your own house quickly.'

"Slowly she gathered herself up and followed me to her own house, settling herself down on the doorstep.

"'Give her the baby,' I said to the distracted father, and gladly he laid the little burden down on its mother's lap. With a few parting words on 'Bearing and Forbearing,' I left the couple alone to make it up. This they evidently did to their mutual satisfaction, as we have heard no more about that or any other quarrels, and if you happen to pass by Harpala's home any evening you will find him busy grinding the masala and taking the heaviest end of cooking the evening meal, whilst his wife with the beloved David is cleaning vegetables, etc.

"On a recent Sunday night, at the evening service, the collection box by some means had been forgotten, and there were neither bonnets, hats nor topis there, so out we rolled the old drum.

"'Now then,' exclaimed the Brigadier, 'all who want to give something to God, throw it on the drum!'

"'Harpala shall be the first to give to God,' said the owner of that name, making a dive for the drum, but another's pice got there before his, so he had to content himself with being second."

* * * *

"Thus Sunshine and Shadow succeed each other in quick succession in a Criminal Settlement. With the Indian criminal you have nothing to work on. Unlike his fallen brother in Europe, he has no recollections of better days. There is no tender chord left by the remembrance of a sainted mother, wife or sister; no Sunday School memories. He only knows that, like Ishmael, every man's hand is against him and his hand is against every man. So far as he knows it has always been thus. He is not the 'Prodigal,' for he has never heard of the forgiving Father. He is not the 'Lost Sheep,' for he was never in the fold, and has never known the loving Shepherd. He is the 'Lost Piece of Silver.' He must have dropped centuries ago. Here he has lain, all unconscious of his own proper place or value. At last the 'Evangel,' the sweet Gospel of Jesus, has come along and is sweeping him out of his corners: there is plenty of dust, blinding dust, but he must be found. And even when this end is accomplished we may well ask, 'Whose Image and superscription is this?' for the Divine imprint is well nigh trampled out. But bring him to the Cleansing Fountain, and then we see the Divine Image reappearing.

HE IS THE LOST PIECE OF SILVER!"

CHAPTER XXVII.

THE PASSION FOR SOULS.

" Souls, souls to win my one desire,—
More Love, more Zeal, more flaming Fire ! "

If asked for the chief characteristic of the Officers in India, whether European or Indian, I should say it is their PASSION FOR SOULS.

The slogan for all, whether in Corps or Settlement, whether dealing with children or greyheads soaked in crime, has been : " Lord, give us souls ! " The mysterious fire which animated them, which inspired their deeds of daring and glad sacrifices, and won the admiration of on-looking multitudes of Hindus and Mahommedans, was, ' Lord, give us their souls ! We must have souls ! Never mind whether we live, or die, or what becomes of us ! Let us see the very image of the Jesus who has done so much for us, stamped upon the changed lives of those to whom we minister ! "

In those great Mass Meeting Melas, where thousands gathered annually, there was no rushing from the hall on the part of the congregation to get to their meals, when the prayer meeting commenced. No ! Every eye would be riveted on the mercy seat as the grand climax and test of everything, and as the weeping stream of penitents picked their way over and across the bodies of the vast congregation bowed in prayer, what a mighty wave of joy would sweep over the hearts of those Officer-Shepherds as they witnessed the glorious harvest of their often-unseen labours poured at the Master's feet. The zeal of His House consumed them. Rivers of living water flowed from them.

And when asked at times, which was our hardest field,

we were able truly to reply that there were no hard fields, for the Spirit of the Lord was moving everywhere among the driest of dry bones, and they were standing on their feet a vast and Spirit-filled host of Blood-washed warrior-witnesses of the Lamb.

And yet in another sense it would be wrong to say there were no hard fields. Yes, there were hard fields—hard in the human sense of losses and crosses to be borne to which human flesh and blood would have said " No ! " Perhaps that was one of the secrets learnt, that where the crosses were the greatest, the triumphs of God's power were the most remarkable.

There is Burma for instance, where, as yet, there have been no great spiritual upheavals, such as we have witnessed in every other portion of our Indian Field. Yet who would say that its field also is not " white unto harvest ? " That fiery band of Burman youths, who met us when we visited Rangoon, who testified and prayed in the open air, and trams, and trains, had been gathered straight from the prisons of the land, and committed to our charge.

The European policeman who had come to plead with us to do something for " the wickedest woman in Rangoon," told us that he had himself received help from The Army in The Old Country, when he remembered the saying among the down and outs :—

" Helter skelter for the Shelter,
There we find Salvation !
There we meet the poor man's friend,
And get a situation ! "

And that Sunday night, " the wickedest woman " walked into The Army meeting, and was amongst the seekers kneeling at the mercy seat. She fell again, alas, a victim of the tempter drink. But it was to The Army that she turned, when we met her at the Calcutta station, while we were waiting for our train. Can we ever forget that scene ? Reeling about amidst the crowd with that daring abandon that marks the drunkard, when he or she care not what people may think or say—singling The Army out for her attentions, and received and shepherded by them without fear or shame. See in front of a first-class carriage window stands Commissioner Dutini, accompanied by Colonel (now Commissioner) Mithri, pouring forth the vials of her righteous wrath on the man who has been the cause of this woman's fresh downfall.

The Army are after her still. They picked her up again after that fall, and one of our recent letters tells how with patient toil, and faith that will not tire or be turned aside, that "wickedest woman" is still being shepherded, to be finally ingathered, we trust, and included in The Army's Harvest Home.

There was the hard field too of those Telugu villages—physically hard and depressing—such poverty, such dirt, such squalor, such lack of the merest necessaries of life, such succession of droughts and floods, such opposition of the high caste, such terrible scourges of cholera, beri-beri, and small pox—but such beautiful blessed harvests of souls. To those who knew the secrets of the dark background of sorrow and suffering, it was a mystery how these thousands could flock to their own particular local Melas with such happy, shining faces—so determined to get a blessing—so apparently oblivious of the death-cloud which often hung like a black pall over their villages.

A few incidents gathered at random here and there from the far-flung portions of our Indian battlefield must suffice to speak for the many others that are left untold. They are but "fragments that remain" from the feeding of the multitudes with those five barley loaves and few small fishes.

The following is from the pen of the late Colonel Yuddha Bai (Bannister):—

"A LIFE-LONG VOW.

"Forty years ago in a small Marathi village there lived a woman—an Indian woman named Rakmi—a woman with as true a mother-heart as that of any mother of another nation. She was fondly proud of the babe that lay upon her breast. But to Indian women as well as English there comes sorrow intermingled with joy. All suddenly Rakmi was smitten dumb—and terrible was the consternation of her friends and relations to behold! The superstitious mind immediately jumped to the conclusion that the gods they worshipped were angry for some reason or other, and straightway every possible form of appeasing their wrath was put into action. Offerings were brought and placed before the speechless idols of wood or stone, and loud were the lamentations and entreaties on behalf of the one smitten. Nothing could the afflicted woman do but lie and think, and this she did *hour after hour*! Then while listening to the noise going on around her, she suddenly looked up—up above the little patch of thatched mud-huts—up into the sea of bright blue sky overhead, and there flashed across her mind the wonderment, whether there was not one other God—a God above all others—who might do *more* than these gods of stone, and give her back her power of speech? "Well, I can but try," she told herself, and kneeling down, she sent forth from her heart a speechless prayer—that if there *was* a true and *living* God, He would hear her and give her healing. Before rising, she made a vow that, if she were healed, she would never fail to fast every Sunday all through her life until her dying day. She then rose, without, however, receiving at once the answer to her prayer. But test to faith only proves faith to be what it is. She fasted—and not in vain—her speech returned, and henceforth she believed there was a true and living God.

"Forty years passed by—a long time to look back upon, and yet every Sunday during them had seen Rakmi keep her vow. The child that was lying upon her breast during the time she received the stroke had died long since, but she lived to see the Muktifauj enter the village, and after for a little while carefully watching these people, she formed the conclusion that the God to whom she had made her vow, and who had given her back her speech, was none other than the God of the Muktifauj. So she was not long in getting saved, and was made a Soldier right away.

"Rakmi cooked for the Officers, and always on Sunday they noticed she would never take any food. After many times urging her to tell them why, she told them this story, and to the end of her life never a Sunday passed but she kept her fast.

"Having once joined the Muktifauj she was not afraid to say so, and in consequence had to endure her share of persecution. Her relatives, immediately on hearing the news, disowned her, turning her adrift into the world of poverty. This was not *all*. The high caste determined to punish her for changing her religion. They caught and killed her goat, her only means of livelihood. But the poor woman only clung the faster to the Muktifauj and its God.

"Some people are so ready to believe that there is no such trait as stability or fidelity in the character of the sons and daughters of India. Some people find it hard to believe that there can be any good in them at all, and yet these very people but poorly practise the faith that Rakmi exercised for forty long years. And few indeed of the same number have even for half the time so faithfully kept any vow that perhaps they may have made in some dark corner of their experience!"

Then there was indeed the hard field of the high caste Indian, so self-sufficient and self-satisfied. Truly "not many mighty, not many noble" from among these yielded to The Army's persuasions. Indeed, we spent but little time on them. And yet how they hovered around, first in hundreds, and latterly in thousands, specially at our great annual Melas. Year after year they were there, and year after year their numbers and interest kept increasing. Who that saw could forget the hungry, wistful look in their eyes and faces?

"Can you perform miracles?" inquired a young Brahmin student of an Officer. "Can you cast out devils? My father can! I have seen him do it. Therefore our religion must be greater, as well as older than yours."

Just then a telegram came summoning him to his father's deathbed. He arrived too late, but eagerly questioned his mother and relatives as to the last moments of his father. "Terrible, terrible!" was the reply. "He gathered us round his deathbed and told us that many years ago he had promised the devil that he would sell his soul to him, if he would only give him the power to work miracles, and to cast out devils. The offer had been accepted, and they had themselves seen him exercise those occult powers. Now the time had come for him to pay the price and the devil had come to claim his soul! He shrieked in agony that the devil was there in the room—

by his bedside, and thus passed away without hope, and without God."

Overpowered with emotion, the student soon hastened back to The Salvation Army, and sought and found his Saviour. A terrible season of persecution followed. But by the power of Christ he remained faithful, and is to-day occupying an important Government position, and testifying by a consecrated life to the saving and keeping power of Christ.

Chellaya Pillai was another of these high-caste trophies. He had been attending regularly the meetings in Madras, and one day when I was at our Headquarters, he rushed into the room, threw himself upon his knees at the table where we were sitting, burst into a flood of tears, and with the perspiration pouring down his face and mingling with his tears, he claimed our Saviour as his own.

He was a B.A., B.L.—a lawyer of the High Court of Madras, with a successful practice, but resolved to sacrifice all and cast in his lot with us. His charming and devoted wife joined him in his sacrifice. But their health proved unequal to the strain of Officership, though one of my last letters to him contained a proposal for them to join our Headquarters Staff and take up a position where there would be less strain upon his health. His heart was in the work, and he would probably have accepted the proposal, when he fell from his horse, and met with an accident, which terminated fatally. His deathbed was glorious. Not a cloud dimmed the sky, and his dying testimony produced a profound impression upon those who gathered round him. The whole town of Cuddapah, where he was then practising, turned out to do honour to the one whom all alike believed in and loved.

But not only on the outside circle of our friends do we number those who have, like Nicodemus and Joseph of Arimathea, claimed and received the second birth, but up and down the ranks of our Officers we have consecrated lives who have left their comfortable surroundings and bright, earthly prospects to follow Christ in a way that is particularly difficult and humanly-speaking repulsive to the high-caste Indian, by mingling with the "Untouchables," and making themselves one with them. One such,

Colonel Muthiah, is now Chief Secretary for the Northern Territory, while another, Lieut.-Colonel Samaraveera has done many years of faithful and successful service in Ceylon, and the leader of the Travancore Training Homes, Lieut.-Colonel S. S. Perera, has for many years been one of our staunchest stand-bys.

Nor should we fail to mention some of those converts of early days from the Anglo-Indian community who have made good, and left their mark upon our Indian work.

Lieut.-Colonel Yisu Patham (Keil) was one of the early converts in Bombay, and sacrificed his position and prospects in the Government Telegraph Department to cast in his lot with the Muktifauj. Ever since the early days of the revivals in Travancore, he has been identified with those great soul sweeps. In the prayer meetings particularly he has been inimitable, and would pour out his soul till his voice failed, and he was compelled reluctantly to hand over the reins to other hands.

From time to time also that hardest of hard fields, the Fakir of India, has responded to the call of Christ. The story of Punja Bhagat, the blind exorcist of Gujarat, is almost as well known to our Indian comrades as that of Weerasooriya, and his name and memory are still cherished in our ranks.

Punja Bhagat was an old blind Fakir of great reputed sanctity and influence. He had performed extraordinary penances, such as sitting between four fires with the blazing sun shining upon him, and he was credited with the power to cast out devils. His theory was that there were sixteen devils which possessed people and caused all kinds of disease. When afflicted persons were brought to him, he would pass his hands mesmerically over them and profess to swallow one devil after another, they having no power to harm him. Between each process he would receive an offering of pice, grain, or fowls. His profession was therefore a lucrative one.

But when he came across The Salvation Army he accepted Christ with the simplicity of a child, and began to proclaim Him to all. Soon after his conversion he received a wonderful baptism of the Holy Ghost.

He hurried back to his village and told his people of

his new-found joy. But instead of accepting his message, they were angry, and said that since he had changed his religion, and forsaken their time-honoured gods and teachings, he could no longer be their "guru" (priest). He replied that he would pray and fast for them until God should change their hearts. Seating himself under an adjoining tree, he poured out his heart to God in prayer. In the evening they came, and offered him food and shelter. He declined both and spent the night in prayer. The following day, they came and begged him to desist, as they would never change their minds, and his efforts would be useless. But he continued his prayers. Another night passed. The following day the villagers came to him, and said, "We have decided to listen to you, though we cannot accept your teaching." Men, women and children gathered round him. His opportunity had come. He poured out his heart upon them, and told them of the wonderful change the salvation of Christ had wrought in him. The power of God fell upon them. The old familiar cry went forth, "What must we do to be saved?" They wept and prayed around their old teacher, and accepted his Saviour as their own.

Punja sent a message to the District leader, then Major now Commissioner Prabhu Das (Mapp), himself a convert of the early meetings in Bombay, urging him to come and carry on the work. On his arrival he found the old man sitting under the tree, but where were the people? Then came a great sound of tom-toms, and music, and singing, and the villagers came in procession to the tree carrying a large basket, covered with a white cloth. Here they had gathered the village idols, and brought them to be surrendered to and destroyed by the Major, as a token that henceforth they would serve Christ alone.

In spite of his age and blindness, Punja became an Officer, and helped to lay the foundations of the work in Gujarat. He had one great desire, and that was that God would permit him to "see" the Founder of The Salvation Army before he died. His prayer was answered. The Founder came. Old Punja was introduced to him. Amongst the thousands who gathered there, none was more full of joy and the Holy Ghost than Punja. Three days after he quietly lay down and passed to his eternal reward.

From a recent number of *All the World* (June 1923)—The Army's Missionary Magazine, we cull the following graphic account of the surrender of the inhabitants of a Mohalla (District) in Lahore:—

"Nearly three years ago," writes Commissioner Prabhu Das (Mapp), "some of our Lahore Officers were moved to go and hold out-door meetings in a district entirely non-Christian. To help with the singing, they took with them a few of the older boys of the Boarding School. They went each Sunday evening for some time, but seemed to make very little impression, except for a certain animation among the children. Oppressed by the great heat, tormented by a variety of insects, distressed by foul smells, our comrades began to wonder whether any good was being done by these meetings.

"Then the unexpected happened. During the week a deputation arrived from the district in which those Sunday meetings were being held. The spokesman asked if The Army could not supply a teacher who would go and instruct them about the Christian religion. 'You have come every week,' one of the speakers said, 'to our Mohalla. Our children have learnt to sing the Christian bhajans (songs), and we ourselves have been impressed by what we have heard. We have decided to give up our idol-worship. Will you please come and instruct us in the Christian religion?'

"Well, the upshot of our deliberations was that they promised to provide a school, and we undertook to supply the teacher; and when we presently arrived to take over the premises and begin the work, great was our surprise and pleasure to behold, at the entrance to the district, a signboard inscribed in Hindustani, 'Muktifauj Mohalla,' together with the English translation—'Salvation Army District.' In the meeting the people sat on the floor and listened most attentively as the story of God's love was told in simple language. You can imagine our feelings on beholding that crowd as, for the first time in their lives, they knelt in worship of the one true God and, with closed eyes and clasped hands, repeated after our Indian Adjutant the Lord's Prayer.

"Thus began their knowledge of the Fatherhood of God and the brotherhood of man; thus began a work that has been going on with growing momentum ever since. A few weeks ago Lieut.-Commissioner Hira Singh (Hoe) *dedicated the fine new Hall those people have provided at their own expense*; they went further than that, for, on behalf of the Mohalla, Captain Lilawati (Hutchins), the Corps Commander, presented a nazarana (thank-offering), which the Commissioner accepted for the furtherance of God's work."

Perhaps one of the greatest trials of faith to one who has had the 'Passion for Souls,' is when a period of stagnation appears to have set in, and the people around us have settled down in a condition of determined lethargy and indifference.

Such had been for some years the case in Ceylon, when, under the vigorous leadership of Lieut.-Colonels Dayal Singh and Dayali (Suttor) formerly of Australia, a revival of a remarkable character was brought about under conditions which differed considerably from the soul-harvests previously described.

"A system of special campaigns was introduced, each covering a period of nine or ten days, a fighting force of about twenty Officers and other workers being gathered together, and a series of all-day meetings conducted, which proved to be very effective.

"The first attack was made upon Moratuwa, this being conveniently near Colombo, so that the Headquarters Staff could the more easily be utilized. A wealthy Singhalese gentleman undertook to meet all the expenses. The effort proved entirely successful. Many of our old friends rallied to our assistance, and more than two hundred seekers came forward in the meetings. Before the Campaign was over the whole neighbourhood was singing Salvation Army songs and choruses."

The Colonel, after an interval of two or three months, allowed for consolidating the results, next turned his attention to what had from the first proved a particularly hard field—the town of Kandy. What followed may best be described in his own words:—

"Those present will never forget the way the Holy Spirit was poured out. A gracious unction from God rested upon the singing, speaking and praying. It was glorious to be present. The power, the joyous delight, the spiritual exaltation and victory were wonderful. The Plan of Campaign was as follows:—

1. Prayer on the part of the whole Staff and Field Officers for two or three weeks beforehand.
2. Half-night of Prayer to launch the Campaign.
3. Daily Prayer Meeting, 8 to 9 a.m.
4. House to house Visitation, 9 to 11 a.m.
5. Singing Practice, new choruses, meeting for Young People, Home League, etc., 2.30 to 4 p.m.
6. Salvation Open-air Meeting, 4.30 to 6 p.m.
7. Illuminated Procession, 7 to 7.30 p.m.
8. Salvation Meeting in Hall from 7.30 to finish.

"The Half-night of Prayer with which the Campaign commenced was well attended, and at its close ten Buddhists and Hindus knelt at the mercy seat. It was a glorious commencement, and showed to us all that God was graciously giving His blessing.

"Next night the crowd had much increased, and the Hall was almost full. The singing was very remarkable for its volume and fervour, Hindus and Buddhists joining in singing Salvation songs. Again a grand scene of Salvation was witnessed, quite a number of seekers coming forward. The interest and enthusiasm were immense, and a spirit of faith and victory pervaded the whole place.

"The Open-air meetings and nightly processions stirred the town, and a number of penitents knelt at the drum-head in the Market. One morning in the Open-air a fine-looking young Hindu stood close up to the ring. He became visibly affected concerning his spiritual condition, and then suddenly raising his arm to its full length and calling upon God, he fell on his knees at the drum and took Christ as his Saviour. Others followed, and the whole proceedings were intensely interesting and impressive.

"The meetings increased in power, interest and influence each night. Every available seat was occupied and many stood. On the last night the hall was jammed. The meeting commenced at 7 p.m. and continued till nearly

11 p.m., and twenty-five souls knelt at the penitent form. Some idea may be gathered of the hold this meeting had upon the crowd from the fact that the Japanese Crown Prince was in Kandy that night, and at 9 p.m. there were processions through the streets in which twenty elephants and several groups of devil-dancers took part. Notwithstanding this our crowd remained with us till nearly eleven.

"One of the days of the campaign was spent at a village near Kandy, and those who were privileged to take part in the visit will never forget that day. It was a day of days. Sounds of holy songs rolled almost continuously up and down the hills and valleys surrounding the village. The Campaigners arrived early in the morning. Some went forth to visit from door to door, while others waited in the Officers' Quarters. Soon a steady stream of penitents began to arrive, asking to be prayed with. Then would be witnessed the sight that charms us most, sinners at the Cross, with a group of red-coated Salvationists pointing them to the Saviour. Charms were cut off, signifying severance from the old life.

"The Officers were compelled to take food in relays, one set pointing sinners to Jesus while the others had food. It was a scene of gladness, and all taking part rejoiced with joy unspeakable. The Lord moved mightily, and we give Him the glory. The next day the Corps Officers, Adjutant Yuddhadaksha and his wife, visited the whole of the converts, and found them firm in their determination to follow Christ. It was all the Lord's doings and it was wonderful in our eyes.

"Altogether over 200 souls sought Christ during the nine days of the campaign, the majority being Buddhists and Hindus. Many of the best educated young men (Buddhists) of Kandy attended the meetings, and also came to see the campaign party off by train when they left for Colombo. A number are offering themselves as candidates.

"It was a delightful sight to see the glowing faces of the early day Soldiers catch the fire, attend every meeting, testify, sing, fish, deal with penitents and in every way enjoy the Salvation fight. The final night was for thanksgiving, and if all had testified who desired to do so, the meeting instead of lasting four hours might easily have continued throughout the night.

"No matter how glowingly one may write about the meetings, the actual power, glory and blessing which abounded on every hand could only be adequately realized by those who were actually present. To God be all the glory!"

The news of these revivals spread far and wide through the Island and pressing invitations came from various places, where friends of The Army undertook to meet all expenses. The next place to be chosen was the town of Galle, and subsequently Matara, both in the extreme south of the Island. In both of these places special pandals were erected by our friends, and in each case the crowds attending the meetings and the numbers of seekers were similar.

Not only was a great impetus given to the work, but as a result of these campaigns many candidates came forward for Officership in The Army, including a remarkable proportion of men as well as women.

* * * *

Why does the Indian Officer, be he European or Indian, love his battlefield? What is its fascination? Why does he so gladly respond to the invitation to go, to remain, or to return?

Because he sees in India's sands the footprints of His Saviour clear and plain—Jesus of Nazareth is there, pointing the way, sharing his every cross, helping him shepherd those myriads of shepherdless sheep.

CHAPTER XXVIII.

BISM ILLAH: IN THE NAME OF GOD!

Who in this world is able to distinguish
The virtuous from the wicked? Both alike
The fruitful earth supports; on both alike
The sun pours down his beams; on both alike
Refreshing breezes blow; and both alike
The waters purify. Not so hereafter.
Then shall the good be severed from the bad.
Then in a region bright with golden lustre,
Centre of light and immortality,
The righteous after death shall dwell in bliss.
Then doth an awful hell await the wicked—
Profound abyss of bitter misery,
Into the depths of which bad men shall fall
Headlong, and mourn their doom for countless years.

Mahabharata.

Mahommedan books usually commence with the inscription, Bism Illah—in the Name of God. I would like mine to end with it. Standing as it were at the window of the past, and gazing back at its happenings, I have often been constrained to say: "This is the Lord's doing; it is marvellous in our eyes." It is not by human might nor power, but by His Spirit. To Him be all the glory!

That the record is very imperfect, I am well aware. So many things have been left unsaid that should have been said. So many beautiful God-consecrated, God-inspired deeds and lives have been left unrecorded that should have been mentioned.

This book is nothing more than a mere sketch at best of forty years that have teemed with similar happenings. It has been necessary to choose from the glorious record of the blessed men and women whose lives and consecration made up the history of this period and field of labour, and many a name remains unrecorded whose diamond-deeds of heroism and love for the Master might well have illuminated these pages.

But what is here recorded is enough to show, I believe, that they were taught of God, and that nothing but His living presence and guidance could have made even this brief outline of our history possible.

Written upon these workers' lives, inspiring them at every step, encouraging them amidst every difficulty, has been this thought: "It is *God* that India needs—*not us.* The balm for India's wounds is the Christ of Calvary—not man—not The Salvation Army—not ourselves!"

And that thought has served to make easy the losses and crosses—nay, as Weerasooriya reminded us: "The Cross is the Attraction."

Not a few beautiful lives have been laid on the altar for India's salvation, but these pages will serve, I trust, to show that their labour in the Lord has not been in vain. What a multitude of their converts have joined them already around the Throne, and are singing the Song of the Lamb! What a multitude of blood-washed souls are on the way! What a rich harvest-field India has been—and is! How it has responded—and is responding—to the call of the Cross—to the clarion voice of those who count not their lives dear! "How beautiful upon the mountains" have been—and are—the feet of those who proclaim good tidings, who say to India—"Thy God reigneth!"

May this brief record of their deeds, these gleanings from their golden harvest, be an inspiration to others to follow in their footsteps, and to tread the same blood-besprinkled, prayer-strewn paths of sacrifice, assured that though no mortal pen may record their deeds, yet no cup of cold water offered to India in the Master's name shall lose His recognition and reward, and the "Well done!" of Him to whom India must needs be nearer and dearer than to ourselves.

Reader! Have you a personal knowledge of this Jesus as your Saviour, and Friend? Nay, more! Is He to you the Rose of Sharon, and the Lily of the Valley, the Chiefest among ten thousand, and the Altogether Lovely?

If so, you will rejoice as you picture in these pages

the same Jesus you know and read about in your Bible—the Jesus of Nazareth, who walked and talked, and lived and loved, and shepherded those whom His Father gave Him in Judæa and Galilee, doing the same for the myriad multitudes of India and Ceylon. You will rejoice with us, as you see the light of His Salvation illuminating thousands of souls once wrapped in age-long darkness. You will recognize in these pages, not the feeble faltering instruments He has deigned to use—not the frail followers—but the glorious Lord of the Harvest, working with His old-time power, mighty to save and to keep! Your heart will surely be warmed with a newly enkindled faith for yourself and for those around you—with a burning zeal for His House and cause to which you have pledged yourself to belong. You will rise up and say, "What He has done through these, He can surely do through me." You will hear that Voice saying, "Whom shall I send, and who will go for Us?" and you will respond, "Here am I! Send me!"

And if, alas, you are still a stranger to that glorious indwelling Presence—the ineffable, unexplainable Breath of the Holy Spirit of Love, Who, whether you realize it or not, yearns over you still with unutterable yearnings—if as yet you have not recognized and realized that eternal destiny of Peace and Purity and Service for which He would fit and fill and thrill you in every cell and fibre of your being—then will you not see in what He has done and is doing for India what He can and seeks to do for *You*?

When we read of apostles and prophets and martyrs and servants of God in the pages of the Bible, or of past ages, we are prone to think they were made of different material from ourselves—that they could not feel, and be, and suffer like ourselves—that their thoughts were not like ours, or that they could do what it is hopeless to think of doing ourselves.

But when we see—as I trust you will see in these pages, Christ's miracles of grace brought up to date—when you read how He has changed the lives and illuminated the souls of men and women, aye, and children, who are in no way different from yourself, will you not be tempted, nay, compelled to say, "This Jesus shall be *mine*! I will choose to serve and follow Him! I will accept His Cross! I will do His will by His grace here on earth, even as I hope hereafter to do it in Heaven!"

If this book should fail in bringing its reader into close personal touch with the Jesus of Nazareth, just as He was, and is, it will fail in attaining the object of its writer. Its pages have been prayed over many times with that object in view.

On the ceilings of the cathedrals and galleries of Italy are many beautiful paintings which have for centuries been the wonder of the world. Artists have lavished their utmost skill in seeking to portray the doings and sufferings of the Great Hero of Calvary. Thousands have gone to see those works of Art and Heart, and have strained their eyes to gaze upwards, as their guides have explained to them the beauties of each scene.

Latterly it has become the custom to furnish each visitor with a hand mirror, which would reflect the picture and bring it down to them, close within their reach. No longer is the upturned gaze into distant space necessary. No longer are the short-sighted, or physically weak, outclassed and left behind. Each and all have the distant scene brought to their own level and placed within their reach.

Thus this book seeks to serve as a mirror of what the present-day Jesus is doing, and has done, for those who "sit in darkness and in the shadow of death." Thus the glorious Heart-work of the Divine Artist has been brought within our reach!

Oh that the mirror may indeed be such a reflection of the Master Mind that each reader may be stirred up to say: "Lord, make me a mirror of Thyself—Thy Will—Thy Wish henceforth be my Command!"

BISM ISA!

IN THE NAME OF JESUS!